TERRORISM, HOT SPOTS AND CONFLICT-RELATED ISSUES

TERRORISM RISK INSURANCE ACT

ANALYSES OF DATA, MARKET, AND PROGRAM ISSUES

TERRORISM, HOT SPOTS AND CONFLICT-RELATED ISSUES

Additional books in this series can be found on Nova's website under the Series tab.

Additional e-books in this series can be found on Nova's website under the e-book tab.

TERRORISM, HOT SPOTS AND CONFLICT-RELATED ISSUES

TERRORISM RISK INSURANCE ACT

ANALYSES OF DATA, MARKET, AND PROGRAM ISSUES

ERNIE L. DUKE
EDITOR

Copyright © 2014 by Nova Science Publishers, Inc.

All rights reserved. No part of this book may be reproduced, stored in a retrieval system or transmitted in any form or by any means: electronic, electrostatic, magnetic, tape, mechanical photocopying, recording or otherwise without the written permission of the Publisher.

For permission to use material from this book please contact us:
Telephone 631-231-7269; Fax 631-231-8175
Web Site: http://www.novapublishers.com

NOTICE TO THE READER

The Publisher has taken reasonable care in the preparation of this book, but makes no expressed or implied warranty of any kind and assumes no responsibility for any errors or omissions. No liability is assumed for incidental or consequential damages in connection with or arising out of information contained in this book. The Publisher shall not be liable for any special, consequential, or exemplary damages resulting, in whole or in part, from the readers' use of, or reliance upon, this material. Any parts of this book based on government reports are so indicated and copyright is claimed for those parts to the extent applicable to compilations of such works.

Independent verification should be sought for any data, advice or recommendations contained in this book. In addition, no responsibility is assumed by the publisher for any injury and/or damage to persons or property arising from any methods, products, instructions, ideas or otherwise contained in this publication.

This publication is designed to provide accurate and authoritative information with regard to the subject matter covered herein. It is sold with the clear understanding that the Publisher is not engaged in rendering legal or any other professional services. If legal or any other expert assistance is required, the services of a competent person should be sought. FROM A DECLARATION OF PARTICIPANTS JOINTLY ADOPTED BY A COMMITTEE OF THE AMERICAN BAR ASSOCIATION AND A COMMITTEE OF PUBLISHERS.

Additional color graphics may be available in the e-book version of this book.

Library of Congress Cataloging-in-Publication Data

ISBN: 978-1-63463-128-0

Published by Nova Science Publishers, Inc. † New York

CONTENTS

Preface		vii
Chapter 1	Terrorism Risk Insurance: Issue Analysis and Overview of Current Program *Baird Webel*	1
Chapter 2	Terrorism Insurance: Treasury Needs to Collect and Analyze Data to Better Understand Fiscal Exposure and Clarify Guidance *United States Government Accountability Office*	19
Chapter 3	The Long-Term Availability and Affordability of Insurance for Terrorism Risk *President's Working Group on Financial Markets*	65
Chapter 4	Memorandum for the Hearing on "The Future of Terrorism Insurance: Fostering Private Market Innovation to Limit Taxpayer Exposure"	105
Chapter 5	Testimony of Sean McGovern, Director, Risk Management and General Counsel, Lloyd's of London. Hearing on "The Future of Terrorism Insurance: Fostering Private Market Innovation to Limit Taxpayer Exposure"	109
Chapter 6	Testimony of Kean Driscoll, Chief Executive Officer, Validus Re. Hearing on "The Future of Terrorism Insurance: Fostering Private Market Innovation to Limit Taxpayer Exposure"	115
Chapter 7	Testimony of Ernest N. Csiszar, Former Director of Insurance, State of South Carolina. Hearing on "The Future of Terrorism Insurance: Fostering Private Market Innovation to Limit Taxpayer Exposure"	119
Chapter 8	Testimony of Dr. John S. Seo, Co-founder & Managing Principal, Fermat Capital Management, LLC. Hearing on "The Future of Terrorism Insurance: Fostering Private Market Innovation to Limit Taxpayer Exposure"	129

Chapter 9	Testimony of Robert P. Hartwig, President and Economist, Insurance Information Institute. Hearing on "The Future of Terrorism Insurance: Fostering Private Market Innovation to Limit Taxpayer Exposure"	**135**
Index		**155**

PREFACE

This book evaluates the extent of available data on terrorism insurance and Treasury's efforts in determining federal exposure; changes in the terrorism insurance market since 2002; potential impacts of selected changes to the Terrorism Risk Insurance Act (TRIA).

Chapter 1 – Prior to the September 11, 2001, terrorist attacks, coverage for losses from such attacks was normally included in general insurance policies without specific cost to the policyholders. Following the attacks, such coverage became very expensive if offered at all. Because insurance is required for a variety of transactions, it was feared that the absence of insurance against terrorism loss would have a wider economic impact. Terrorism insurance was largely unavailable for most of 2002, and some have argued that this adversely affected parts of the economy.

Congress responded to the disruption in the insurance market by passing the Terrorism Risk Insurance Act of 2002 (TRIA; P.L. 107-297). TRIA created a temporary three-year Terrorism Insurance Program in which the government would share some of the losses with private insurers should a foreign terrorist attack occur. This program was extended in 2005 (P.L. 109-144) and 2007 (P.L. 110-160). The amount of government loss sharing depends on the size of the insured loss. In general terms, for a relatively small loss, private industry covers the entire loss. For a medium-sized loss, the federal role is to spread the loss over time and over the entire insurance industry; the government assists insurers initially but then recoups the payments through a broad levy on insurance policies afterwards. For a large loss, the federal government would cover most of the losses, although recoupment is possible in these circumstances as well. Insurers are required to make terrorism coverage available to commercial policyholders, but TRIA does not require policyholders to purchase the coverage. The prospective government share of losses has been reduced over time, but the 2007 reauthorization expanded the program to cover losses from acts of domestic terrorism. The TRIA program is currently slated to expire at the end of 2014.

The specifics of the current program are as follows: (1) terrorist act must cause $5 million in insured losses to be certified for TRIA coverage; (2) the aggregate insured losses from a certified act of terrorism must be $100 million in a year for the government coverage to begin; and (3) an individual insurer must meet a deductible of 20% of its annual premiums for the government coverage to begin. Once these thresholds are passed, the government covers 85% of insured losses due to terrorism. If the insured losses are under $27.5 billion, the Secretary of the Treasury is required to recoup 133% of government outlays. As insured losses rise above $27.5 billion, the Secretary is required to recoup a progressively reduced amount of the outlays. At some high insured loss level, which will depend on the exact distribution of losses, the Secretary would no longer be required to recoup outlays, but retains the discretionary authority to do so.

Since TRIA's passage, the private industry's willingness and ability to cover terrorism risk have increased. According to industry surveys, prices for terrorism coverage have generally trended downward, with approximately 60% of commercial policyholders purchasing coverage over the past few years. This relative market calm has been under the umbrella of TRIA coverage, and it is unclear how the insurance market would react to the expiration of the federal program.

In the 113th Congress, five bills (H.R. 508, H.R. 1945, H.R. 2146, S. 2244, and H.R. 4871) have been introduced to amend the TRIA statute. S. 2244 passed the Senate on a vote of 93-4 on July 17, 2014. H.R. 4871 was reported by the House Financial Services Committee on July 16, 2014. Both bills would extend the TRIA program, but have a number of differences, particularly the length (seven years for S. 2244 vs. five years for H.R. 4871) and the program trigger (remaining at $100 million in S. 2244 vs. increasing to $500 million for non-Nuclear, Chemical, Biological, or Radiological [NCBR] terrorist events in H.R. 4871).

Chapter 2 – Congress passed TRIA in 2002 to help ensure the availability and affordability of terrorism insurance for commercial property and casualty policyholders after the September 11, 2001, terrorist attacks. TRIA was amended and extended twice and currently will expire at the end of 2014. Under TRIA, Treasury administers a program in which the federal government and private sector share losses on commercial property and casualty policies resulting from a terrorist attack. Because the federal government will cover a portion of insured losses, the program creates fiscal exposures for the government. GAO was asked to review TRIA.

This report evaluates (1) the extent of available data on terrorism insurance and Treasury's efforts in determining federal exposure, (2) changes in the terrorism insurance market since 2002, and (3) potential impacts of selected changes to TRIA. To address these objectives, GAO analyzed insurance data, information from 15 insurers selected primarily based on size of insurer, interviewed Treasury staff and industry participants, updated prior work, and developed examples to illustrate potential fiscal exposure under TRIA.

Chapter 3 – The Terrorism Risk Insurance Act of 2002, as amended (TRIA), requires U.S. insurers to make insurance available for losses resulting from acts of terrorism, and provides a federal government backstop for the insurers' resulting financial exposures. TRIA established in the U.S. Department of the Treasury (Treasury) the Terrorism Risk Insurance Program (TRIP), which is responsible for administering the essential components of TRIA.

Section 108(e) of TRIA requires the President's Working Group on Financial Markets (PWG) to conduct, on an ongoing basis, an analysis of the long-term availability and affordability of insurance for terrorism risk, and to report to Congress regarding the PWG's findings. The PWG previously reported to Congress in 2006 and again in 2010 (the 2006 PWG Report and 2010 PWG Report, respectively). The analysis and conclusions in the 2006 PWG Report and the 2010 PWG Report were based on consultations with industry participants and comments responding to Federal Register notices. In addition, Treasury provided an assessment of TRIA to Congress on June 30, 2005. The 2005 Treasury report relied in part on surveys of various stakeholders conducted by an independent research firm under Treasury auspices.

To assist the PWG's analysis in connection with this report (this Report), on July 16, 2013, Treasury published a notice and request for comment (the PWG Notice), in reply to which 29 written comments were submitted. Submissions in reply to the PWG Notice are available at treasury.gov/initiatives/fio.

This Report draws upon the comments received in response to the PWG Notice, as well as from direct engagement by PWG member staff (staff) with a range of stakeholders, including consumer advocates, insurers, reinsurers, industry services firms, state insurance regulators, commercial insurance policyholders, the National Association of Insurance Commissioners (NAIC), and industry trade associations. Most comments submitted to the PWG addressed whether and to what extent uncertainty concerning TRIA's scheduled expiration at the end of 2014 affects the affordability and availability of terrorism risk insurance, which is referenced in this Report.

Chapter 4 – Memorandum for the Hearing on "The Future of Terrorism Insurance: Fostering Private Market Innovation to Limit Taxpayer Exposure" before the House Committee on Financial Services, Subcommittee on Housing and Insurance, held on November 13, 2013.

Chapter 5 – This is the Testimony of Sean McGovern, Director, Risk Management and General Counsel, Lloyd's of London. Hearing on "The Future of Terrorism Insurance: Fostering Private Market Innovation to Limit Taxpayer Exposure" before the House Committee on Financial Services, Subcommittee on Housing and Insurance, dated November 13, 2013.

Chapter 6 – This is the Testimony of Kean Driscoll, Chief Executive Officer, Validus Re. Hearing on "The Future of Terrorism Insurance: Fostering Private Market Innovation to Limit Taxpayer Exposure" before the House Committee on Financial Services, Subcommittee on Housing and Insurance, dated November 13, 2013.

Chapter 7 – This is the Testimony of Ernest N. Csiszar, Former Director of Insurance, State of South Carolina. Hearing on "The Future of Terrorism Insurance: Fostering Private Market Innovation to Limit Taxpayer Exposure" before the House Committee on Financial Services, Subcommittee on Housing and Insurance, dated November 13, 2013.

Chapter 8 – This is the Testimony of Dr. John S. Seo, Co-founder & Managing Principal, Fermat Capital Management, LLC. Hearing on "The Future of Terrorism Insurance: Fostering Private Market Innovation to Limit Taxpayer Exposure" before the House Committee on Financial Services, Subcommittee on Housing and Insurance, dated November 13, 2013

Chapter 9 – This is the Testimony of Robert P. Hartwig, President and Economist, Insurance Information Institute. Hearing on "The Future of Terrorism Insurance: Fostering Private Market Innovation to Limit Taxpayer Exposure" before the House Committee on Financial Services, Subcommittee on Housing and Insurance, dated November 13, 2013.

In: Terrorism Risk Insurance Act
Editor: Ernie L. Duke

ISBN: 978-1-63463-128-0
© 2014 Nova Science Publishers, Inc.

Chapter 1

TERRORISM RISK INSURANCE: ISSUE ANALYSIS AND OVERVIEW OF CURRENT PROGRAM[*]

Baird Webel

SUMMARY

Prior to the September 11, 2001, terrorist attacks, coverage for losses from such attacks was normally included in general insurance policies without specific cost to the policyholders. Following the attacks, such coverage became very expensive if offered at all. Because insurance is required for a variety of transactions, it was feared that the absence of insurance against terrorism loss would have a wider economic impact. Terrorism insurance was largely unavailable for most of 2002, and some have argued that this adversely affected parts of the economy.

Congress responded to the disruption in the insurance market by passing the Terrorism Risk Insurance Act of 2002 (TRIA; P.L. 107-297). TRIA created a temporary three-year Terrorism Insurance Program in which the government would share some of the losses with private insurers should a foreign terrorist attack occur. This program was extended in 2005 (P.L. 109-144) and 2007 (P.L. 110-160). The amount of government loss sharing depends on the size of the insured loss. In general terms, for a relatively small loss, private industry covers the entire loss. For a medium-sized loss, the federal role is to spread the loss over time and over the entire insurance industry; the government assists insurers initially but then recoups the payments through a broad levy on insurance policies afterwards. For a large loss, the federal government would cover most of the losses, although recoupment is possible in these circumstances as well. Insurers are required to make terrorism coverage available to commercial policyholders, but TRIA does not require policyholders to purchase the coverage. The prospective government share of losses has been reduced over time, but the 2007 reauthorization expanded the program to cover losses from acts of domestic terrorism. The TRIA program is currently slated to expire at the end of 2014.

---

[*] This is an edited, reformatted and augmented version of a Congressional Research Service publication R43125, prepared for Members and Committees of Congress, dated R42716.

The specifics of the current program are as follows: (1) terrorist act must cause $5 million in insured losses to be certified for TRIA coverage; (2) the aggregate insured losses from a certified act of terrorism must be $100 million in a year for the government coverage to begin; and (3) an individual insurer must meet a deductible of 20% of its annual premiums for the government coverage to begin. Once these thresholds are passed, the government covers 85% of insured losses due to terrorism. If the insured losses are under $27.5 billion, the Secretary of the Treasury is required to recoup 133% of government outlays. As insured losses rise above $27.5 billion, the Secretary is required to recoup a progressively reduced amount of the outlays. At some high insured loss level, which will depend on the exact distribution of losses, the Secretary would no longer be required to recoup outlays, but retains the discretionary authority to do so.

Since TRIA's passage, the private industry's willingness and ability to cover terrorism risk have increased. According to industry surveys, prices for terrorism coverage have generally trended downward, with approximately 60% of commercial policyholders purchasing coverage over the past few years. This relative market calm has been under the umbrella of TRIA coverage, and it is unclear how the insurance market would react to the expiration of the federal program.

In the 113th Congress, five bills (H.R. 508, H.R. 1945, H.R. 2146, S. 2244, and H.R. 4871) have been introduced to amend the TRIA statute. S. 2244 passed the Senate on a vote of 93-4 on July 17, 2014. H.R. 4871 was reported by the House Financial Services Committee on July 16, 2014. Both bills would extend the TRIA program, but have a number of differences, particularly the length (seven years for S. 2244 vs. five years for H.R. 4871) and the program trigger (remaining at $100 million in S. 2244 vs. increasing to $500 million for non-Nuclear, Chemical, Biological, or Radiological [NCBR] terrorist events in H.R. 4871).

INTRODUCTION

Prior to the September 2001 terrorist attacks on the United States, insurers generally did not exclude or separately charge for coverage of terrorism risks. The events of September 11, 2001, changed this as insurers realized the extent of possible terrorism losses. Estimates of insured losses from the 9/11 attacks are over $40 billion in current dollars, the largest insured losses from a non-natural disaster on record. These losses were concentrated in business interruption insurance (34% of the losses), property insurance (30%), and liability insurance (23%).[1]

Although primary insurance companies, those who actually sell and service the insurance policies bought by consumers, suffered losses from the terrorist attacks, the heaviest insured losses were absorbed by foreign and domestic reinsurers—the insurers of insurance companies. Because of the lack of public data on, or modeling of, the scope and nature of the terrorism risk, reinsurers felt unable to accurately price for such risks and largely withdrew from the market for terrorism risk insurance in the months following September 11, 2001. Once reinsurers stopped offering coverage for terrorism risk, primary insurers, suffering equally from a lack of public data and models, also withdrew, or tried to withdraw, from the market. In most states, state regulators must approve policy form changes. Most state regulators agreed to insurer requests to exclude terrorism risks from commercial policies, just as these policies had long excluded war risks. Terrorism risk insurance was soon unavailable or extremely expensive, and many businesses were no longer able to purchase insurance that would protect them in future terrorist attacks. Although the evidence is largely anecdotal, some were concerned that the lack of coverage posed a threat of serious harm to the real estate, transportation, construction, energy, and utility sectors, in turn threatening the broader economy.

In November 2002, Congress responded to the fears of economic damage due to the absence of commercially available coverage for terrorism with passage of the Terrorism Risk Insurance Act[2] (TRIA). TRIA created a three-year Terrorism Risk Insurance Program to provide a government reinsurance backstop in the case of terrorist attack. The TRIA program was amended and extended in 2005[3] and 2007.[4] Following the 2007 amendments, the TRIA program is set to expire at the end of 2014. (A side-by-side of the original law and the two reauthorization acts is in *Table 1*.)

The executive branch has been skeptical about the TRIA program in the past. Bills to expand TRIA were resisted by then-President George W. Bush's Administration,[5] and previous presidential budgets under President Obama called for changes in the program that would have had the effect of scaling back the TRIA coverage.[6] Congress declined to act on these budgetary proposals at the time and no such legislative proposals were contained in the President's FY2013 or FY2014 budget proposal. The FY2015 budget "proposes to extend the Terrorism Risk Insurance Program and to implement programmatic reforms to limit taxpayer exposure and achieve cost neutrality"[7] but does not detail what these reforms might be.

The insurance industry largely continues to support TRIA,[8] as do commercial insurance consumers in the real estate and other industries that have formed a "Coalition to Insure Against Terrorism" (CIAT).[9] Not all insurance consumers support renewal of TRIA, however, with the Consumer Federation of America questioning the need for the program.[10]

Although the April 2013 bombing in Boston was termed an "act of terror," by the President,[11] whether the bombing is considered as such under TRIA depends on a certification by the Secretary of the Treasury in conjunction with the Attorney General and the Secretary of State. Such certification has not been issued. The Massachusetts Department of Insurance has collected information on insured losses from the Boston bombing and the losses from TRIA covered lines of insurance appear to be under the $5 million threshold established in the act.[12] (See precise criteria under the TRIA program on page 6.)

TRIA IN THE 113TH CONGRESS

The Terrorism Risk Insurance Act of 2002 Reauthorization Act of 2013 (H.R. 508)

Representative Michael Grimm along with nine cosponsors introduced H.R. 508 on February 5, 2013. The bill is a reauthorization of the existing TRIA program that would extend the program five years, until the end of 2019. It would also extend the deadline for mandatory recoupment seven years, until September 30, 2024. The bill has been referred to the House Committee on Financial Services.

The Fostering Resilience to Terrorism Act of 2013 (H.R. 1945)

Representative Bennie Thompson along with one cosponsor introduced H.R. 1945 on May 9, 2013. The bill would extend the expiration date of the program 10 years, until the end of 2024, and would extend the deadline for mandatory recoupment seven years, until September 30, 2024. The Secretary of Homeland Security would be added as the lead authority responsible for certifying an act of terrorism and required to provide information and reports on terrorism risks and best practices to foster resilience in the face of terrorism. The Secretary of the Treasury would remain in the certification process but as a concurring party, not the lead authority, and the program in general would remain under the authority of the Treasury. H.R. 1945 has been referred to the House Committee on Financial Services and the House Committee on Homeland Security.

Terrorism Risk Insurance Program Reauthorization Act of 2013 (H.R. 2146)

Representative Michael Capuano along with 20 cosponsors introduced H.R. 2146 on May 23, 2013. The bill is a reauthorization of the existing TRIA program that would extend the program 10 years, until the end of 2024, as well as extend the deadline for mandatory recoupment 10 years, until September 30, 2027. In addition, the President's Working Group on Financial Markets is to continue filing reports on the market conditions, with reports required in 2017, 2020, and 2023. The bill has been referred to the House Committee on Financial Services.

Terrorism Risk Insurance Program Reauthorization Act of 2014 (S. 2244)[13]

Senator Charles Schumer along with eight cosponsors introduced S. 2244 on April 10, 2014. The bill would extend the current TRIA program seven years, until December 31, 2021, as well as decrease the federal loss sharing amount and increase the amount to be retained by the industry and recouped by the government. The Senate Committee on Banking, Housing, and Urban Affairs marked up S. 2244 on June 3, 2014, and ordered the amended bill favorably reported on a vote of 22-0.[14] The full Senate took up the bill on July 17, 2014, amending it and passing it on a vote of 93-4.

S. 2244 as passed by the Senate would decrease the federal loss sharing gradually from 85% to 80%. It would increase the insurance marketplace aggregate retention amount by $2 billion per year until it reaches $37.5 billion from the current $27.5 billion, extend the various dates for mandatory recoupment by seven years, and increase the amount to be recouped to 135.5% of federal payments compared with the current 133%. Treasury would be required to issue a study on improving the certification process and final rules governing the process. GAO would be required to issue a study on the viability of upfront premiums. S. 2244 as passed also would create an advisory committee on risk-sharing mechanisms. In addition to these provisions related to terrorism risk insurance, it also included a section relating to the membership of the Federal Reserve Board of Governors and a second title nearly identical to the text of the National Association of Registered Agents and Brokers Reform Act, which previously passed the full Senate as Title II of S. 1926 and the House of Representatives as H.R. 1155.[15]

TRIA Reform Act of 2014 (H.R. 4871)[16]

H.R. 4871 was introduced by Representative Randy Neugebauer and one cosponsor on June 17, 2014. The bill would extend the TRIA program five years while generally reducing the government's exposure to future TRIA losses, increasing post-event recoupment, and making several other changes to the program. Among the provisions are

- gradual reduction of federal share of losses from 85% to 80%;
- gradual increase in program trigger from $100 million to $500 million;
- increase in the maximum of the mandatory recoupment amount to the total of insurer deductibles under the program (currently approximately $36 billion) and removal of a provision that decreases mandatory recoupment in the case of very large attacks;
- increase to mandatory recoupment from 133% to 150% of the federal share of losses;
- separate treatment of Nuclear, Chemical, Biological, and Radiological (NCBR) terrorist attacks with lower trigger ($100 million) and higher federal loss sharing (85%).

The House Committee on Financial Services marked up H.R. 4871 beginning June 19, 2014, and ordered the bill favorably reported on June 20, 2014, by a vote of 32-27.[17] During the markup, a second title was added containing the text of the National Association of Registered Agents and Brokers Reform Act (H.R. 1155), which previously passed both the committee and the full House of Representatives.[18] The committee rejected a substitute amendment by Representative Maxine Waters, which would have replaced the text with a straightforward 10-year reauthorization of the current program, on a vote of 27-31.

Congressional Hearings

The House Committee on Financial Services and the Senate Committee on Banking, Housing, and Urban Affairs have held hearings on terrorism insurance, including the following:

- "Reauthorizing TRIA: The State of the Terrorism Risk Insurance Market, Part II," Senate Committee on Banking, Housing, and Urban Affairs, February 25, 2014.[19]
- "The Future of Terrorism Insurance: Fostering Private Market Innovation to Limit Taxpayer Exposure," House Financial Services' Subcommittee on Housing and Insurance, November 13, 2013.[20]
- "Reauthorizing TRIA: The State of the Terrorism Risk Insurance Market," Senate Committee on Banking, Housing, and Urban Affairs, September 25, 2013.[21]
- "The Terrorism Risk Insurance Act of 2002," House Committee on Financial Services, September 19, 2013.[22]

GOALS AND SPECIFICS OF THE CURRENT TRIA PROGRAM

The original TRIA legislation's stated goals were to (1) create a temporary federal program of shared public and private compensation for insured terrorism losses to allow the private market to stabilize; (2) protect consumers by ensuring the availability and affordability of insurance for terrorism risks; and (3) preserve state regulation of insurance. Although Congress has amended specific aspects of the original act, the general operation of the program largely follows the original statute. The changes to the program have largely reduced the government coverage for terrorism losses, except that the 2007 amendments expanded coverage to losses due to domestic terrorism, rather than limiting the program to foreign terrorism.

Federal Government Sharing of Terrorism Losses

To meet the *first* goal, the TRIA program creates a mechanism through which the federal government could share insured commercial property/casualty[23] losses with the private insurance market. The role of federal loss sharing depends on the size of the insured loss. For a relatively small loss, there is no federal sharing. For a medium-sized loss, the federal role is to spread the loss over time and over the entire insurance industry, providing assistance up front but then recouping the payments through a broad levy on insurance policies afterwards. For a large loss, the federal government is to pay most of the losses, although recoupment is possible in these circumstances as well.

The precise criteria under the current TRIA program are as follows:

1. An individual act of terrorism must be certified jointly by the Secretary of the Treasury, Secretary of State, and Attorney General; losses must exceed $5 million in the United States or to U.S. air carriers or sea vessels for an act of terrorism to be certified.
2. The federal government shares in an insurer's losses due to a certified act of terrorism only if "the aggregate industry insured losses resulting from such certified act of terrorism"[24] exceed $100 million.
3. The federal program covers only commercial property and casualty insurance, and excludes by statute several specific lines of insurance.[25]
4. Each insurer is responsible for paying out a certain amount in claims—known as its deductible—before receiving federal coverage. An insurer's deductible is proportionate to its size, equaling 20% of an insurer's annual direct earned premiums for the commercial property/casualty lines of insurance specified in TRIA.
5. Once the $100 million aggregate loss threshold and 20% deductible are passed, the federal government is to cover 85% of each insurer's losses above its deductible until the amount of losses totals $100 billion.
6. After $100 billion in aggregate losses, there is no federal government coverage and no requirement that insurers provide coverage.
7. In the years following the federal sharing of insurer losses, but prior to September 30, 2017, the Secretary of the Treasury is required to establish surcharges on

property/casualty insurance policies to recoup 133% of some or all of the outlays to insurers under the program. If losses are very high, the Secretary has the authority to assess surcharges, but is not required to do so. (See "Recoupment Provisions" below for more detail.)

Initial Loss Sharing

The initial loss sharing under TRIA can be seen in *Figure 1*, adapted from a report by the Congressional Budget Office (CBO). The exact amount of the 20% deductible at which TRIA coverage would begin depends on how the losses are distributed among insurance companies. In the aggregate, 20% of the direct-earned premiums for all of the property/casualty lines specified in TRIA totaled approximately $36 billion according to 2012 data supplied by the National Association of Insurance Commissioners (NAIC). TRIA coverage is likely, however, to begin under this amount as the losses from an attack are unlikely to be equally distributed among insurance companies.

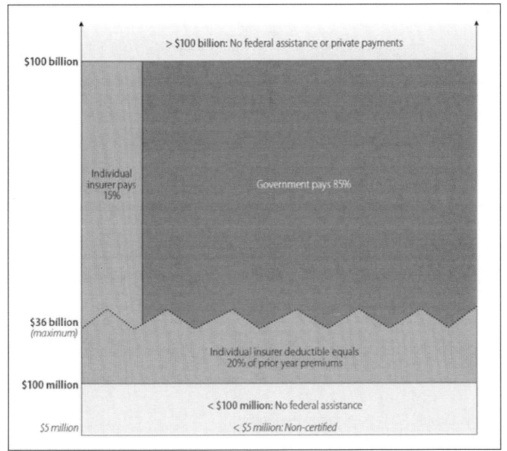

Source: Congressional Research Service, adapted from Congressional Budget Office, Federal Reinsurance for Terrorism Risks: Issues in Reauthorization, August 1, 2007, p. 12.

Note: Aggregate of all individual insurer deductibles totaled approximately $36 billion in 2012, according to the NAIC data and CRS calculations.

Figure 1. Initial Loss Sharing Under Current TRIA Program.

Recoupment Provisions

The precise amount to be recouped is determined by the interplay between a number of different factors in the law and in the insurance marketplace. The general result of the recoupment provisions is that, for attacks that result in under $27.5 billion[26] in insured losses, the Treasury Secretary is required to recoup 133% of the government outlays through surcharges on property/casualty insurance policies. For events with insured losses over $27.5 billion, the Secretary has discretionary authority to recoup all the government outlays and may be required to partially recoup the government outlays depending on the size of the attacks and the amount of uncompensated losses paid by the insurance industry. (See the Appendix for more information on exact recoupment calculations.) The mandatory recoupment is required to occur prior to the end of FY2017. Since the latest reauthorization was passed in 2007, this requirement resulted in all recoupment being completed within a 10-year timeframe. For an attack causing large insured loses, however, this requirement could result in high surcharges being applied for a relatively short time.

Program Administration

The administration of the TRIA program was originally left generally to the Secretary of the Treasury. This was changed somewhat in the Dodd-Frank Wall Street Reform and Consumer Protection Act of 2010.[27] The act created a new Federal Insurance Office (FIO) to be located in the Department of the Treasury. Among the duties specified for the FIO in the legislation was to assist the Secretary in the administration of the Terrorism Insurance Program.[28]

TRIA Consumer Protections

TRIA addresses the *second* goal, to protect consumers, by requiring those insurers that offer the lines of insurance covered by TRIA to make terrorism insurance available prospectively to their commercial policyholders. This coverage may not differ materially from coverage for other types of losses. Each terrorism insurance offer must reveal both the premium charged for terrorism insurance and the possible federal share of compensation. Policyholders are not, however, required to purchase coverage. If the policyholder declines to purchase terrorism coverage, its insurer can exclude terrorism losses. The law itself does not limit what insurers can charge for terrorism risk insurance, though state regulators typically have the authority under state law to modify excessive, inadequate, or unfairly discriminatory rates.

Preservation of State Insurance Regulation

TRIA's *third* goal, to preserve state regulation of insurance, is expressly accomplished in Section 106(a), which provides "Nothing in this title shall affect the jurisdiction or regulatory authority of the insurance commissioner [of a state]." The Section 106(a) provision has two exceptions: (1) the federal statute preempts any state definition of an "act of terrorism" in favor of the federal definition and (2) state rate and form approval laws for terrorism insurance were preempted from enactment to the end of 2003. In addition to these exceptions, Section 105 of the law also preempts state laws with respect to insurance policy exclusions for acts of terrorism.

COVERAGE FOR NUCLEAR, CHEMICAL, BIOLOGICAL, AND RADIOLOGICAL TERRORISM

A terrorist attack with some form of NCBR[29] weapon would often be considered the most likely type of attack causing large scale losses. The current TRIA statute does not specifically include or exclude NCBR events; thus, the TRIA program in general would cover insured losses from terrorist actions due to NCBR as it would for an attack by conventional means. The term *insured losses*, however, is a meaningful distinction. Except for workers compensation insurance, most insurance policies that would fall under the TRIA umbrella include exclusions that would likely limit insurer coverage of an NCBR event, whether it was due to terrorism or to some sort of accident, although these exclusions have never been legally tested in the United States after a terrorist event.[30] If these exclusions are invoked and do indeed limit the insurer losses due to NCBR terrorism, they would also limit the TRIA coverage of such losses. Language that would have specifically extended TRIA coverage to NCBR events was offered in the past,[31] but was not included in legislation as enacted. In 2007, the Government Accountability Office (GAO) was directed to study the issue and a GAO report was issued in 2008.[32] H.R. 4871 provides for higher federal cost sharing and a lower program trigger in the event of an NCBR attack, but does not specifically address NCBR exclusions. Other TRIA extension bills in the 113th Congress have not specifically addressed NCBR events.

BACKGROUND ON TERRORISM INSURANCE

Insurability of Terrorism Risk

Stripped to its most basic elements, insurance is a fairly straightforward operation. An insurer agrees to assume an indefinite future risk in exchange for a definite current premium from a consumer. The insurer pools a large number of risks such that at any given point in time, the ongoing losses will not be larger than the current premiums being paid, plus the residual amount of past premiums that the insurer retains and invests, plus, in a last resort, any borrowing against future profits if this is possible. For the insurer to operate successfully and avoid bankruptcy, it is critical to accurately estimate the probability of a loss and the severity of that loss so that a sufficient premium can be charged. Insurers generally depend upon huge databases of past loss information in setting these rates. Everyday occurrences, such as automobile accidents or natural deaths, can be estimated with great accuracy. Extraordinary events, such as large hurricanes, are more difficult, but insurers have many years of weather data, coupled with sophisticated computer models, with which to make predictions.

Terrorism risk is seen by many to be so fundamentally different from other risks, making it essentially uninsurable by the private insurance market and thus requiring a government solution. The argument that terrorism risk is uninsurable typically focuses on lack of public data about both the probability and severity of terrorist acts. The reason for the lack of historical data would generally be seen as a good thing—very few terrorist attacks are attempted and fewer have succeeded. This, however, does not assuage the fiduciary duty of an insurance company president not to put a company at risk by insuring against an event that could bankrupt the firm. As a replacement for large amounts of historical data, insurers turn to various forms of models similar to those used to assess future hurricane losses. Even the best model, however, can only partly replace good data, and terrorism models are still relatively new compared with hurricane models.

One prominent insurance textbook identifies four ideal elements of an insurable risk: (1) a sufficiently large number of insureds to make losses reasonably predictable; (2) losses must be definite and measurable; (3) losses must be fortuitous or accidental; and (4) losses must not be catastrophic (i.e., it must be unlikely to produce losses to a large percentage of the risks at the same time).[33] Terrorism risk in the United States would appear to fail the first criterion. It also likely fails the third due to the malevolent human actors behind terrorist attacks, whose motives, means, and targets of attack are constantly in flux. Whether it fails the fourth criterion is largely decided by the underwriting actions of insurers themselves (i.e., whether the insurers insure a large number of risks in a single geographic area that would be affected by a terrorist strike). Unsurprisingly, insurers generally have sought to limit their exposures in particular geographic locations with a conceptually higher risk for terrorist attacks, making terrorism insurance more difficult to find in those areas.

International Experience with Terrorism Risk Insurance[34]

Although the U.S. experience with terrorism is relatively limited, other countries have dealt with the issue more extensively and have developed their own responses to the challenges presented by terrorism risk. Spain, which has seen significant terrorist activity by Basque separatist movements, insures against acts of terrorism via a broader government-owned reinsurer that has provided coverage for catastrophes since 1954.

The United Kingdom, responding to the Irish Republican Army attacks in the 1980s, created Pool Re, a privately owned mutual insurance company with government backing, specifically to insure terrorism risk. In the aftermath of the September 11, 2001, attacks, many foreign countries reassessed their terrorism risk and created a variety of approaches to deal with the risk.

The UK greatly expanded Pool Re, whereas Germany created a private insurer with government backing to offer terrorism insurance policies. Germany's plan, like TRIA in the United States, was created as a temporary measure. It has been extended since its inception and is now set to expire at the end of 2015.[35] Not all countries, however, concluded that some sort of government backing for terrorism insurance was necessary. Canada specifically considered, and rejected, creating a government program following September 11, 2001.

Previous U.S. Experience with "Uninsurable" Risks

Terrorism risk post-2001 is not the first time the United States has faced a risk perceived as uninsurable in private markets that Congress chooses to address through government action. During World War II, for example, Congress created a "war damage" insurance program, and there are current programs insuring against aviation war risk[36] and flood losses,[37] respectively.

The closest previous analog to the situation with terrorism risk may be the federal riot reinsurance program created in the late 1960s. Following large scale riots in American cities in the late 1960s, insurers generally pulled back from insuring in those markets, either adding policy exclusions to limit their exposure to damage from riots or ceasing to sell property damage insurance altogether. In response, Congress created a riot reinsurance program as part of the Housing and Urban Development Act of 1968.[38] The federal riot reinsurance program offered reinsurance contracts similar to commercial excess reinsurance. The government agreed to cover some percentage of an insurance company's losses above a certain deductible in exchange for a premium paid by that insurance company. Private reinsurers eventually returned to the market, and the federal riot reinsurance program was terminated in 1985.

THE TERRORISM INSURANCE MARKET

Post-9/11 and Pre-TRIA

The September 2001 terrorist attacks, and the resulting billions of dollars in insured losses, caused significant upheaval in the insurance market. Even before the attacks, the insurance market was showing signs of a cyclical "hardening" of the market in which prices typically rise and availability is somewhat limited. The unexpectedly large losses caused by terrorist acts exacerbated this trend, especially with respect to the commercial lines of insurance most at risk for terrorism losses. Post-September 11, insurers and reinsurers started including substantial surcharges for terrorism risk, or, more commonly, they excluded coverage for terrorist attacks altogether. Reinsurers could take these steps rapidly because reinsurance contracts and rates are generally unregulated. Primary insurance contracts and rates are more closely regulated by the individual states, and the exclusion of terrorism coverage for the individual purchaser of insurance required regulatory approval at the state level in most cases. States acted fairly quickly, and, by early 2002, 45 states had approved insurance policy language prepared by the Insurance Services Office, Inc. (ISO, an insurance consulting firm), excluding terrorism damage in standard commercial policies.[39]

The lack of readily available terrorism insurance caused fears of a larger economic impact, particularly on the real estate market. In most cases, lenders prefer or require that a borrower maintain insurance coverage on a property. Lack of terrorism insurance coverage could lead to defaults on existing loans and a downturn in future lending, causing economic ripple effects as buildings are not built and construction workers remain idle.

The 14-month period after the September 2001 terrorist attacks and before the November 2002 passage of TRIA provides some insight into the effects of a lack of terrorism insurance. Some examples in September 2002 include the Real Estate Round Table releasing a survey finding that "$15.5 billion of real estate projects in 17 states were stalled or cancelled because of a continuing scarcity of terrorism insurance"[40] and Moody's Investors Service downgrading $4.5 billion in commercial mortgage-backed securities.[41] This picture, however, was not uniform. For example, in July 2002, *The Wall Street Journal* reported that "despite concerns over landlords' ability to get terrorism insurance, trophy properties were in demand."[42] The Congressional Budget Office concluded in 2005 that "[TRIA] appears to have had little measurable effect on office construction, employment in the construction industry, or the volume of commercial construction loans made by large commercial banks," but CBO also notes that variety of economic factors at the time "could be masking positive macroeconomic effects of TRIA."[43]

After TRIA

The "make available" provisions of TRIA addressed the availability problem in the terrorism insurance market, as insurers were required by law to offer commercial terrorism coverage. There was significant uncertainty, however, as to how businesses would react, because there was no general requirement to purchase terrorism coverage[44] and the pricing of terrorism coverage was initially high. Initial consumer reaction to the terrorism coverage offers was relatively subdued. Marsh, Inc., a large insurance broker, reports that only 27% of their clients bought terrorism insurance in 2003. This take-up rate, however, climbed relatively quickly to 49% in 2004 and 58% in 2005. Since 2005, the take-up rate has remained near 60%, with Marsh reporting 62% in 2012.[45]

The price for terrorism insurance has appeared to decline over the past decade, although available pricing data are based on surveys; thus, the level of pricing may not always be comparable between sources. The 2014 report by the President's Working Group on Financial Markets shows a high of above 7% for the median terrorism premium as a percentage of the total property premium in 2003, with a generally downward trend, and the latest values around 3%.[46] These values were reported by Aon, another major insurance broker. While the trend may be downward, there has been variability, particularly across industries. For example, Marsh reported rates in 2009 as high as 24% of the property premium for financial institutions and as low as 2% in the food and beverage industry.[47] This variability dropped in the report by Marsh as the rates for 2012 vary from 7% in the transportation industry and the hospitality and gaming industry to 1% in the energy and mining industry.[48]

The willingness of insurers to cover terrorism risk, as well as their financial capability to do so, has increased over the past decade. From the late 2001 and 2002 marketplace, where terrorism coverage was essentially unavailable, recent estimates from the insurance broker Guy Carpenter are that between $6 billion and $8 billion in terrorism reinsurance capacity is available in the U.S. market.[49] The combined policyholder surplus among all U.S. property/casualty insurers was $674.0 billion at the end of 2013, up from $293.5 billion at the start of 2002.[50] This amount, however, backs all policies in the United States and is subject to depletion in a wide variety of events. Extreme weather losses could particularly draw capital away from the terrorism insurance market, as such weather events share some risk characteristics with large terrorist attacks.

EVOLUTION OF TERRORISM RISK INSURANCE LAWS

Table 1 presents a side-by-side comparison of the original TRIA law, along with the reauthorizing laws of 2005 and 2007.

Table 1. Side-by-Side of Terrorism Risk Insurance Laws

Provision	15 U.S.C. 6701 Note (P.L. 107-297)	P.L. 109-144	P.L. 110-160
Title	Terrorism Risk Insurance Act of 2002	Terrorism Risk Insurance Extension Act of 2005	Terrorism Risk Insurance Program Reauthorization Act of 2007
Expiration Date	December 31, 2005 (§108(a))	December 31, 2007 (§2)	December 31, 2014 (§3(a))
"Act of Terrorism" Definition	For an act of terrorism to be covered under TRIA, it must be a violent act committed on behalf of a foreign person or interest as part of an effort to coerce the U.S. civilian population or influence U.S. government policy. It must have resulted in damage within the United States or to a U.S. airliner or mission abroad. Terrorist act is to be certified by the Secretary of the Treasury in concurrence with the Attorney General and Secretary of State. (§102(1)(A))	No Change	Removed requirement that a covered act of terrorism be committed on behalf of a foreign person or interest. (§2)
Limitation on Act of Terrorism Certification in Case of War	Terrorist act would not be covered in the event of a war, except for workers compensation insurance. (§102(1)(B)(I))	No Change	No Change
Minimum Damage To Be Certified	Terrorist act must cause more than $5 million in property and casualty insurance losses to be certified. (§102(1)(B)(ii))	No Change	No Change
Aggregate Industry Loss Requirement/Program Trigger	No Provision	Created a "program trigger" that would prevent coverage under the program unless "aggregate industry losses resulting from such certified act of terrorism" exceed $50 million in 2006 and $100	No Change. Program trigger remains at $100 million until 2014. (§3(c))

Table 1. (Continued)

Provision	15 U.S.C. 6701 Note (P.L. 107-297)	P.L. 109-144	P.L. 110-160
		million for 2007. (§6)	
Insurer Deductible	7% of earned premium for 2003, 10% of earned premium for 2004, 15% of earned premium for 2005. (§102(7))	Raised deductible to 17.5% for 2006 and 20% for 2007. (§3)	No Change. Deductible remains at 20% until 2014. (§3(c))
Covered Lines of Insurance	Commercial property/casualty insurance, including excess insurance, workers' compensation, and surety but excluding crop insurance, private mortgage insurance, title insurance, financial guaranty insurance, medical malpractice insurance, health or life insurance, flood insurance, or reinsurance. (§102(12))	Excluded commercial auto, burglary and theft, professional liability (except for directors and officers liability), and farm owners multiple peril from coverage. (§3)	No change from P.L. 109-144
Mandatory Availability	Every insurer must make terrorism coverage that does not differ materially from coverage applicable to losses other than terrorism. (§103(c))	No Change. Mandatory availability extended through 2007. (§2(b))	No Change. Mandatory availability extended through 2014. (§3(c))
Insured Loss Shared Compensation	Federal share of losses will be 90% for insured losses that exceed the applicable insurer deductible. (§103(e))	Reduced federal share of losses to 85% for 2007. (§4)	No Change. Federal share remains at 85% through 2014.
Cap on Annual Liability	Federal share of compensation paid under the program will not exceed $100 billion and insurers are not liable for any portion of losses that exceed $100 billion unless Congress acts otherwise to cover these losses. (§103(e))	No Change	Removed the possibility that a future Congress could require insurers to cover some share of losses above $100 billion if the insurer has met its individual deductible. Requires insurers to clearly disclose this to policy holders. (§4(a) and §4(d))
Payment Procedures if Losses Exceed $100,000,000,000	After notice by the Secretary of the Treasury, Congress determines the procedures for payments if losses exceed $100 billion. (§103(e)(3))	No Change	Required Secretary of the Treasury to publish regulations within 240 days of passage regarding payments if losses exceed $100 billion. (§4(c))
Aggregate Retention Amount Maximum	$10 billion for 2002-2003, $12.5 billion for 2004, $15 billion for 2005 (§103(6))	Raises amount to $25 billion for 2006 and $27.5 billion for 2007.	No Change. Aggregate retention remains at $27.5 billion through

Provision	15 U.S.C. 6701 Note (P.L. 107-297)	P.L. 109-144	P.L. 110-160
		(§5)	2014.
Mandatory Recoupment of Federal Share	If insurer losses are under the aggregate retention amount, a mandatory recoupment of the federal share of the loss will be imposed. If insurer losses are over the aggregate retention amount, such recoupment is at the discretion of the Secretary of the Treasury. (§103(e)(7))	No Change	Increases total recoupment amount to be collected by the premium surcharges to 133% of the previously defined mandatory recoupment amount. (§4(e)(1)(A))
Recoupment Surcharge	Surcharge is limited to 3% of property-casualty insurance premium and may be adjusted by the Secretary to take into account the economic impact of the surcharge on urban commercial centers, the differential risk factors related to rural areas and smaller commercial centers, and the various exposures to terrorism risk across lines of insurance. (§103(e)(8))	No Change	Removes 3% limit for mandatory surcharge. (§4(e)(2)(A))

Source: The Congressional Research Service using public laws obtained from the Government Printing Office through http://www.congress.gov.

Notes: Section numbers for the initial TRIA law are as codified in 15 U.S.C. §6701 note. Section numbers for P.L. 109-144 and P.L. 110-160 are from the legislation as enacted.

APPENDIX. CALCULATION OF TRIA RECOUPMENT AMOUNTS

Table A-1 contains illustrative examples of how the recoupment for the government portion of terrorism losses under TRIA might be calculated in the aggregate for various sizes of losses. The amount of the deductible in the chart is simply assumed to be 30% of the insured losses for illustrative purposes. Without knowing the actual distribution of losses due to a terrorist attack, it is impossible to know what the actual deductible will be. The conclusions of the chart with regard to recoupment, however, hold across different actual deductible amounts.

The specific provisions of the law define the "insurance marketplace aggregate retention amount" (Column F) as the lesser of $27.5 billion or the total amount of insured losses (Column A). The "mandatory recoupment amount" (Column G) is defined as the difference between $27.5 billion and the aggregate insurer losses that were not compensated for by the program (i.e., the total of the insurers' deductible (Column B) and their 15% loss share

(Column C)). If the aggregate insured loss is less than $27.5 billion, the law requires recoupment of 133% of the government outlays (Column H). For insured losses over $27.5 billion, the mandatory recoupment amount decreases, thus the Secretary would be required to recoup less than 133% of the outlays. Depending on the precise deductible amounts, the uncompensated industry losses (Column D) may eventually rise to be greater than $27.5 billion, which would then mean that the mandatory recoupment provisions would not apply. The Secretary would still retain discretionary authority to apply recoupment surcharges no matter what level uncompensated losses reached.

Table A-1. Example of TRIA Recoupment Calculations
($ billions)

Column A	Column B	Column C	Column D	Column E	Column F	Column G	Column H
Theoretical Insured Losses	Theoretical Insurer Deductible	Insurer 15% share of Insured Losses (0.15x(A-B))	Insurance Industry Un-compen-sated losses (B+C)	Government 85% share of Insured Losses (0.85x(A-B))	Aggregate Retention Amount (A or $27.5)	Mandatory Recoupment Amount (F-D)	Amount Required to be Recouped (Gx1.33)
$0.1	$0.03	$0.01	$0.04	$0.06	$0.1	$0.06	$0.08
$0.5	$0.15	$0.05	$0.2	$0.3	$0.5	$0.3	$0.4
$1.0	$0.3	$0.1	$0.4	$0.6	$1.0	$0.6	$0.8
$5.0	$1.5	$0.5	$2.0	$3.0	$5.0	$3.0	$4.0
$10.0	$3.0	$1.1	$4.1	$6.0	$10.0	$6.0	$7.9
$20.0	$6.0	$2.1	$8.1	$11.9	$20.0	$11.9	$15.8
$27.5	$8.3	$2.9	$11.1	$16.4	$27.5	$16.4	$21.8
$30.0	$9.0	$3.2	$12.2	$17.9	$27.5	$15.4	$20.4
$50.0	$15.0	$5.3	$20.3	$29.8	$27.5	$7.3	$9.6
$75.0	$22.5	$7.9	$30.4	$44.6	$27.5	$0	$0
$100.0	$30.0	$10.5	$40.5	$59.5	$27.5	$0	$0

Source: U.S. Treasury, TRIA statute as amended; calculations by CRS.

Notes: Totals may not sum due to rounding. For illustrative purposes, the deductible size set at 30% of the insured loss size; actual deductible will vary depending on the distribution of events.

End Notes

[1] Insurance Information Institute, Terrorism Risk: A Constant Threat, March 2014, available at http://www.iii.org/assets/docs/pdf/terrorism_white_paper_0320141.pdf.

[2] P.L. 107-297; 116 Stat. 2322, codified at 15 U.S.C. §6701 note. For more information, see CRS Report RS21444, The Terrorism Risk Insurance Act of 2002: A Summary of Provisions, by Baird Webel.

[3] P.L. 109-144; 119 Stat. 2660. For more information, see CRS Report RL33177, Terrorism Risk Insurance Legislation in 2005: Issue Summary and Side-by-Side, by Baird Webel.

[4] P.L. 110-160; 121 Stat 1839. For more information, see CRS Report RL34219, Terrorism Risk Insurance Legislation in 2007: Issue Summary and Side-by-Side, by Baird Webel.

[5] See, for example, the Statement of Administration Policy on H.R. 2761 dated December 11, 2007, available at http://www.whitehouse.gov/sites/default/files/omb/legislative/sap/110-1/hr2761sap-h.pdf.

[6] See, for example, Office of Management and Budget, Analytical Perspectives, Budget of the United States, Fiscal Year 2011, p. 184, http://www.gpo.gov/fdsys/pkg/BUDGET-2011-PER/pdf/BUDGET-2011-PER.pdf.

[7] U.S. Department of the Treasury, FY2015 Congressional Justification, Departmental Summary, p. 5, available at http://www.treasury.gov/about/budget-performance/CJ15/00.%20FY%202015%20Exec%20Summary%20for%20CJ.pdf.

[8] See, for example, American Insurance Association, "AIA Statement On Introduction Of TRIA Legislation," press release, February 5, 2013, http://www.aiadc.org/aiadotnet/docHandler.aspx?DocID=355930.

[9] See the CIAT website at http://www.insureagainstterrorism.org.

[10] Consumer Federation of America, "Growing Insurer Surplus Calls into Question Industry Need for Congressional Renewal of Terrorism Insurance," May 8, 2013, available at http://consumerfed.org/news/666.

[11] The White House, "Statement by the President," press release, April 16, 2013, http://www.whitehouse.gov/the-pressoffice/2013/04/16/statement-president.

[12] According to information provided by the Massachusetts Department of Insurance to the Congressional Research Service (CRS), the incurred losses on TRIA-eligible lines of insurance totaled approximately $2.6 million as of August 2013, with $1.2 million of this having been paid out. Estimated health insurance losses totaled more than $20 million; health insurance, however, is not covered under TRIA.

[13] For more detail on S. 2244 and other legislation see CRS Report R43619, Terrorism Risk Insurance Legislation: Issue Summary and Side-by-Side Analysis, by Baird Webel.

[14] The written report (S.Rept. 113-199) was filed on June 26, 2014.

[15] For more information see CRS Report R43095, Insurance Agent Licensing: Overview and Background on Federal "NARAB" Legislation, by Baird Webel.

[16] For more detail on H.R. 2871 and other legislation see CRS Report R43619, Terrorism Risk Insurance Legislation: Issue Summary and Side-by-Side Analysis, by Baird Webel.

[17] H.Rept. 113-523 was filed on July 16, 2014.

[18] For more information see CRS Report R43095, Insurance Agent Licensing: Overview and Background on Federal "NARAB" Legislation, by Baird Webel.

[19] See http://www.banking.

[20] See http://financialservices.house.gov/calendar/eventsingle.aspx?EventID=360497.

[21] See http://www.banking 425a-89dd-793fcb049190.

[22] See http://financialservices.house.gov/calendar/eventsingle.aspx?EventID=349518.

[23] Commercial insurance is generally insurance purchased by businesses in contrast to personal lines of insurance, which is purchased by individuals. This means damage to individual homes and autos would not be covered under the TRIA program. Property/casualty insurance includes most lines of insurance except for life insurance and health insurance.

[24] 15 U.S.C. §6701 note, Section 103(e)(1)(B).

[25] Named lines of insurance that are not covered are federal crop insurance, private crop or livestock insurance, private mortgage insurance, title insurance, financial guaranty insurance of single-line guaranty insurers, medical malpractice, flood insurance, reinsurance, and all life insurance products.

[26] This $27.5 billion figure is the current one and has been in effect since 2007. At the beginning of the TRIA program, this started at $10 billion and increased over time.

[27] P.L. 111-203, 124 Stat. 1376.

[28] Section 502 of P.L. 111-203, codified at 31 U.S.C. §313(c)(1)(D).

[29] There is some variance in the acronym used for such attacks. The U.S. Department of Defense, for example, uses "CBRN," rather than NCBR, in its Dictionary of Military and Associated Terms; see p. 86 at http://www.scribd.com/doc/25603718/The-DOD-Lexicon-JP1-02.

[30] It should be noted that insurers might have attempted to exclude the September 11, 2001, losses under existing war risk exclusions, but did not generally attempt to do so.

[31] See, for example, H.R. 2761 (110th Congress) as passed by the House on September 19, 2007, and H.Rept. 110-318, available at http://www.gpo.gov/fdsys/pkg/CRPT-110hrpt318/pdf/CRPT-110hrpt318.pdf.

[32] U.S. Government Accountability Office, TERRORISM INSURANCE: Status of Coverage Availability for Attacks Involving Nuclear, Biological, Chemical, or Radiological Weapons, GAO-09-39, December 12, 2008, at http://gao.gov/products/GAO-09-39.

[33] Emmett J. Vaughan and Therese Vaughan, Fundamentals of Risk and Insurance (Hoboken, NJ: John Wiley & Sons, 2003), p. 41.

[34] More information on foreign countries' programs can be found in pages 8-11 of the testimony of Erwann O. MichelKerjan before the U.S. Congress, House Committee on Financial Services, Subcommittee on Insurance, Housing and Community Opportunity, TRIA at Ten Years: The Future of the Terrorism Risk Insurance Program, 112th Cong., 2nd sess., September 11, 2012. See http://financialservices.house.gov/uploadedfiles/hhrg-112-ba04-wstate-emichelkerjan20120911.pdf.

[35] Extremus Versicherungs AG, "Verlaengerung der Staatshaftung fuer Terroranschlaege," press release, undated; available at http://www.extremus.de/index.php/aktuelles/pressemeldungen.

[36] For more information, see http://www.faa.gov/about/office_org/headquarters_offices/apl/aviation_insurance/.

[37] For more information, see CRS Report R40650, *National Flood Insurance Program: Background, Challenges, and Financial Status*, by Rawle O. King.

[38] P.L. 90-448; 82 Stat. 476. The act also created state "Fair Access to Insurance Requirements" (FAIR) plans and a Federal Crime Insurance Program.

[39] Jeff Woodward, "The ISO Terrorism Exclusions: Background and Analysis," *IRMI Insights*, February 2002, available at http://www.irmi.com/expert/articles/2002/woodward02.aspx.

[40] "Terror Insurance Drag on Real Estate Still Climbing," *Real Estate Roundtable*, September 19, 2003, available at http://www.rer.org/media/newsreleases/TRIA_Survey_15billion_Sept19_2002.cfm.

[41] "Moody's Downgrades Securities on Lack of Terrorism Insurance," *Wall Street Journal*, September 30, 2002, p. C14.

[42] "Office-Building Demand Rises Despite Vacancies," *Wall Street Journal*, July 24, 2002, p. B6.

[43] Congressional Budget Office, *Federal Terrorism Reinsurance: An Update*, January 2005, pp. 10-11, available at http://www.cbo.gov/publication/16210.

[44] Although there is no requirement in federal law to purchase terrorism coverage, businesses may be required by state law to purchase the coverage. This is particularly the case in workers compensation insurance. Market forces, such as requirements for commercial loans, may also compel purchase of terrorism coverage.

[45] Marsh, Inc., 2013 Terrorism Risk Insurance Report, May 2013, p. 9.

[46] President's Working Group on Financial Markets, *The Long-Term Availability and Affordability of Insurance for Terrorism Risk*, April 2014, p. 26.

[47] Marsh, Inc., The Marsh Report: Terrorism Risk Insurance 2010, p. 14.

[48] Marsh, Inc., 2013 Terrorism Risk Insurance Report, May 2013, p. 12.

[49] Testimony of Edward B. Ryan, Aon Benfield, before the U.S. Congress, House Committee on Financial Services, Subcommittee on Insurance, Housing and Community Opportunity, *TRIA at Ten Years: The Future of the Terrorism Risk Insurance Program*, 112th Cong., 2nd sess., September 11, 2012. See http://financialservices.house.gov/ uploadedfiles/hhrg-112-ba04-wstate-eryan-20120911.pdf, p. 3.

[50] AM Best, Best's Aggregates & Averages, Property-Casualty, 2002 Edition, p. 2 and AM Best Statistical Study, "U.S. Property/Casualty—2013 Financial Results," March 24, 2014, p. 1.

In: Terrorism Risk Insurance Act
Editor: Ernie L. Duke

ISBN: 978-1-63463-128-0
© 2014 Nova Science Publishers, Inc.

Chapter 2

TERRORISM INSURANCE: TREASURY NEEDS TO COLLECT AND ANALYZE DATA TO BETTER UNDERSTAND FISCAL EXPOSURE AND CLARIFY GUIDANCE[*]

United States Government Accountability Office

WHY GAO DID THIS STUDY

Congress passed TRIA in 2002 to help ensure the availability and affordability of terrorism insurance for commercial property and casualty policyholders after the September 11, 2001, terrorist attacks. TRIA was amended and extended twice and currently will expire at the end of 2014. Under TRIA, Treasury administers a program in which the federal government and private sector share losses on commercial property and casualty policies resulting from a terrorist attack. Because the federal government will cover a portion of insured losses, the program creates fiscal exposures for the government. GAO was asked to review TRIA.

This report evaluates (1) the extent of available data on terrorism insurance and Treasury's efforts in determining federal exposure, (2) changes in the terrorism insurance market since 2002, and (3) potential impacts of selected changes to TRIA. To address these objectives, GAO analyzed insurance data, information from 15 insurers selected primarily based on size of insurer, interviewed Treasury staff and industry participants, updated prior work, and developed examples to illustrate potential fiscal exposure under TRIA.

---

[*] This is an edited, reformatted and augmented version of the United States Government Accountability Office publication, GAO-14-445, dated May 2014.

WHAT GAO RECOMMENDS

Treasury should collect and analyze data on the terrorism insurance market to assess the market, estimate fiscal exposure under different scenarios, and analyze the impacts of changing program parameters. Treasury agreed with these recommendations.

WHAT GAO FOUND

Comprehensive data on the terrorism insurance market are not readily available and Department of the Treasury (Treasury) analysis to better understand federal fiscal exposure under various scenarios of terrorist attacks has been limited. Treasury compiled some market data from industry sources, but the data are not comprehensive. Federal internal control standards state that agencies should obtain needed data and analyze risks, and industry best practices indicate that analysis of the location and amount of coverage helps understand financial risks. However, without more data and analysis, Treasury lacks the information needed to help ensure the goals of the Terrorism Risk Insurance Act (TRIA) of ensuring the availability and affordability of terrorism risk insurance and addressing market disruptions are being met and to better understand potential federal spending under different scenarios.

Available data show that terrorism insurance premiums and other market indicators are stable. For example, estimated terrorism insurance premiums have been relatively constant since 2010. Insurers told GAO that, in 2012, terrorism insurance premiums made up on average less than 2 percent of commercial property and casualty premiums. According to industry participants, prices for terrorism coverage have declined, the percentage of businesses buying coverage seems to have leveled recently, and insurers' ability to provide it has remained constant.

Insurers and other industry participants cited concerns about the availability and price of terrorism coverage if TRIA expired or was changed substantially, but some changes could reduce federal fiscal exposure. Some insurers GAO contacted said they would stop covering terrorism if TRIA expired. Changes such as increasing the deductible or threshold for required recoupment of the government's share of losses through surcharges on all commercial policyholders could reduce federal fiscal exposure. Most insurers GAO contacted expressed concerns about solvency and ability to provide coverage if their deductible or share of losses increased. Insurers were less concerned about increases to the thresholds for government coverage to begin or to the required recoupment of the government's share of losses.

ABBREVIATIONS

ISO	Insurance Services Office, Inc.
NAIC	National Association of Insurance Commissioners
NBCR	nuclear, biological, chemical, or radiological weapons
PWG	President's Working Group on Financial Markets
TRIA	Terrorism Risk Insurance Act

May 22, 2014

The Honorable Randy Neugebauer
Chairman
Subcommittee on Housing and Insurance
Committee on Financial Services
House of Representatives

The Honorable Ed Royce
Chairman
Committee on Foreign Affairs
House of Representatives

The terrorist attacks of September 11, 2001, which resulted in reported total insured losses of roughly $43 billion (2013 dollars), drastically changed the way insurers viewed the risk of terrorism.[1] Insurers must be able to predict the frequency and severity of insured losses with some reliability to best manage financial risk. Unpredictable and infrequent events, such as terrorist attacks, can cause severe losses that substantially deplete insurers' capital. If a company determines that the risk of loss is unacceptably high relative to the premiums it can charge, the company may cease offering coverage. This was the case after September 11, 2001, when insurers generally stopped covering terrorism risk.

In November 2002, Congress enacted the Terrorism Risk Insurance Act of 2002 (TRIA) to help ensure the continued availability and affordability of commercial property and casualty insurance for terrorism risk and address concerns that the lack of terrorism insurance could have significant effects on the economy.[2] TRIA requires the Department of the Treasury (Treasury) to administer a program in which the government would share some of the losses with private insurers in the event of a certified act of terrorism.[3] In addition to requiring insurers to make terrorism coverage available to commercial policyholders, the program creates a public-private loss-sharing mechanism—through which private insurers pay deductibles and copayments (or coshares) in the event of a terrorist attack and the government shares a portion of the losses.[4] The amount of government loss sharing depends on the size of the insured loss. The program was intended to be temporary (3 years), but was extended and modified twice—in 2005 and 2007—and expires on December 31, 2014. As of May 2014, no certified acts of terrorism had occurred to trigger the program. As a result, the program has not received any claims from insurers and made no payments.

Recently, policymakers and insurance industry experts have debated the role of the federal government in supporting insurance coverage for acts of terrorism. Some have raised questions about whether the program hinders the development of the private market and continues to expose the government (and thus taxpayers) to insurance losses on private property. Others in the insurance sector have stated that insurers would be unwilling to cover terrorism risk without the government program in place. In addition, some have indicated that because of recoupment the program was designed to be budget neutral under most circumstances (with the exception of very high insured losses that may result from a large-scale attack). Finally, recent congressional hearings focused on possible changes to the current program and debated the appropriate time frame of any potential reauthorization.

You asked us to review the program and market for terrorism risk insurance. This report (1) evaluates the extent of available data and Treasury's efforts in determining the government's exposure, (2) describes changes in the terrorism insurance market since 2002, and (3) evaluates potential impacts of selected changes to TRIA.

To address these objectives, we obtained information and interviewed representatives from Treasury and the National Association of Insurance Commissioners (NAIC).[5] We reviewed applicable laws, regulations, and information about loss sharing created by the program and any corresponding government recoupment. Additionally, we obtained and reviewed available data on premiums, capacity, pricing, and take-up rates (the percentage of businesses buying terrorism coverage) from 2003 through 2013 from insurance brokers Marsh and McLennan Companies, Inc. (Marsh) and Aon plc, the largest insurance brokers in the United States, and A.M. Best, an insurance rating agency. We interviewed representatives from Marsh, Aon, and A.M. Best about their data collection methods and reviewed related documentation to help ensure we had a clear understanding of their data and any limitations. The data from these sources, although not containing information from all insurers that provide terrorism coverage, capture a large portion of this segment of the insurance market. We found the data from these sources are the best available and are sufficiently reliable for our purposes.

We also obtained information as part of a questionnaire we sent to 15 insurance companies (insurers), all of which had businesses purchase terrorism coverage from them in 2012. The 15 companies are not representative of the entire market, but represented a major portion— roughly 40 percent of the commercial property and casualty market by direct earned premium volume for 2012, according to SNL Financial data.[6] Through the questionnaire and follow-up interviews, we obtained proprietary data from the insurers about their terrorism coverage, premium volume, and underwriting decisions. Additionally, we obtained their views on potential modifications to TRIA and how any modifications would affect the market. For the purposes of this report, we aggregated and summarized responses from these insurers. Their responses may or may not be representative of all insurers in the property and casualty market, but their experiences and views offer insights directly into this group of insurers. We also interviewed industry participants about terrorism insurance, such as representatives from insurance trade associations, terrorism risk modeling firms, rating agencies, and insurance brokers.[7] Finally, we developed illustrative examples to help demonstrate estimated changes in the magnitude of fiscal exposure under different, hypothetical parameters for the terrorism risk insurance program. To develop these examples, we consulted with experts from terrorism risk modeling firms, reviewed relevant literature, and made several assumptions. The illustrative examples are not specific determinations of federal fiscal exposure under TRIA. Appendix I of this report contains more detailed information about our objectives, scope, and methodology.

We conducted this performance audit from July 2013 to May 2014 in accordance with generally accepted government auditing standards. Those standards require that we plan and perform the audit to obtain sufficient, appropriate evidence to provide a reasonable basis for our findings and conclusions based on our audit objectives. We believe that the evidence obtained provides a reasonable basis for our findings and conclusions based on our audit objectives.

BACKGROUND

From an insurance standpoint, measuring and predicting terrorism risk is challenging. According to standard insurance theory, four major principles contribute to the ability of insurers to estimate and cover future losses: the law of large numbers, measurability, fortuity, and the size of the potential losses.[8] When determining whether to offer coverage for a particular risk and at what price, insurers evaluate whether sufficient information exists about each of these principles. To underwrite insurance—that is, decide whether to offer coverage and what price to charge—insurers consider both the likelihood of an event (frequency) and the amount of damage it would cause (severity). As we have reported, measuring and predicting losses associated with terrorism risks can be particularly challenging for reasons including lack of experience with similar attacks, difficulty in predicting terrorists' intentions, and the potentially catastrophic losses that could result from terrorist attacks.[9] Increasingly, insurers use sophisticated modeling tools to assess terrorism risk, but there have been very few terrorist attacks, so there are little data on which to base estimates of future losses, in terms of frequency or severity, or both.[10]

When Congress passed TRIA in 2002, its purposes included making terrorism insurance widely available and affordable for businesses. As required by TRIA, insurers must make terrorism coverage available to commercial policyholders, although commercial policyholders are not required to buy it. As shown in table 1, many lines of commercial property and casualty insurance are eligible for TRIA, but the legislation specifically excludes certain lines. For example, the law excludes personal property and casualty insurance, as well as health and life insurance.

TRIA requires an insurer to make terrorism coverage available to its policyholders for insured losses that does not differ materially from the terms, amounts, and other coverage limitations applicable to losses arising from events other than acts of terrorism. For example, an insurer offering $100 million in commercial property coverage must offer $100 million in coverage for property damage from a certified terrorist attack. Insurers can charge a separate premium to cover terrorism risk, although some include the price in their base rates for all-risk policies.[11]

Public-Private Loss Sharing under TRIA

Under the current program, Treasury would reimburse insurers for a share of losses associated with certain certified acts of foreign or domestic terrorism. A single terrorist act must cause at least $5 million in insured losses to be certified; separately, the aggregate industry insured loss from certified acts must be at least $100 million for government coverage to begin (program trigger). If an event were to be certified as an act of terrorism and the insured losses exceed the program trigger, then an individual insurer that experienced losses would pay a deductible of 20 percent of its previous year's direct earned premiums in TRIA-eligible lines (insurer deductible). After the insurer pays its deductible, the federal government would reimburse the insurer for 85 percent of its losses and the insurer would be responsible for the remaining 15 percent (coshare). Annual coverage for losses is limited—

aggregate industry insured losses in excess of $100 billion are not covered by private insurers or the federal government (cap). See figure 1 for an illustration of these program parameters.

The amount of federal loss-sharing varies with the amount of industry insured losses, as the following shows:

- In general, for an event with insured losses of less than $100 million, private industry covers the entire loss and the federal government faces no responsibility to cover losses.
- In general, for an event with insured losses from $100 million to $100 billion private industry and the federal government initially share the losses, but TRIA includes a provision for mandatory recoupment of the federal share of losses when private industry's uncompensated insured losses are less than $27.5 billion. Treasury must impose policyholder premium surcharges on all property and casualty insurance policies until total industry payments reached the mandatory recoupment amount or the government is fully repaid, whichever comes first.[12] The mandatory recoupment amount is the difference between $27.5 billion and the aggregate amount of insurers' uncompensated insured losses. This industry aggregate retention amount was set in the 2005 reauthorization for the year 2007 at $27.5 billion and extended as applicable for all future years under the program by the 2007 reauthorization.[13] When the amount of federal assistance exceeds any mandatory recoupment amount, TRIA also allows for discretionary recoupment, if Treasury determines additional amounts should be recouped. Under TRIA, any discretionary recoupment would be based on the ultimate cost to taxpayers, the economic conditions in the marketplace, the affordability of insurance for small and medium-sized businesses, and any other factors Treasury considered appropriate.

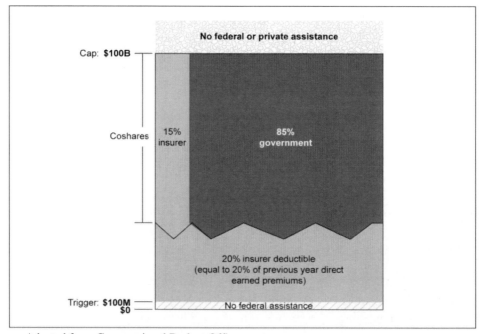

Source: Adapted from Congressional Budget Office.

Note: The insurer deductible is a jagged line because only those insurers that experience losses would pay a deductible and as a result, the amount would vary depending on the number of affected insurers.

Figure 1. Initial Loss-Sharing under the Terrorism Risk Insurance Act.

Table 1. Terrorism Risk Insurance Act Eligible Insurance Lines

Insurance line	Description
Aircraft (all perils)	Covers aircraft hulls, contents, and owners' and manufacturers' liability to passengers, airports, and third parties.
Allied lines	Property insurance usually bought in conjunction with fire insurance; it includes wind, water damage, explosion, riot, vandalism and other coverage, and business interruption.
Boiler and machinery	Insurance for the malfunction or breakdown of boilers, machinery, and electrical equipment, and associated business interruption.
Commercial multiperil (liability and nonliability)	Package policy for the entire commercial enterprise that includes various risk exposures, frequently including fire, allied lines, and business interruption. It can be purchased with or without liability portion.
Fire	Coverage protecting property against damage from losses caused by a fire or lightning and loss of use (that is, business interruption).
Inland marine	Coverage for shipments that do not involve ocean transport. Covers articles in transit by all forms of land and air transportation as well as bridges, tunnels, and other means of transportation and communication.
Ocean marine	Coverage of all types of vessels and watercraft, for property damage to the vessel and cargo, business interruption, and for marine-related liabilities.
Insurance line	Description
Other liability	Covers the policyholder against liability resulting from negligence, carelessness, or failure to act that causes property damage and personal injury to others.
Products liability	Protects manufacturers' and distributors' exposure to lawsuits from a defective condition causing bodily injury or property damage through the use of the product.
Workers' compensation	Covers an employer's liability for medical care and physical rehabilitation of injured workers and helps to replace lost wages while they are unable to work. State laws, which vary significantly, govern the amount of benefits paid and other compensation provisions.

Sources: Code of Federal Regulations (31 C.F.R. § 50.5(u)) and GAO analysis of Treasury information.

As initially enacted, one of the purposes of TRIA was to provide a transitional period in which the insurance market could determine how to model and price terrorism risk. Congress reauthorized TRIA twice—in 2005 and 2007. As shown in table 2, the reauthorizations changed several aspects of the terrorism risk insurance program, including the insurer deductible, lines of insurance covered, and types of terrorist acts covered (added domestic terrorism). TRIA covers insured losses resulting from an act of terrorism, which is defined, in part, as a "violent act or an act that is dangerous" to human life, property, or infrastructure. The act is silent about losses from attacks with nuclear, biological, chemical, or radiological weapons (NBCR) or from cyber terrorism.[14]

Table 2. Selected Coverage Provisions in the Terrorism Risk Insurance Act and Its Reauthorizations

	Terrorism Risk Insurance Act of 2002 (Pub. L. No. 107-297)	Terrorism Risk Insurance Extension Act of 2005 (Pub. L. No. 109-144)	Terrorism Risk Insurance Program Reauthorization Act of 2007 (Pub. L. No. 110-160)
Program trigger	$5 million[a]	$50 million (2006) $100 million (2007)	$100 million
Insurer deductible	7% (2003) 10% (2004) 15% (2005)	17.5% (2006) 20% (2007)	20%
Coshare	Insurers 10% Government 90%	Insurers 10% Government 90% (2006) Insurers 15% Government 85% (2007)	Insurers 15% Government 85%
Terrorist acts covered	Foreign	Foreign	Foreign and domestic
Examples of commercial property and casualty insurance lines excluded	Crop, private mortgage, and life insurance	Crop, private mortgage, and life insurance, commercial automobile, burglary and theft, and professional liability	Crop, private mortgage, and life insurance, commercial automobile, burglary and theft, and professional liability

Source: GAO.

[a] TRIA as initially enacted in 2002 did not include a specific program trigger, but an act of terrorism could not be certified without more than $5 million in property and casualty insurance losses resulting from the act. Without a certified act of terrorism, TRIA is not activated.

Program Administration and Reporting Requirements

TRIA authorizes Treasury to administer the Terrorism Insurance Program. Specifically, the Terrorism Risk Insurance Program Office within Treasury's Office of Domestic Finance administers the program and manages day-to-day operations, with oversight and assistance from the Federal Insurance Office, according to Treasury officials.[15] In 2004, Treasury issued regulations to implement TRIA's procedures for filing claims for payment of the federal share of compensation for insured losses.[16] Upon certification of an act of terrorism, Treasury will activate a web-based facility for receiving claims from insurers and responding to insurers that seek assistance. According to Treasury, currently five staff work directly on the program and the program is assisted by others in Treasury. Staff responsibilities include managing contractors in place to process claims in the event of an attack and making any necessary changes to program regulations. According to Treasury, the spending for this program has generally declined since 2003 (see figure 2).

TRIA mandates various studies and data compilation efforts. For example, TRIA requires GAO, Treasury, and the President's Working Group on Financial Markets (PWG) to complete various studies related to terrorism risk insurance.[17] We have completed and submitted to Congress several mandated studies on TRIA.[18] Treasury completed an assessment of the program and submitted a report to Congress in 2005.[19] PWG must periodically report on terrorism market conditions (in 2006, 2010, and 2013).[20] TRIA also requires Treasury to annually compile information on the terrorism risk insurance premium rates of insurers for the preceding year. In the event that information is not otherwise available to Treasury, Treasury may require each insurer to submit that information to NAIC. We discuss data compilation requirements in more detail later in this report.

State Regulation of Insurance

Insurance in the United States is primarily regulated at the state level.[21] The insurance regulators of the 50 states, the District of Columbia, and the U.S. territories created and govern NAIC, which is the standard-setting and regulatory support organization for the U.S. insurance industry. Through NAIC, state insurance regulators establish standards and best practices, conduct peer review, and coordinate their regulatory oversight. According to NAIC, insurers set the rates for terrorism coverage, and state law requires insurers to file those rates (and to file insurance forms) with state regulators. Generally state insurance regulators receive information from insurers regarding the products the insurers plan to sell in the state. States vary with regard to timing and depth of the reviews of the insurers' rates and contractual language. Many state laws have filing and/or review exemptions that apply to large commercial policyholders. For exempt commercial policyholders, state insurance regulators perform neither rate nor form reviews because it is presumed that these large businesses have a better understanding of insurance contracts and pricing than the average personal-lines consumer and as such, are able to effectively negotiate price and contract terms with the insurers.

COMPREHENSIVE DATA ON TERRORISM INSURANCE ARE NOT READILY AVAILABLE AND TREASURY'S ANALYSIS TO BETTER UNDERSTAND FISCAL EXPOSURE HAS BEEN LIMITED

Comprehensive data on the terrorism risk insurance market are not readily available. In general, individual insurers maintain data on the terrorism coverage they underwrite. While Treasury has obtained some market data from industry sources, those data are limited because they do not include information from the entire industry. Federal internal control standards state that agencies should identify and obtain relevant and needed data to be able to meet program goals. TRIA requires Treasury to annually compile information on the terrorism risk insurance premium rates of insurers, and if the information is not available permits Treasury to require insurers to submit that information to NAIC, but Treasury has not taken either action. Without comprehensive market data, including the number of insurers in the market and whether differences exist in pricing or take-up rates, Treasury may not have a full understanding of the terrorism risk insurance market and be unable to assess whether TRIA's program goals of helping to ensure the continued widespread availability and affordability of terrorism risk insurance and addressing market disruptions are being met. Furthermore,

Treasury has conducted limited analysis of the federal government's fiscal exposure under different scenarios of potential terrorist attacks. Analyzing such risks is a federal internal control standard and insurance industry best practice. Without additional analyses, Treasury does not have enough information to help understand the potential magnitude of federal fiscal exposure in the event of a certified terrorist attack, and will not be in the position to provide Congress with analysis to inform decisions about reauthorization, including any changes that would limit exposure.

Terrorism Insurance Data Available from Industry Sources Are Limited

Comprehensive market data on terrorism insurance, including premiums and the number of insurers underwriting terrorism risk, are not readily available.[22] In general, individual insurers maintain data on the terrorism coverage they underwrite, including data on the percentage of policies with terrorism coverage and premiums for such coverage. However, these data are proprietary and are not publicly available. Further, NAIC manages an electronic system that many insurance companies use to file premium rates and policy language with state regulators for approval. But NAIC officials stated that they generally cannot extract terrorism coverage information from it, such as the number of insurers providing such coverage or the prices charged.[23] Moreover, using the property and casualty information NAIC collects likely would overestimate any numbers on terrorism insurance because not all policies provide terrorism coverage. NAIC officials told us that obtaining a complete view of the terrorism insurance market would require reviewing insurers' filings with each state.

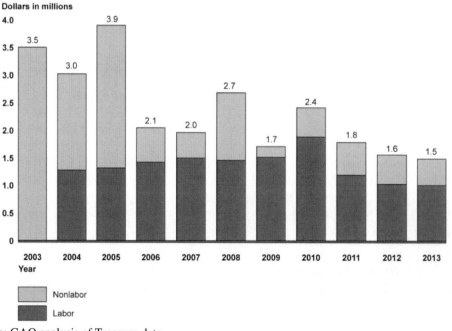

Source: GAO analysis of Treasury data.

Figure 2. Terrorism Risk Insurance Program Spending History, 2003-2013.

Many insurance industry organizations are important sources of data on the terrorism insurance market, but data from these sources are also limited in some respects. For example, although A.M. Best, an insurance-rating and information organization, and the Insurance Services Office, Inc. (ISO), an advisory organization and data and analytics provider, collect premium information from their clients, these data are not publicly available and may not be representative of the entire industry.[24] Insurance brokers also compile market data such as pricing, take-up rates, and coverage by industry sector from their clients. Similarly, some of these data are not publicly available and are not representative of the entire market.

Terrorism Insurance Information Treasury Collects Is Not Comprehensive, and Treasury Does Not Require Insurers to Provide Data

Treasury officials told us they periodically consulted with industry participants to obtain information about the terrorism insurance market, such as take-up rates, pricing, and capacity, but noted that the industry relies on the two largest insurance brokers for this information. However, as discussed above, the information that brokers compile is not comprehensive because it does not include detailed data on terrorism coverage from the insurance industry as a whole. In addition, PWG also solicited comments from the insurance industry on the availability and affordability of terrorism risk insurance for three studies mandated by TRIA. For example, according to Treasury officials, 29 entities submitted comments for the 2014 PWG report. In addition, Treasury conducted numerous interviews with industry participants. However, the comments PWG solicited and received from industry participants for these studies generally were anecdotal representations from the organizations that chose to submit information, rather than comprehensive data representing the entire industry.[25] Treasury officials acknowledged that their information on the terrorism insurance market could be supplemented with more detailed information.

Furthermore, TRIA requires Treasury to annually compile information on the terrorism insurance premium rates of insurers, and if the information is not available, also permits Treasury to require insurers to submit that information to NAIC, but Treasury has not taken either action.[26] According to Treasury officials, Treasury has not compiled information on an annual basis, and has not collected market data on terrorism risk insurance directly from insurers. Treasury officials told us this was because the agency has periodically collected market data on terrorism risk insurance for the three PWG reports from industry sources, which has been sufficient for purposes of responding to TRIA's reporting requirements.[27] If the premium rate information was not otherwise available, TRIA states that Treasury may require each insurer to submit the information to NAIC, which then would make the information available to Treasury.[28] Treasury officials noted that the premium rate data TRIA requires Treasury to compile may not be the only helpful data points for understanding the terrorism insurance market and said that additional baseline data would be crucial for a more detailed analysis. The officials said they may seek additional market data and evaluate whether the sources previously used were adequate.

While TRIA states that Treasury has the authorities necessary to carry out the terrorism risk insurance program, including prescribing regulations and procedures to effectively administer and implement it, whether these authorities allow Treasury to collect comprehensive market data directly from insurers is unclear. However, federal internal control standards state that agencies should identify and obtain relevant and needed data to be able to meet program goals.[29] As stated earlier, the purposes of the terrorism insurance program include helping to ensure the continued widespread availability and affordability of property and casualty insurance for terrorism risk and addressing market disruptions. Without comprehensive, nationwide market data, including the number of insurers in the market and whether differences exist in pricing or take-up rates for companies of different sizes, industries, or geographic locations, Treasury might not have a full understanding of the terrorism risk insurance market, including how changing program parameters may impact the market. Treasury may also be unable to assess whether the program is meeting its goals of helping to ensure the continued widespread availability and affordability of terrorism risk insurance and addressing market disruptions.

Treasury Performs Limited Analysis to Help Estimate Federal Fiscal Exposure under TRIA

Treasury has conducted limited analysis to help estimate the potential magnitude of the federal government's fiscal exposure under TRIA under different scenarios of potential terrorist attacks. We developed a conceptual framework for fiscal exposures to aid discussion of long-term costs and uncertainties that present risks for the federal budget.[30] Fiscal exposures vary widely by source, extent of the government's legal commitment, and magnitude. Fiscal exposures may be explicit (the government is legally required to fund the commitment) or implicit (exposures arise not from a legal commitment, but from current policy, past practices, or other factors that may create the expectation for future spending).[31] The government's legal commitment to pay losses when a certified terrorist event occurs makes the terrorism risk insurance program an explicit exposure. The amount of federal spending resulting from the fiscal exposure under the terrorism risk insurance program depends on the extent of insured losses.

In 2009, Treasury contracted with ISO to develop and implement a method for estimating total average annual insured terrorism losses in the aggregate for TRIA-eligible lines, review certain material, and advise on the appropriateness of its use for projecting potential payout rates of the federal share of insured losses.[32] The study provides estimates (both gross and net) of the federal share of losses and was used to aid Treasury in its development of a federal budget item for the terrorism risk insurance program.[33] ISO representatives stated that it was important to understand that the study provides an estimate of average annual losses in any given year, but in years with losses, the numbers likely would be significantly higher than the average. ISO representatives also noted that the study had some data limitations and relied on assumptions such as take-up rates for terrorism coverage that could affect the results of the analysis. This is the only study Treasury has commissioned that examines the potential overall fiscal exposure of the terrorism risk insurance program to the federal government.

In addition to the ISO study, Treasury officials provided us with a hypothetical loss scenario that shows private-sector and federal loss sharing under a specific set of circumstances.[34] According to Treasury officials, this example was not an official work product and they emphasized that they developed the example purely to illustrate the recoupment calculations and it should not be considered as a projection of the fiscal exposure of a terrorist event to the government. The exact amount of government spending or the government's obligation is difficult to predict because, among other factors, it depends on the distribution of losses among insurers. For example, the aggregated 20 percent deductible equaled $37 billion (20 percent of direct earned premiums for TRIA-eligible lines), according to our analysis of SNL Financial's 2012 insurance data. However, losses from a terrorist attack are highly unlikely to affect all insurers or be distributed evenly among all insurers. As a result, if fewer insurers had losses, the deductible amount would be lower and the government's share of losses likely would be triggered at an amount less than the aggregated industry deductible. Therefore, the government's spending or obligation likely would begin at an amount less than the industry's aggregated deductible.[35]

Federal internal control standards state that agencies should identify and analyze risks associated with achieving program objectives, and use this information as a basis for developing a plan for mitigating the risks.[36] For example, because the amount of the government's fiscal exposure varies according to the specific program's design and characteristics, estimates could be developed to better understand the potential costs of changes to certain program parameters under various scenarios of potential terrorist attacks.[37] This could increase the attention given to fiscal exposures, while also providing decision makers relevant information to consider when determining the best way to achieve various policy goals or design a program.[38] According to the insurers and other industry participants we spoke to, insurers' best practices also show that an insurer's analysis of the location and amount of coverage written is prudent for understanding the financial risks of a potential terrorist attack of a specific size. Insurers work with terrorism risk modeling firms to help understand their potential financial exposure from a future terrorist attack.[39] For example, to help illustrate how an insurer would be financially affected after a terrorist event and how losses would be shared between the private sector and the federal government under TRIA, some industry participants have developed hypothetical scenarios. According to a study published by the Wharton Risk Management and Decision Processes Center, insurers use such scenarios to determine their maximum exposure to a range of possible attacks.[40] Ultimately, the amount of fiscal exposure created by TRIA will be determined by the program parameters and the specific circumstances of a future attack (such as the number of insurers affected and number of businesses that had purchased terrorism coverage). However, these scenarios can be used to help understand risk and the impact of the financial losses under TRIA under specific scenarios of potential terrorist events, and to analyze losses if TRIA were not renewed (that is, if the private sector would be responsible for all losses). In addition to information on the type of attack (for example, damage from 2-to-10 ton truck bombs), these scenarios can rely on estimates of insurers' market share and direct premiums earned, among other data points. For public policy purposes, in 2014 the Reinsurance Association of America developed a model to help participants evaluate various loss scenarios. We also have developed hypothetical examples to help illustrate the potential magnitude of the federal government's fiscal exposure, which will be discussed later in this report.

Treasury officials said that they have conducted limited analysis on the government's fiscal exposure under TRIA because the amount of the government's fiscal exposure is ultimately determined by program parameters and the risk modeling and exposure analyses used by insurers are not entirely applicable in understanding how to reduce federal exposure. According to Treasury officials, insurers manage risk by first understanding and then limiting their exposures by insurance line or geographic location. Fiscal exposure under TRIA is limited by the program parameters and the circumstances of a future attack (such as number of insurers affected and number of businesses that had purchased terrorism coverage). Treasury officials also said that the amount of fiscal exposure is difficult to determine because it is shaped by variables, such as geography, type of event, and number of affected insurers. However, Treasury officials acknowledged that hypothetical analyses that provide illustrative analyses and estimate the potential total amount of losses may be helpful in understanding fiscal exposure. Without analyzing comprehensive market data on the type and amount of coverage provided from all insurers participating in the market, Treasury does not have enough information to help understand potential federal spending under various scenarios of potential terrorist attacks. In addition, Treasury is not in the position to provide Congress with analysis to inform decisions about reauthorization and the future structure of the program, including any changes that would limit exposure, one of the goals that Treasury recently articulated in its 2015 budget justification.

INSURANCE MARKET FOR TERRORISM RISK HAS STABILIZED

Available data on the market for terrorism risk insurance generally indicate a stable market in recent years. Total terrorism insurance premiums, which make up a small percentage of insurers' overall premiums, increased after the original act and reached a high in 2007, then declined, and have stabilized since 2010. Insurers report capacity to provide terrorism coverage over the past decade has remained unchanged. In general, prices appeared to have decreased as the number of businesses buying terrorism coverage (take-up rates) increased from 2003 to 2006, but have been constant since 2010. The transference of terrorism risk through reinsurance or alternatives to reinsurance, such as insurance-linked securities (catastrophe bonds), has remained limited.

Terrorism Insurance Premiums Have Stabilized and Made up a Small Percentage of Overall Premiums

Available data show terrorism insurance premiums have stabilized over the past few years (see figure 3).[41] For instance, total premiums generally increased through 2007, then declined, and stabilized from 2010 through 2012. In 2012, the most recent year for which data are available,[42] estimated terrorism insurance premiums were $1.7 billion, down from a high of $2 billion in 2007. A.M. Best's estimates about $17 billion was collected for terrorism insurance premiums from 2004 through 2012. Furthermore, terrorism insurance premiums collected on workers' compensation and commercial property insurance lines each made up about 40 percent of the estimated total terrorism insurance premiums, with the remaining 20 percent from all other commercial lines. These proportions remained relatively stable in recent years.

Based on our analysis of A.M. Best and SNL Financial insurance data, trends in terrorism insurance premiums have not differed markedly from trends in other commercial insurance line premiums. For example, premiums for all commercial property and casualty lines showed the same pattern—increases until 2007, declines from 2007 through 2010, and then increases in 2011 and 2012. Commercial property and casualty generally follows an insurance industry cycle, characterized by periods of soft market conditions—a market with abundant willingness to write new policies (capacity), increasing competition, and rates (prices) that grow marginally or decrease—followed by periods of hard market conditions— in which capacity is relatively low, competition decreases, rates increase, and capital is scarce. This cyclical nature of the property and casualty industry likely plays a role in the hardness or softness of the terrorism insurance market. For example, the similarity in trends in premiums indicates that the terrorism insurance market is closely related to the overall commercial property and casualty market. The 2007-2009 financial crisis affected the overall commercial property and casualty market and most likely affected the terrorism insurance market in similar ways. For instance, the financial crisis generally affected commercial property and casualty insurers through decreased net income, as underwriting and investment results deteriorated.[43] However, making an accurate assessment of the terrorism insurance market is challenging. According to industry participants, uncertainty surrounding the two previous TRIA reauthorizations—whether the program would be reauthorized and if so, with what changes—led to periods of market instability.

Insurers told us their terrorism insurance premiums made up a very small amount of their overall premiums. As previously mentioned, we obtained information from 15 insurers as part of a questionnaire. According to the responses, on average terrorism insurance premiums made up less than 2 percent of commercial property and casualty premiums, or roughly $1.7 billion in calendar year 2012 (the range for the 15 insurers was 0.7 to 3 percent).[44] An insurer told us terrorism insurance premiums have not significantly affected overall capital levels because premiums collected for terrorism risk have been low and insurers use some of the terrorism insurance premiums to account for reinsurance, expenses, and taxes.

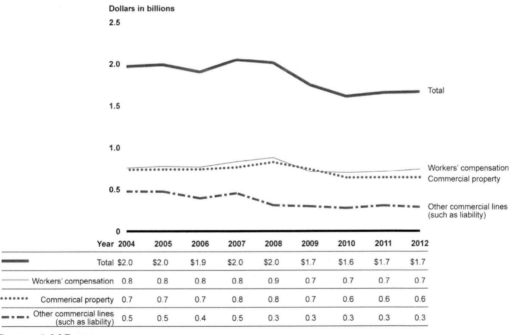

Source: A.M.Best.

Figure 3. Estimated Terrorism Insurance Premiums by Total and Selected Insurance Lines, 2004–2012.

A.M. Best and SNL Financial data also indicate that, in terms of the share of total premium, coverage for terrorism risk is concentrated among the largest insurers.[45] In the case of terrorism insurance premiums, according to A.M. Best data, 10 insurers made up roughly 70 percent of premium volume (see table 3). The same 10 insurers accounted for 44 percent of premiums in all insurance lines subject to TRIA and 39 percent of premiums in all commercial property and casualty lines. An industry representative with whom we spoke said only the largest insurers have the ability to underwrite large terrorism risks and hence account for a large portion of the industry's terrorism insurance premiums. The composition of the terrorism insurance market resembles other insurance markets that the Federal Insurance Office has characterized as concentrated. For example, according to the Federal Insurance Office's 2013 annual report, 10 insurers made up 47 percent of the property and casualty market (both commercial and personal) and 72 percent of the life and health insurance market, in 2012—both of which the report characterizes as concentrated markets.[46]

Although we present an estimated number of insurers that provide coverage for terrorism risk, identifying the precise number of insurers in this market is difficult because of the lack of comprehensive data. As noted previously, insurers are not required to report data about terrorism risks to Treasury or NAIC. As shown in table 3, according to SNL Financial data, more than 800 insurers reported premiums in insurance lines subject to TRIA and therefore, by law, offered coverage.[47] A.M. Best's survey data provides further context for this market. For 2012, A.M. Best estimated more than 200 insurers provided coverage for terrorism risk. Insurers providing coverage in the insurance lines subject to TRIA must offer terrorism coverage, but businesses are not required to buy it. Therefore, the number of insurers offering coverage in the insurance lines subject to TRIA (more than 800) and the number of insurers covering terrorism risk and collecting terrorism insurance premiums (estimated at more than 200) will differ.

Capacity Has Remained the Same, Prices Declined, and Take-up Rates Flattened in Recent Years

Capacity

According to an insurance broker, capacity seems to have improved, but insurers report that capacity has remained the same and that they limit capacity as needed to manage their overall exposure. Capacity is the amount that insurers are willing to allocate to underwrite a specific risk. Terrorism coverage typically is embedded in an all-risk property policy and therefore available terrorism capacity is tied to overall capacity for all-risk property policies. According to information from an insurance broker, the reported market capacity for terrorism risk seems to have increased.[48] According to an Aon report, in 2013 about $14 billion per risk was available to any one insured for an all-risk property policy.[49] This amount increased from $13.5 billion in 2010 and $8 billion in 2005. This represents the amount of coverage an insurer is willing to provide to any one insured. However, the actual capacity for terrorism risk is much lower than $14 billion per risk because the amounts above encompass capacity for risks in addition to acts of terrorism. According to Aon, non-terrorism-related exposures, such as natural catastrophes (earthquake and windstorm), can vastly decrease the available capacity for terrorism risk.

Table 3. Estimated Number of Insurers and Percentage of Premiums, 2012

	Estimated number of insurers	Percentage of premiums earned by Top 10 insurers	Percentage of premiums earned by Top 20 insurers
Premiums in all commercial property and casualty insurance lines	1,091	39%	53%
Premiums in commercial property and casualty insurance lines subject to TRIA	867	44%	58%
Premiums for terrorism coverage	226	70%	75%

Source: GAO analysis of A.M. Best and SNL Financial insurance data.

Note: We defined the top insurers by their direct earned premiums in 2012 in the insurance lines subject to the Terrorism Risk Insurance Act. The top insurers in insurance lines subject to TRIA differ slightly from the top insurers in the commercial property and casualty market as a whole. Insurers means insurance groups—A.M. Best and SNL Financial report data by groups.

Moreover, individual insurers' capacity to underwrite terrorism will differ, and insurers told us they would limit capacity as needed based on their aggregate terrorism exposures, geographic concentration of terrorism exposures, and terrorism exposures relative to other natural catastrophe exposures. Most insurer representatives with whom we spoke reported that capacity to provide terrorism coverage over the past decade remained constant and 6 out of the 15 insurers stated that they limited capacity as needed to manage their overall exposures. About half of the insurers told us TRIA enabled them to provide capacity for terrorism risks, but TRIA also was the reason why capacity has remained relatively unchanged—because insurers managed their exposures based on the program parameters. In general, insurers assume some financial risk when covering terrorism risk, but they also employ various underwriting standards to manage the risk and limit potential financial exposures. As we previously reported, insurers' willingness to provide coverage in certain areas may change frequently as new clients or properties are added to or removed from their book of business.[50]

In response to our questionnaire, most insurers told us they determined the amount of coverage they were willing to provide in defined geographic areas, depending on their risk tolerance. These amounts are sometimes called coverage limits (capacity limits) and are managed in relation to overall terrorism exposures. Almost all insurers told us factors such as loss estimates from terrorism models, aggregation of exposures in defined areas, proximity of exposures to high-profile targets or buildings, and individual property characteristics affect their terrorism underwriting decisions. Insurers may decide to limit capacity; that is, decide not to underwrite certain coverage, if taking on the additional risk would exceed their internal capacity limits. A few insurers that we interviewed also told us that over the past decade they have benefitted from significant improvements to their data systems and models that track terrorism exposures; in turn, the better systems and models have improved their ability to make sound underwriting decisions when renewing or writing new policies.

Pricing

Prices have declined and insurers say TRIA has allowed them to offer coverage at prices policyholders are willing to pay. Insurers may charge an additional premium for terrorism coverage, as TRIA does not provide specific guidance on pricing. According to data from Marsh, prices for terrorism coverage, as part of a commercial property policy, generally declined over the past decade (see figure 4).[51] These data are not necessarily reflective of the entire market, but represent the best available data on pricing.[52] While prices slightly increased from 2003 to 2004, prices steadily declined since 2006. In 2013, the nationwide median amount that businesses paid per million dollars of coverage for terrorism insurance was $27. Using the 2013 nationwide median rate, a company purchasing $100 million in coverage for property damage would have paid approximately $2,700 in terrorism insurance premiums.

In addition, prices that businesses pay will vary depending on company size, location, and industry. For example, prices will typically decrease as the size of the company increases (size measured in terms of insured value and prices measured in millions of dollars of coverage), are typically higher in the Northeast, and higher in certain industry subsectors (such as construction, power and utilities, and media) due to perceived or actual risk exposure to terrorism.[53] But because comprehensive pricing data are not readily available, it is difficult to clearly understand how prices differ by company size, location, or industry.

According to data from Marsh, from 2003 to 2013, companies paid approximately from 4 to 9 percent of their total property premium for terrorism coverage (see figure 5). Analyzing the price of terrorism coverage as a part of overall property premiums allows companies to understand how terrorism coverage affected their overall property insurance budget. Businesses paid no more than approximately 5 percent of their total property premium for terrorism coverage since 2011.[54] Using the 2013 data, a company purchasing $100 million in property coverage would have paid approximately 4 percent of its $67,500 overall property premiums for terrorism coverage (or $2,700).

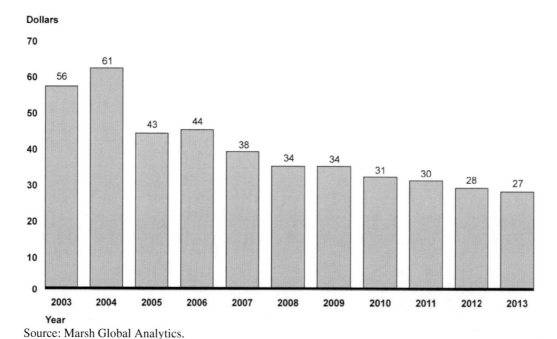

Source: Marsh Global Analytics.

Figure 4. Terrorism Insurance Pricing, 2003–2013 (Median Rates per Million Dollars of Coverage).

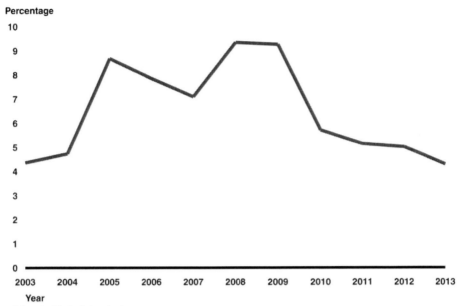

Source: Marsh Global Analytics.

Figure 5. Terrorism Insurance as a Percentage of Overall Property Premiums, 2003–2013.

Insurers told us TRIA allows them to offer coverage at prices their policyholders are willing to pay. Insurers said their primary concern for covering terrorism risks was limiting their exposures (that is, capacity) because the losses could be huge under certain types of terrorist attacks and that pricing was secondary. TRIA addresses insurers' primary concerns about the size of potential losses—it provides a structure in which insurers know, before an event, what their losses could be because the deductible and coshare are defined by law and losses are capped. For most insurance products, insurers typically use the potential frequency and severity of events to calculate premiums that are commensurate with the risks. Because the frequency and severity of terrorism are difficult to predict, the limits established in TRIA, which cap the potential severity of losses to insurers, make underwriting the risk and determining a price for terrorism coverage easier for insurers.

Furthermore, most insurers said their companies' experiences with collecting terrorism insurance premiums and providing terrorism coverage over the past decade have had minimal or no impact on their pricing strategy. Insurer responses suggest this is mainly because terrorism is so different from other perils. For example, one insurer noted that with natural catastrophes, insurers have a long history y of experience writing and pricing (based on claims), but this is not the case with terrorism.

Another insurer noted that terrorism risk provides too few data points to inform pricing and underwriting decisions. Additionally, one insurer told us it is a very competitive market and they do not charge terrorism insurance premiums that would cover their potential losses from a terrorist attack. For example, this insurer noted that if insurers did charge premiums that would cover potential losses, businesses would not buy it.

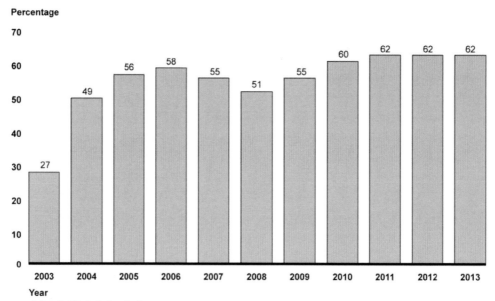

Source: Marsh Global Analytics.

Note: Take-up rates measure the percentage of businesses buying terrorism insurance as part of a commercial property policy.

Figure 6. Terrorism Insurance Take-Up Rates, 2003–2013.

Take-up Rates

Take-up rates—which are the percentage of businesses buying terrorism coverage and help measure the demand for terrorism risk insurance—increased from 2003 to 2006 and have remained relatively constant (and above 60 percent) since 2010, according to data from Marsh (see figure 6). According to Treasury and NAIC, neither collects this type of information. Take-up rate data for businesses buying terrorism coverage as part of commercial property policies are only available from insurance brokers.[55] The take-up rate for businesses buying terrorism coverage as part of workers' compensation policies is 100 percent because state laws require businesses to purchase workers' compensation insurance and do not permit insurers to exclude terrorism from workers' compensation policies.

Take-up rates will vary depending on company size, location, and industry. For example, larger companies are more likely to purchase coverage than smaller companies, the Northeast has the highest take-up rates, and certain industry subsectors have higher take-up rates than others (for example, media, education, and financial institutions).[56] According to our questionnaire results, overall take-up rates for insurers varied significantly (from 26 to 100 percent). One respondent noted that analyzing insurers' overall take-up rates can be misleading and it is more appropriate to look at take-up rates for terrorism coverage in each line of insurance subject to TRIA. According to our questionnaire results, the lines of insurance with the highest take-up rates for terrorism coverage are commercial multiperil and inland marine, and the lines with the lowest take-up rates for terrorism coverage are aircraft and boiler and machinery.[57] However, because Treasury and NAIC do not collect take-up rate data from insurers, it is difficult to thoroughly analyze take-up rates by line of insurance.

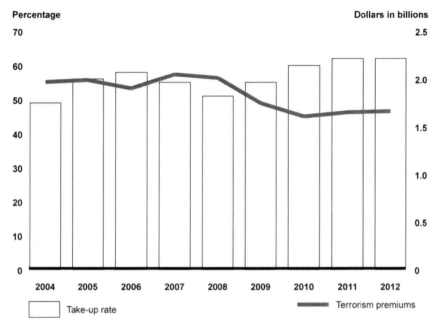

Source: A.M. best and Marsh Global Analytics.

Figure 7. Comparison of Terrorism Insurance Premiums and Take-up Rates, 2004–2012.

According to industry participants, take-up rates may have reached a plateau—that is, most businesses that want the coverage already have purchased it. From 2003 through 2013, take-up rates doubled, while prices declined by 50 percent.[58] In more recent years, take-up rates remained relatively constant, although prices continued to decline (as shown in figures 4 and 6). Since 2010, both take-up rates and estimated terrorism insurance premiums have been relatively stable (see figure 7).

The changing proportions of new versus renewal policies covering terrorism risk offer further evidence that demand may be leveling off. On the basis of our questionnaire results, the majority of policies are renewals rather than new issuances, and this has stayed the same over the past several years (on average, about 83 percent renewals in 2008 and in 2012).

Use of Reinsurance and Insurance-Linked Securities for Significant Amounts of Terrorism Risk Remains Limited

The transference of terrorism risk—namely, through reinsurance and alternatives to reinsurance such as insurance-linked securities—has been limited.[59] Reinsurance capacity for terrorism risk has increased, but remains small relative to the federal reimbursements available through TRIA.[60] For example, according to industry participants about $6 billion to $10 billion in terrorism reinsurance capacity was available in the United States in 2013, which was an increase from the $4 billion to $6 billion available several years ago, but was still small compared with the federal assumption of 85 percent of losses (up to $100 billion of aggregate industry exposure minus items such as the insurer deductibles) in TRIA.[61] Without TRIA, current reinsurance capacity would be insufficient to respond to a large-scale terrorist attack, in particular up to the limits the government program provides, according to a reinsurance trade association representative. Additionally, terrorism reinsurance capacity is small in relation to capacity for other perils. For example, the total amount of reinsurance capacity available for natural catastrophe risks in the United States in 2012 ranged from $90 billion to $120 billion.

Several factors limit the market for reinsurance of terrorism risk. For instance, unlike primary insurers, reinsurers are not subject to TRIA and therefore are not required to offer primary insurers coverage for terrorism risk. According to industry representatives, reinsurers face the same challenges as primary insurers—that is, terrorism risk is difficult to model and price, which also contributes to a limited market. Finally, insurers told us they typically purchase terrorism reinsurance as part of a multiperil policy that covers terrorism risk in addition to other risks.[62] To help manage their exposures to concentrated losses, reinsurers frequently write terrorism coverage with specific limits for individual properties rather than reinsure a share of an insurance company's overall holdings.

According to brokers and reinsurers, terrorism reinsurance prices generally have declined by 50 percent over the past decade and more. Reasons these industry participants cite for the price declines include the passage of time since the September 11 attacks, the lack of subsequent terrorist attacks resulting in significant losses, decreased demand from primary insurers, and increased supply of reinsurance.[63] However, the location of exposures also affects the price of terrorism reinsurance. For example, reinsurance coverage is more expensive for exposures in densely populated urban areas than less densely populated areas.

Although individual insurers' reinsurance patterns vary, insurers have been reinsuring a limited amount of their terrorism risk and retaining roughly 80 percent of it according to the 2010 PWG report. Insurers make decisions on how much reinsurance to purchase based on their perception of risk, price of coverage, ability to manage risk, and other factors. One insurer contributing to this report commented that terrorism risk reinsurance remains insufficient to serve the market's current risk exposure.[64] According to our questionnaire results, 13 insurers purchased reinsurance for terrorism risk and 2 did not. Some responding insurers that purchased reinsurance for terrorism risk noted an increase in their purchasing levels, some noted a decrease, and still others noted fluctuations in their purchasing patterns. One insurer purchased terrorism reinsurance coverage continuously since 2002 and increased its limits as capacity became available and pricing became more affordable. Two insurers said that their purchases of terrorism reinsurance decreased over time. The two insurers that did not purchase reinsurance for terrorism noted that while some reinsurers were willing to provide a modest capacity for terrorism risk, the cost was prohibitive for them. Additionally, insurers noted that potential modifications to TRIA would affect their demand for reinsurance. For example, potential modifications that would increase insurers' deductible and coshare amounts would result in increased demand from primary insurers for reinsurance, but supply might stay the same.

As an alternative to reinsurance, insurance-linked securities have remained a limited option for covering terrorism risk. Specifically, catastrophe bonds, insurance-linked securities that typically cover natural catastrophes, have been used over the past 20 years mainly because of the large amount of resources available in capital markets.[65] Catastrophe bonds are risk-based securities that pay relatively high interest rates and provide insurance companies with a form of reinsurance to pay losses from natural catastrophes. A catastrophe bond offering typically is made through an investment entity that may be sponsored by an insurance or reinsurance company. The investment entity issues bonds or debt securities for purchase by investors, thus spreading risk. Catastrophe bonds, by tapping into the securities markets, offer the opportunity to expand the pool of capital available to cover a particular risk. Some insurers and reinsurers issue catastrophe bonds because they allow for risk transfer and may lower the costs of insuring against the most severe catastrophes (compared with traditional reinsurance).[66]

Although catastrophe bonds have become more common, two have been issued to date that cover terrorism risk and neither is explicitly a terrorism risk bond that covers risks included under TRIA. Each is a multi-event bond associated with the risks of natural disaster, pandemic, or terrorist attack.[67] However, these bonds are mortality bonds and therefore would be an alternative for a life insurance policy (which is not a line of insurance eligible for TRIA) and not an alternative to commercial property and casualty insurance. As of April 2014, no property and casualty terrorism bonds have been issued.

Industry representatives mentioned various challenges to issuing catastrophe bonds covering terrorism risk.

- Investors generally avoid risks not widely underwritten in reinsurance markets and therefore lack interest in such catastrophe bonds.[68]
- Investors are reluctant to make investments in which losses may be correlated with widespread financial market losses (as was the case with terrorism losses after September 11, 2001) as well as low returns or payouts.[69]
- Rating agencies have not been willing to use terrorism loss models that estimate the probability of terrorism events (probabilistic models) for rating purposes and at least for terrorism risk investors tend to avoid risks that cannot be credibly modeled and rated.[70]

The difficulty of modeling terrorism represents an additional overall challenge to the development of the private market for terrorism insurance. Models used to estimate terrorism risk have become more sophisticated in estimating the severity of specific events in recent years.

However, they remain fundamentally different from those used to assess natural hazard risks, which estimate both the severity and probability. For example, according to the Reinsurance Association of America, terrorism modeling is primarily a means for underwriters to measure how much they have at risk in a given geographic area and losses from a specific type of event (that is, the severity of an event), not to estimate the probability of such events.[71] Terrorism risk is unlike other catastrophic risks—such as earthquake or hurricane—in that terrorists can alter their behavior, which makes it hard to model the probability of potential events with the level of accuracy required to accurately price the coverage. There are relatively few instances on which to base probability estimates for acts of terror in the United States, which means that such estimates lack actuarial credibility. Additionally, insurers and modeling firms have no access to data used internally by U.S. intelligence and counterterrorism agencies. Moreover it may be impossible to build a model that provides a valid representation of all individuals and groups that might decide to try to use terrorism as a tactic against the United States. In addition, as opposed to other types of risks that are random to some extent, terrorist acts are intentional and terrorists continually attempt to defeat loss prevention and mitigation strategies.

TRIA EXPIRATION OR MODIFICATION COULD AFFECT AVAILABILITY OF TERRORISM COVERAGE AND FEDERAL FISCAL EXPOSURE, BUT ADDITIONAL CLARIFICATION OF COVERED RISKS IS NEEDED

Insurers and other industry participants cited concerns about the availability and price of terrorism coverage if TRIA expired or was changed substantially, but some changes could reduce the government's fiscal exposure. For example, some insurers we interviewed said they would stop covering terrorism risks if TRIA expired. In addition, most of the insurers we interviewed, including larger and smaller insurers, cited potential consequences associated with increasing the deductible or coshare, such as impacts on pricing, the need to reevaluate risk and capacity, and threats to their solvency in the event of a large industry loss. These concerns are consistent with points industry participants raised before previous reauthorizations of the program. However, several insurers told us they were less concerned about an increase to the aggregate retention amount or program trigger. Further, we found that increasing the deductible, coshare, or industry aggregate retention amount could reduce the government's fiscal exposure under certain terrorist event scenarios. Responses to our questionnaire revealed that insurers were uncertain about whether TRIA covers risks from a cyber terrorism attack. Without clarification of the coverage of cyber risks, some insurers may not offer cyber coverage and the coverage may not be as available.

Insurers May Limit Terrorism Insurance if TRIA Expires, but Long-Term Impacts of Expiration Are Difficult to Determine

The long-term impact of expiration of the terrorism risk insurance program's authority is difficult to determine, but according to insurers, in the short run, the availability of terrorism coverage may become more limited. Some insurers told us that they will stop providing terrorism coverage if TRIA expires on December 31, 2014. As indicated by responses to our questionnaire and other surveys of insurers, some insurers already made regulatory filings or issued notices to policyholders indicating that terrorism coverage would be excluded from policies in force beginning on January 1, 2015, if TRIA expired. For example, one insurer said that if TRIA were not renewed, the company would either exclude terrorism coverage or not underwrite businesses in states that prohibit terrorism exclusions.[72] Insurers could further limit terrorism exposures, particularly in geographic areas considered at high risk for attacks.

Because some states prohibit excluding certain risks, if a large-scale event occurred in the absence of TRIA, some insurers could face higher risk of insolvency or have more incentives to leave the market. For example, New York state insurance law prohibits terrorism exclusions for property and casualty policies that include standard fire coverage. In some other states, property insurers must cover losses from fire regardless of the cause of the fire, including a terrorist attack, even if the policyholder declined terrorism coverage. Thus, if TRIA expired, insurers operating in these states still would have to cover damage from fire following a terrorist attack. Such situations might leave some insurers bearing risks they could not adequately reinsure and leave them at increased risk for insolvency. Some insurers might decide their exposures were too great without TRIA and exit the market or decline to insure commercial property altogether.[73]

Some industry observers have noted that, in the long term if no large losses occur, the private insurance market might be able to address the need for terrorism coverage without support from the program. The amount of insurance and reinsurance written is related, in part, to the amount of surplus held by insurers and reinsurers.[74] Over time, the private insurers and reinsurers might develop additional terrorism capacity if there are no losses due to terrorism. If capacity did not increase in the terrorism insurance and reinsurance markets, the insurance-linked securities market might develop and insurers might increasingly attempt to access capital markets to help spread terrorism risk. One capital markets participant said that in the past catastrophic shocks have led to more interest in insurance-linked securities and accelerated issuance of natural catastrophe bonds and that the expiration of the program could similarly foster interest in bonds for terrorism risk. However, insurers and reinsurers continue to question whether the market can accurately price terrorism risk. As a result, insurers and reinsurers might continue to believe they were unable to accurately price for such risks and leave the market for terrorism risk insurance (as happened after September 11, 2001). Furthermore, because losses would no longer be capped, rating agencies might downgrade ratings for insurers and reinsurers, affecting the companies' ability to raise capital. In the long term, policyholders (businesses) also might increase terrorism mitigation and deterrence efforts. For example, businesses might locate some operations away from high-risk areas, invest in mitigation measures (retrofitting properties to better withstand an attack or improve evacuation measures), or both.[75]

In the case of workers' compensation, businesses unable to find coverage from insurers would have to obtain coverage from state funds, which might be more expensive than coverage from primary insurers.[76] For example, representatives of one industry association told us that after the September 11, 2001, attacks, participation in state funds in New York, Washington, D.C., and Virginia increased, as some businesses were unable to find workers' compensation coverage from primary insurers. Over time, businesses were able to leave the state funds and find coverage in the primary market, but workers' compensation insurers became more selective about the number of employers they insured in a particular location.

Finally, past experience following disasters suggests that the federal government may provide assistance to businesses after a terrorist event in the absence of a federal terrorism insurance program. For example, following the September 11, 2001, terrorist attacks, we reported in 2003 that Congress committed at least $18.5 billion to individuals, businesses, and government entities in the New York City area for initial response efforts, compensation for disaster-related costs and losses, infrastructure restoration and improvement, and economic revitalization.[77] As we reported in 2009, many federal agencies and program components administer supplemental programs and funding, reprogram funds, or expedite normal procedures after a disaster.[78] For example, forms of disaster assistance available from federal agencies include grants, loans, loan guarantees, temporary housing, counseling, technical assistance to state and local governments, and rebuilding or recovery projects. Following the April 2013 bombings in Boston, the federal government issued an emergency declaration for the state of Massachusetts that made federal assistance for equipment, resources, or protection available as needed. In 2012, we reported that the growing number of major disaster declarations contributed to an increase in federal expenditures for disaster assistance.[79] For fiscal years 2004 through 2011, the federal government obligated more than $80 billion in disaster relief, about half of which followed Hurricane Katrina. And about $50 billion in federal assistance supported rebuilding efforts after Superstorm Sandy.[80]

Certain Modifications to TRIA Could Affect Availability of Terrorism Coverage, but Insurers Said Other Changes May Not Significantly Affect the Market

As previously discussed, each of the program parameters—program trigger, deductible, coshare, and industry aggregate retention amount— have changed since the program was enacted. It is not clear what impact these past changes have had on insurers in the market, but insurers told us that they generally preferred no additional changes. According to responses from our questionnaire, 11 of 15 insurers said that the TRIA program trigger (currently $100 million) could be increased without significantly changing their ability to provide coverage.[81] In particular, 6 of those 11 insurers noted their companies would be able to offer terrorism coverage if the program trigger were raised up to $500 million, while of the remaining 5 insurers, 4 said they could offer coverage if the trigger were raised up to $1 billion and one insurer said that the trigger could be increased to more than $1 billion. Insurers said that they could continue offering coverage under an increased trigger amount because their current deductibles under the program were higher than the program trigger and increasing the trigger would not impact their share of losses.

For example, using 2012 data, the 10 largest insurers in TRIA-eligible lines all had deductibles much greater than $100 million. As stated previously, while government coverage is triggered once aggregate industry losses exceed $100 million, individual insurers that experienced losses would first pay their deductibles and only then be eligible to receive federal reimbursement for 85 percent of their losses. One insurer explained it was less concerned with changes to the program trigger than to the deductible and coshare percentages, because changes to the latter were more likely to have direct impacts on insurers' liquidity and result in significant market disruptions. Further, we found that increases to the program's parameters could reduce federal fiscal exposure in certain situations, as long as the private sector's share of losses is below the industry aggregate retention amount of $27.5 billion. As previously discussed, TRIA includes a provision for mandatory recoupment of the federal share of losses when private industry's uncompensated insured losses are less than the industry aggregate amount of $27.5 billion. Insurers that responded that they preferred that no change be made to the program trigger cited concerns about capacity limitations, increased terrorism insurance premiums, and an increase in the cost for terrorism reinsurance if the trigger were increased.

Most of the insurers said that increases to the current deductible (20 percent of previous year's direct earned premium) or private-sector coshare (currently at 15 percent) could affect insurer capacity and pricing. For example, insurers commented that an increase in either of these parameters would result in their companies reevaluating their risk, and likely reducing their capacity or increasing policyholders' premiums. One insurer said that it had adjusted its terrorism risk-management program according to the current program, and that any increases almost certainly would result in the company taking risk-mitigation actions, including reducing terrorism exposures, to offset the increased risk to the company's surplus. In addition, insurers stated that increasing the deductible or private-sector coshare would bring many companies under rating agency scrutiny for risk concentrations, which likely would result in industry-wide reductions in terrorism exposure. However, some insurers (3 of 15) told us that their companies could absorb a higher deductible amount, including one insurer that told us its company could absorb an increase in the deductible up to 29 percent. However, this same insurer cautioned that such an increase likely would result in increased premiums for terrorism coverage and decreased take-up rates.

Insurers also expressed concerns about impacts on their solvency if the deductible or coshare percentages were increased. For example, insurers commented that such increases could affect rating agency assessments of companies' financial strength. Representatives of A.M. Best told us that they use a stress test of different scenarios to measure insurers' financial strength and notified 34 insurers their ratings could be negatively affected without a sufficient action plan as a result of failing the stress test.[82] Insurers told us that increasing the deductible or private-sector coshare— and thus the amount of losses insurers would be responsible for paying— could adversely affect insurers' liquidity and solvency in the event of large terrorism losses given the levels of surplus available from which to pay these losses. Industry participants consider deductible in relation to surplus as a metric to help understand how much of the company's surplus would be at stake to pay the TRIA deductible amount in the event of a certified act of terrorism.[83] (Insures also must have surplus available to cover unexpectedly large losses in all other lines of insurance they underwrite.) We found the TRIA deductible has generally represented an increasing portion of insurers' surplus. Under the current program parameters, in 2012 the industry-wide TRIA deductible made up approximately 17 percent of estimated surplus of insurers potentially exposed to terrorism risk.[84] Deductibles remained at 15 percent or higher of estimated surplus since 2005 (see figure 8).

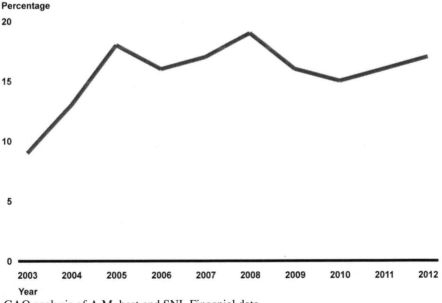

Source: GAO analysis of A.M. best and SNL Finacnial data.

Figure 8. Terrorism Risk Insurance Act Deductible as a Percentage of Estimated Surplus, 2003–2012.

Smaller insurers' surplus would be affected more than larger insurers' surplus in the event of a large terrorism loss. For example, according to our analysis of 2012 SNL Financial insurance data, on average, smaller insurers' TRIA deductible amounts made up 23 percent of surplus compared with 12 percent for larger insurers (that is, the 10 largest commercial property and casualty insurers in TRIA-eligible lines).[85] However, some larger insurers' surplus also would be at heightened risk. For example, the TRIA deductible amounts represented from 7 to 19 percent of surplus of larger insurers. If the deductible was increased to 35 percent, surplus at stake (using 2012 data and holding the estimate for surplus constant) would nearly double to 30 percent, greatly increasing the possibility of insurer insolvencies due to certified terrorism losses.

In contrast to insurer responses on the program deductible and coshare percentages, some insurers told us that the industry could absorb an increase to the industry aggregate retention amount.[86] According to responses from our questionnaire, 7 out of 15 insurers said the industry aggregate retention amount should stay the same and 5 said it could be increased.[87] Two insurers that said increasing the retention amount was reasonable because the industry has grown. For example, one insurer commented that the $27.5 billion amount was roughly based on 20 percent of industry premiums for TRIA-eligible lines in 2006. This insurer stated that because of growth in premiums, the insurance industry was capable of assuming a higher aggregate retention.[88] Another insurer commented that surplus for the property and casualty industry has grown by approximately 20 percent since the 2007 reauthorization; therefore, the insurance industry might be able to absorb an increase in the amount based on the growth in surplus, which would be approximately $33 billion.[89] However, 7 insurers reported that they preferred to maintain the current industry aggregate retention amount and most of those insurers cited concerns about the impact a higher retention amount would have on policyholders, due to the surcharges that would be added to policyholder premiums in the event of recoupment.[90] One industry participant noted that according to experience in other lines of insurance, any surcharge that resulted in a premium increase of more than 2 percent might result in policyholders deciding not to purchase this coverage.

Changes to Program Parameters Could Reduce Federal Fiscal Exposure under Certain Circumstances

Changes to program parameters not only would affect insurers but also estimates for fiscal exposure under TRIA. The legal commitment to pay a share of the losses when a certified terrorist attack occurs makes the program an explicit fiscal exposure for the U.S. government.[91] The amount of federal spending resulting from this exposure depends on the extent of covered losses incurred as a result of a certified attack. Because the potential amounts of fiscal exposure and loss sharing would depend on the specifics of a certified act of terrorism, we developed illustrative examples to help demonstrate estimated changes in the magnitude of fiscal exposure when the deductible, coshare, or industry aggregate retention amounts were individually changed.[92] We found that increasing the insurer deductible, coshare, or aggregate retention amount could reduce the government's fiscal exposure in certain situations (see figure 9). More specifically, as the deductible or coshare percentages increase, the government's overall share of losses decreases, but only when the private sector's share of losses exceeds $27.5 billion (because of mandatory recoupment).[93]

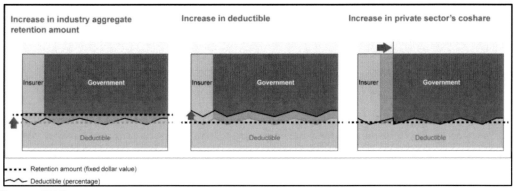

Source: GAO.

Figure 9. Potential Impacts of Increases to the Industry Aggregate Retention Amount and Insurers' Deductible and Coshare Related to the Terrorism Risk Insurance Act.

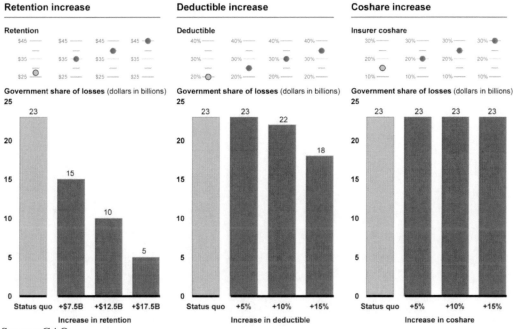

Source: GAO.

Note: This example assumes a terrorist attack that occurred in 2012, resulted in $50 billion of insured losses, and affected the 10 largest commercial property and casualty insurers in TRIA-eligible insurance lines. The example assumes all 10 insurers have an equal market share and that the event will have an equal impact on the TRIA-eligible insurance lines.

Figure 10. Examples of Reductions in Estimated Fiscal Exposure by Increasing Program Parameters, $50 Billion Terrorism-Related Insured Loss Event.

Increasing the industry aggregate retention amount would have a greater impact on reducing fiscal exposure than increasing either the deductible or coshare percentages by certain specified amounts (see figure 10). The potential reduction to federal exposures was most pronounced in our scenario with a $50 billion loss and an increased retention amount.

Such a scenario would approximate current-dollar losses similar to those that resulted from the September 11, 2001, terrorist attacks. Potentially, every $1 increase in the retention amount can result in an equal $1 decrease in federal exposure, when the insured losses are more than the industry aggregate retention amount of $27.5 billion. The insurers' share of losses increases with any decrease in federal fiscal exposures.

According to this $50 billion loss scenario, under the current program parameters the government's share of losses after mandatory recoupment would be $23 billion. If the industry aggregate retention amount were increased to $35 billion, as suggested by increased surplus levels in the industry, federal exposure could decrease to $15 billion (see figure 10). To achieve similar levels of reduction in the government's share of losses, the deductible would have to be raised from 20 to more than 35 percent. There was no observable change to federal exposure when the coshare was increased in this $50 billion loss example because of the mandatory recoupment amount.[94]

The impact of changing the industry aggregate retention amount compared to changes to the deductible or coshare is even more evident under our $75 billion loss scenario (see figure 11).

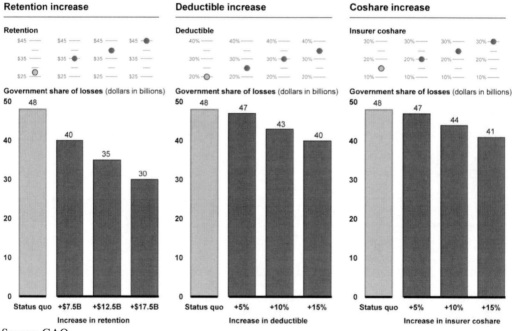

Source: GAO.

Note: This example assumes a terrorist attack that occurred in 2012, resulted in $75 billion of insured losses, and affected the 10 largest commercial property and casualty insurers in TRIA-eligible insurance lines. The example assumes all 10 insurers have an equal market share and that the event will have an equal impact on the TRIA-eligible insurance lines.

Figure 11. Examples of Reductions in Estimated Fiscal Exposure by Increasing Program Parameters, $75 Billion Terrorism-Related Insured Loss Event.

Most Insurers Not Willing to Cover NBCR Outside of Workers' Compensation Policies

As we have previously reported, insurers generally have attempted to limit their exposure to nuclear, biological, chemical, or radiological (NBCR) risks by excluding nearly all NBCR events from property and casualty coverage. According to industry representatives, property and casualty insurers believe they have excluded NBCR coverage by interpreting existing exclusions in their policies to apply to NBCR risks, but some of the exclusions could be challenged in courts.[95] In 2004 Treasury issued an interpretive letter that clarified that the act's definition of insured loss does not exclude losses resulting from NBCR attacks or preclude Treasury from certifying a terrorist attack involving NBCR weapons.[96] According to Treasury's interpretive letter, the program covers insured losses from NBCR events resulting from a certified act of terrorism, if the coverage for those perils is provided in the policy issued by the insurer.

While Treasury has confirmed that NBCR losses would qualify for loss sharing under TRIA, we found insurers generally excluded coverage for NBCR risks.[97,98] Several insurers told us that they do not underwrite NBCR risks because of the lack of data to assess frequency and severity, which makes it difficult to determine an accurate price for the coverage. One insurer told us that NBCR events are uninsurable because of the scale of losses, difficulties in modeling, and the deliberate nature of the acts. Several insurers also told us they generally exclude NBCR risk where state law permits.

However, insurers are generally required to cover NBCR losses for workers' compensation policies, and may provide NBCR coverage in other limited circumstances. For instance, two insurers we interviewed provide NBCR coverage in limited circumstances. One insurer told us that the company covers NBCR risks in its general liability policies, and another said some of its environmental policies include NBCR coverage. As stated previously, workers' compensation insurers generally include NBCR coverage because states generally prohibit the exclusion of any peril for workers' compensation.[99] Also, certain states require insurers to cover fire following an event, regardless of the cause of the fire. Thus, an NBCR event that leads to a fire may activate a fire policy providing coverage to a policyholder.

Other options for NBCR coverage exist. For instance, NBCR coverage can be obtained through the use of captive insurers accessing the TRIA program and we previously reported that some large businesses elected this coverage route.[100] There also is a limited stand-alone terrorism insurance market for NBCR, but high prices have prevented most businesses from purchasing coverage.[101] And, although reinsurance companies traditionally excluded NBCR, about two-thirds of reinsurance companies offered some coverage for NBCR events, according to a 2010 survey.[102]

Some insurers told us that expanding TRIA to require insurers to make NBCR coverage available would result in significant disruptions to the market. Some insurers said that an NBCR event could render the insurance industry insolvent. Another insurer told us that underwriting NBCR risks would decrease its capacity to underwrite other types of insurance. Several insurers did not support changing TRIA to require coverage for NBCR events because, in their opinion, NBCR was not an insurable risk. One insurer said effective underwriting and pricing of NBCR exposure was not possible and attempting to do so would be contrary to basic principles of insurance underwriting and pricing.[103] One company told us that significant market disruptions would occur if NBCR coverage were mandatory. Additionally, one insurer told us that reinsurance capacity for NBCR risks was minimal and, as a result, the ability of any insurer to offer NBCR coverage was limited.

Insurers Reported Numerous Obstacles Involved in Charging for Federal Reinsurance

According to responses to our questionnaire, 10 of 15 insurers said that they did not favor establishing a prefunding mechanism (such as a pool) in place of the current post funding mechanism under TRIA (recoupment). For example, a prefunding mechanism could potentially allow insurers to set aside tax-deductible reserves for terrorist events or the creation of risk-sharing pools. One insurer supported a prefunding mechanism and four other insurers did not provide comments on the advantages and disadvantages associated with a prefunding mechanism. Insurers not in favor of a mechanism to charge for federal reinsurance cited a number of obstacles that would need to be considered, such as the following:

- Increased administrative costs. Several insurers commented that a prefunding mechanism would require additional resources and staff to administer. For example, one insurer said that Treasury would have to expand its staff and augment their expertise to administer a prefunding mechanism. This insurer also noted that Treasury would have to collect and analyze exposure and other pricing data, utilize terrorism risk models, obtain staff with actuarial and underwriting expertise, conduct audits of insurers, and manage a billing process.
- Difficulties funding a reinsurance pool. Insurers noted challenges in accumulating sufficient reserves for a pool, and effectively managing the pool. For example, one insurer commented that the federal government likely would not be able to accumulate enough funds for such a pool. Insurers also cited other challenges involved in prefunding federal reinsurance, such as decreases in the purchase of terrorism insurance due to its increased cost or lack of coverage after an event depletes the fund.
- Challenges in estimating the frequency of terrorist attacks. The unpredictability of terrorist attacks and the inability to effectively underwrite against terrorism risk would need to be considered. One insurer commented that any prefunding mechanism would be purely speculative and contribution amounts would bear little relationship to the likely losses from an event. Additionally, because it is difficult to assess the potential frequency and severity of a terrorism event (key components in pricing or funding for risk), insurers commented that postfunding (recoupment) was the preferable approach for terrorism risk.
- Increased cost to policyholders. Insurers commented that if a prefunding mechanism were established, it likely would result in increased costs, such as administrative costs and increased costs to policyholders. For example, one insurer told us that as users of such a mechanism, its costs for such a mechanism would be passed to policyholders. This insurer also noted that additional costs may cause policyholders to forgo terrorism coverage; therefore, in their view a prefunding mechanism could

contravene the purpose of TRIA—to encourage the availability and affordability of terrorism coverage for policyholders that want to insure against terrorism exposure.

While Some Insurers Cover Cyber Terrorism Risks, Others Not Certain If TRIA Covers This Risk

Some uncertainty exists in the market about whether TRIA covers cyber terrorism risks. According to industry participants, cyber attacks could involve a wide spectrum of potential threats that could impact property, critical communications, and utility and transportation infrastructure, among other unconventional threats. Industry participants also pointed out that cyber events have the ability to impact numerous lines of insurance coverage. While TRIA does not explicitly exclude coverage of cyber risks (or other specific perils) it also does not explicitly cover it. Program guidance and other official communications have been silent on this point—thus, allowing for confusion or uncertainties about coverage. According to our questionnaire, 8 of 15 insurers considered losses resulting from cyber terrorism as covered by TRIA as long as the insurer underwrote cyber terrorism coverage as part of the underlying policy. However, our questionnaire also revealed uncertainty about such TRIA coverage. For example, 7 other insurers said that, based on their understanding of TRIA, they did not know if losses resulting from cyber terrorism would be covered by TRIA. Insurers commented that more clarity about the treatment of cyber terrorism under the program would be helpful to eliminate any uncertainty in the insurance industry about coverage of this type of risk.

Insurers also commented that because cyber terrorism is an emerging risk there was some uncertainty about what the term encompassed. For example, one insurer noted that there is no statutory definition for cyber terrorism and that depending on the definition of cyber terrorism the program may or may not be triggered; therefore, the insurer said that a consistent definition would be needed. Another insurer said it was unsure if the industry has had a consistent approach to defining and covering cyber terrorism in policies and suggested that a technical working group or clarification from Treasury could help make this clearer. Some insurers, industry associations, and brokers also noted that because cyber terrorism risk is a new and evolving risk that recently has come into focus, some clarification about how this risk would be covered under TRIA would be helpful and could help increase capacity in the market. For example, in its comments to PWG, Aon noted a lack of cyber insurance capacity in certain industries, such as large energy, utility, gas, and water entities. In addition, in their 2013 statement to PWG, the American Academy of Actuaries stated that cyber terrorism is a significant risk, and that clarification is important because of the nation's ever-increasing dependence on technology, including for commerce and business administration.

As discussed earlier in this report, Treasury issued an interpretive letter in 2004 that clarified whether losses from an NBCR event would be covered under TRIA.[104] In addition, our work on fiscal exposures demonstrates the importance of complete information about fiscal exposures.[105] Specifically, a more complete understanding of the sources of fiscal exposure and the way they change can provide enhanced control and oversight over federal resources. Treasury acknowledged that there has been growth in the cyber insurance market. Treasury officials said that they have not issued any clarifications because clarification was unnecessary and explicitly listing TRIA-covered events may create unnecessary coverage disputes. While TRIA does not explicitly prohibit coverage of cyber terrorism risk, neither does it explicitly allow it. However, without clarification of the coverage of cyber risks, some insurers may not offer cyber coverage or may not explicitly exclude coverage. As a result, coverage may not be as available. Additionally, inclusion of cyber risks affects the government's fiscal exposure under TRIA, and without gathering information from the industry to help provide clarity surrounding the definition and coverage of this risk, the federal government would not have an understanding of the potential impact of losses from a cyber attack.

CONCLUSION

Congress enacted TRIA and its reauthorizations to help ensure the availability and affordability of insurance for terrorism risk and provide a transitional period in which the private insurance market could determine how to model and price terrorism risk. However, Treasury has not collected comprehensive data directly from insurers. Federal internal control standards state that agencies should identify and obtain relevant and needed data to be able to meet program goals. Obtaining comprehensive data is necessary to thoroughly analyze the market. While Treasury stated that the information available from other sources has been sufficient for purposes of responding to TRIA's reporting requirements, more data and periodic assessments of the market would help Treasury assess whether the program goals of ensuring the continued widespread availability and affordability of terrorism risk insurance and addressing market disruptions are being met, and advance decision making about any potential program changes and the impact of those program changes on the market.

Moreover, Treasury has performed limited analyses of the potential amount of fiscal exposure the program represents. While no terrorist attacks have triggered TRIA, the program still creates an explicit fiscal exposure for the government because the government is legally required to make payments for certified terrorist events. According to industry best practices, analysis of exposures is important for understanding the financial risks of a potential terrorist attack. In addition, federal internal control standards state the importance of analyzing risks to programs, and our prior work on fiscal exposures highlights how estimates could be developed to better understand fiscal exposures. By enhancing its data analyses, Treasury would be in a better position to estimate the amount of fiscal exposure under various scenarios of potential terrorist attacks and to inform Congress of the potential fiscal implications of any program changes. By better understanding fiscal exposure, Treasury can aid Congress in monitoring the financial condition of the program and its potential impact on the federal budget over the longer term.

In the last few years, demand for terrorism insurance may have leveled off, as indicated by available data. However, insurers are concerned about how a new type of terrorist threat, cyber attacks, would be treated under the program and some industry sectors have experienced difficulty obtaining coverage. Some terrorism risk insurers told us they do not know whether losses resulting from cyber terrorism would qualify for coverage under TRIA, which may impact their decision to cover it. In the past, Treasury issued an interpretive letter to clarify the treatment of NBCR risks under the program. TRIA is silent on cyber threats. Clarification of the coverage of cyber risks could spur additional capacity in the market for this type of risk. Additionally, clarification of cyber risks could help estimates of the government's fiscal exposure more accurately reflect the potential risks.

RECOMMENDATIONS FOR EXECUTIVE ACTION

We recommend that the Secretary of the Treasury take the following three actions:

- Collect the data needed to analyze the terrorism insurance market. Types of data may include terrorism coverage by line of insurance and terrorism insurance premiums earned. In taking this action, Treasury should determine whether any additional authority is needed and, if so, work with Congress to ensure it has the authority needed to carry out this action.
- Periodically assess data collected related to terrorism insurance, including analyzing differences in terrorism insurance by company size, geography, or industry sector; conducting hypothetical illustrative examples to help estimate the potential magnitude of fiscal exposure; and analyzing how changing program parameters may impact the market and fiscal exposure.
- Gather additional information needed from the insurance industry related to how cyber terrorism is defined and used in policies, and clarify whether losses that may result from cyber terrorism are covered under TRIA—clarification could be made through an interpretative letter or revisions to program regulations, some combination or any other vehicle that Treasury deems appropriate.

AGENCY COMMENTS AND OUR EVALUATION

We provided a draft of this report for review and comment to the Department of the Treasury (Treasury), including the Federal Insurance Office, and National Association of Insurance Commissioners (NAIC). We received written comments from Treasury. NAIC did not provide written comments. Treasury and NAIC also provided technical comments, which we incorporated as appropriate. In its written comments, Treasury agreed with our recommendations on collecting and assessing data to analyze the terrorism insurance market, but with respect to our recommendation about clarifying guidance on coverage of cyber terrorism, said that it did not believe advance determination of such an event would be helpful or appropriate.

Treasury agreed to collect the data needed to analyze the terrorism insurance market and to periodically assess these data for certain purposes, such as for differences in terrorism insurance by company size, geography, or industry sector and effects on the market for terrorism risk insurance of changing program parameters. Treasury also noted that collecting and analyzing market data would not provide a basis to meaningfully estimate the fiscal exposure of the government under the program and that the amount of federal payments to insurers resulting from acts of terrorism hinges on multiple variables that cannot be predicted with precision. As discussed in the report, limitations of modeling the probability of this type of risk exist, but we maintain that estimating the potential magnitude of fiscal exposure under various hypothetical scenarios of terrorist attacks could help inform Congress of the potential fiscal implications of any program changes, including changes that could limit federal fiscal exposure. Further, accounting for insurers' deductibles and recoupment in these estimates could aid Treasury in monitoring the potential impact of the program on the federal budget over the longer term. In light of Treasury's response, we have revised our draft recommendation to clarify what types of analyses to conduct and to specify that illustrative examples of different terrorist attack scenarios could be used for the analysis of the potential magnitude of fiscal exposure.

Regarding our third recommendation that Treasury should clarify whether losses that may result from cyber terrorism are covered under TRIA, Treasury stated that TRIA does not preclude federal payments for a cyber terrorism event if it meets the statutory criteria for an act of terrorism. Treasury also stated that while the agency will continue to monitor this issue as it develops and collect applicable market data as necessary, it does not believe that providing an advance determination of when a cyber event is an act of terrorism would be helpful or appropriate. As discussed in the report, clarification of whether losses from a cyber terrorism event could be eligible for coverage under TRIA is needed because of existing uncertainties regarding this coverage. Such clarification would not necessarily require an advance determination of what types of cyber events would qualify as acts of terrorism under the statute. As we discussed in the report, 7 of the 15 insurers responding to our questionnaire did not know if losses resulting from cyber terrorism would be covered by TRIA. In addition, a large broker noted a lack of cyber insurance capacity in certain industries. Due to the uncertainties that exist about what this emerging risk encompasses and whether losses resulting from a cyber terrorism event would qualify for coverage under TRIA, clarification would be helpful to spur additional market capacity for this risk, consistent with the program's goals of ensuring availability and affordability of terrorism risk insurance. In light of Treasury's response, we revised our draft recommendation to specify the type of information to be gathered from the industry to help inform Treasury's decision regarding guidance on cyber terrorism.

Daniel Garcia-Diaz
Director, Financial Markets and Community Investment

APPENDIX I. OBJECTIVES, SCOPE, AND METHODOLOGY

The objectives of our report were to (1) evaluate the extent of available data and the U.S. Department of the Treasury's (Treasury) efforts in determining the government's exposure for the terrorism risk insurance program, (2) describe changes in the terrorism insurance market since 2002, and (3) evaluate potential impacts of selected changes to the Terrorism Risk Insurance Act (TRIA).

For each of our objectives, we reviewed relevant laws, particularly the Terrorism Risk Insurance Act of 2002, its amendments, and implementing regulations.[106] We also reviewed relevant literature and past reports on terrorism risk, including the Congressional Research Service's reports on the current program and recent legislation.[107] Additionally, we reviewed reports our previous reports on TRIA and updated our work accordingly.[108] We reviewed reports to Congress from the President's Working Group on Financial Markets (PWG).[109] We also reviewed comments submitted from the public to PWG for their most recent TRIA report. We interviewed federal officials and staff from Treasury, the National Association of Insurance Commissioners, and the Congressional Budget Office. We also interviewed several industry participants (such as representatives from insurance trade associations, terrorism risk modeling firms, rating agencies, and insurance brokers) to obtain information for all our objectives.

Because detailed information on terrorism insurance was not publicly available, we developed a questionnaire to solicit information applicable to all our objectives from 15 insurers from which businesses had purchased terrorism coverage in 2012. The 15 companies—10 of the largest U.S. commercial property and casualty insurers in lines subject to TRIA (by premium volume) and 5 additional insurers recommended to us by an insurance broker, trade association, or both—represented roughly 40 percent of the commercial property and casualty market (by direct earned premium volume for 2012), according to SNL Financial data.[110] We included questions about coverage, premium volume, and underwriting decisions. We also obtained views on potential modifications to TRIA and how they might affect the market, which we took into account when developing questions. We worked with a GAO specialist to draft questions. To minimize errors arising from differences in how questions might be interpreted and reduce variability in responses, we conducted pretests with two different organizations in January 2014. On the basis of feedback, we revised the questionnaire to improve organization and clarity. We then sent the questionnaire to the 15 insurers in January 2014. Some questions required close-ended responses, such as providing a specific percentage or checking boxes. Other questions were open-ended, allowing the insurers to provide more in-depth responses on how changes to TRIA might affect them. Since the 15 insurers we contacted were selected on a nonprobability basis, the findings are only applicable to the 15 companies that we interviewed and do not generalize to even the commercial property and casualty insurers that sold terrorism coverage in 2012. They do offer insight into how some private market insurers currently view parameters and topics under consideration related to government-backed terrorism insurance.

We took steps to verify the information gathered in the questionnaire and analyzed the results. We initially reviewed returned questionnaires to ensure company representatives had provided complete and consistent responses. After we received the completed, written responses, we held teleconferences with representatives from each insurer to discuss, clarify, or amend responses, as appropriate. We aggregated the responses and presented summary information in this report. We used standard descriptive statistics to analyze quantitative responses and performed content analysis on the open-ended responses to identify common themes. Where possible, we corroborated insurers' responses with information or analysis from other sources. On the basis of our questionnaire design and these follow-up procedures, we determined that the data used in this report were sufficiently reliable for our purposes. Finally, GAO data analysts independently verified all data analysis programs and calculations for accuracy.

To evaluate the extent of comprehensive data, we obtained and reviewed information on the availability of data on the terrorism insurance market and Treasury's efforts to help estimate federal exposure under TRIA. We reviewed previous reports to Congress from PWG and Treasury on TRIA. In addition, we interviewed and obtained information from officials and staff at Treasury's Federal Insurance Office and Terrorism Risk Insurance Program

Office. To obtain information on Treasury's efforts in determining federal exposure, we reviewed a study from the Insurance Services Office, Inc. that provided an estimate of average annual losses under TRIA in any given year. We also reviewed documents from Treasury, and information on exposure analyses from risk modeling companies, such as RMS and AIR Worldwide. We spoke to insurers, brokers, and terrorism risk modeling firms to better understand how they analyze information about terrorism exposures and obtain information about the industry's best practices. Finally, we reviewed our work on fiscal exposures to help determine any explicit exposures created by TRIA.[111] For example, a certified terrorism attack would represent an explicit exposure because some payment by the federal government would be legally required.

To describe changes in the terrorism risk insurance market, we obtained and analyzed available information on premiums, capacity, pricing, and take-up rates (the percentage of businesses buying terrorism coverage). We obtained information on terrorism insurance premiums from 2004 through 2012 from A.M. Best, an insurance rating agency, which had collected this information as part of its annual Supplemental Rating Questionnaire. A.M. Best provided aggregated data to us.[112] To compare terrorism premiums with premiums collected for other insurance lines, we obtained data from SNL Financial on premiums earned for commercial property and casualty insurers for all commercial lines and for lines subject to TRIA. Additionally, we obtained capacity, pricing, and take-up rate information from 2003 through 2013 from two insurance brokers— Marsh and McLennan (Marsh) and Aon—as available. Marsh provided nationwide pricing and take-up rate data, while Aon had information on capacity. Marsh and Aon are the largest business insurance brokers in the United States. We interviewed representatives from Marsh and Aon to ensure we had a clear understanding of which insurers the data represented and how the brokers obtain information from their data systems. All data presented in this report from Marsh and Aon solely represent their clients, cannot be generalized to the entire market, and are attributed accordingly. Based on this, we determined that the data used in this report from the insurance brokers were sufficiently reliable for our purposes. To obtain information on the reinsurance market and insurance-linked securities, we interviewed representatives from the Reinsurance Association of America and Fermat Capital Management. We also reviewed reports from industry participants, such as Swiss Re, Munich Re, and Aon Benfield on the status of the reinsurance and insurance-linked securities markets. Finally, as part of our questionnaire, we asked insurers whether they purchased reinsurance for terrorism risk and how reinsurance purchasing patterns have changed over the last decade.

To evaluate the potential impact of selected changes to TRIA, we identified certain changes to the program's parameters based on our analysis of the program's structure, review of relevant literature, testimonies from congressional hearings, and prior changes made in the TRIA reauthorizations. On the basis of these, we asked the 15 insurers who received our questionnaire for their input on how selected changes would affect the insurance market for terrorism risk. For example, we asked insurers to categorize the greatest changes to program parameters and how such changes could affect each company's capacity, pricing, and take-up rates. We asked insurers to categorize the greatest change to the aggregate industry retention amount (currently, $27.5 billion) that, in their opinion, the industry could handle. We also asked insurers if their companies underwrote nuclear, biological, chemical, or radiological risks or cyber risks and what metrics or factors Congress would need to consider if changes were made to TRIA related to losses as a result of these types of risks. Finally, we asked insurers to indicate what metrics and factors Congress would need to consider if the federal government were to establish a prefunding mechanism (in place of the current postfunding mechanism—recoupment). We obtained information from A.M. Best on estimated policyholder surplus of insurers potentially exposed to terrorism from 2003 through 2012, to compare, industry-wide, the TRIA deductible amounts with estimates of policyholder surplus. We also compared the average TRIA deductible as a percentage of estimated policyholder surplus, for the 10 largest commercial property and casualty insurers (in insurance lines subject to TRIA), with all other insurers, as well as the range for the 10 largest insurers. We performed this analysis to help determine whether any differences existed for large versus small insurers in terms of their TRIA deductible amounts as a percentage of surplus.

We also developed examples to illustrate the impact of certain changes to the current program on the federal government's fiscal exposure. To develop the examples, we consulted with experts from terrorism risk modeling firms and reviewed relevant literature. Additionally, to develop the examples, we made assumptions for the number of insurers affected, and their direct earned premiums, market share, insurance lines, and total loss amount. We used SNL Financial insurance data and information from A.M. Best to help develop these assumptions. We compared what federal losses would be under the current program parameters (status quo) with those after making changes to the current program. For example, we compared changing the deductible from 20 to 35 percent and changing the insurers' coshare from 15 to 30 percent, in intervals of 2 to 3 percent. We analyzed the federal share of losses for variously sized terrorist attacks ($25 billion, $50 billion, $75 billion, and $100 billion) before and after recoupment, using the current law's aggregate industry retention amount ($27.5 billion).[113] To help assess the reliability of our analysis, we verified that our results were consistent with a model developed by the Reinsurance Association of America.

We conducted this performance audit from July 2013 through May 2014, in accordance with generally accepted government auditing standards. Those standards require that we plan and perform the audit to obtain sufficient, appropriate evidence to provide a reasonable basis for our findings and conclusions based on our audit objectives. We believe that the evidence obtained provides a reasonable basis for our findings and conclusions based on our audit objectives.

End Notes

[1] Insurance Information Institute, (accessed on March 4, 2014) http://www.iii.org/facts_statistics/terrorism.html.

[2] Pub. L. No. 107-297, 116 Stat. 2322 (2002). TRIA was reauthorized in 2005 and again in 2007, see Terrorism Risk Insurance Extension Act of 2005, Pub. L. No. 109-144, 119 Stat. 2660 (2005) and Terrorism Risk Insurance Program Reauthorization Act of 2007, Pub. L. No. 110-160, 121 Stat. 1839 (2007). In this report, we collectively refer to the original act and its reauthorizations as TRIA.

[3] TRIA states that the Secretary of the Treasury, in concurrence with the Secretary of State and the Attorney General of the United States, shall determine whether an event should be certified as an act of terrorism, based on certain criteria.

[4] Insurance lines of business are divided into two parts: (1) property and casualty and (2) life and health. Property and casualty insurance is further divided into personal and commercial lines. For example, personal lines include automobile, homeowners, and renters insurance for individuals. The major commercial lines include multiple perils, fire, liability, and workers' compensation. TRIA solely applies to commercial property and casualty lines of insurance.

[5] NAIC is a voluntary association of the heads of insurance departments from the 50 states, District of Columbia, and five territories.

[6] SNL Financial, through a partnership with NAIC, provides comprehensive statutory financial data for the insurance industry.

[7] For the purposes of this report, "industry participants" refers to those entities with a role in the insurance industry.

[8] Emmett J. Vaughan and Therese Vaughan, *Fundamentals of Risk and Insurance*, 9th ed. (Hoboken, NJ: John Wiley and Sons, 2003). Specifically, (1) there must be a sufficiently large number of homogeneous units exposed to random losses to make future losses reasonably predictable; (2) the loss must be definite and measurable; (3) the loss must be accidental, or resulting from chance; and (4) the loss must not be catastrophic; that is, it must not affect a very large percentage of an insurance company's policyholders at the same time or be extraordinarily large relative to the exposure.

[9] GAO, *Terrorism Insurance: Measuring and Predicting Losses from Unconventional Weapons Is Difficult, but Some Industry Exposure Exists*, GAO-06-1081 (Washington, D.C.: Sept. 25, 2006).

[10] Insurance Information Institute, *Terrorism Risk and Insurance*, August 2013.

[11] Before September 11, 2001, insurers generally did not exclude or separately charge for coverage of terrorism risks. After September 11, insurers started including substantial charges to cover terrorism risk, or, excluded the coverage (with the exception of workers' compensation—states require that workers' compensation insurance cover terrorism and do not permit exclusions).

[12] The federal government will collect an amount equal to 133 percent of the mandatory recoupment amount.

[13] The industry aggregate retention amount is the lesser of $27.5 billion or the aggregate amount for all insurers of insured losses due to acts of terror during the calendar year. Throughout the report, the $27.5 billion figure is utilized to encompass the industry aggregate retention definition.

[14] GAO, *Terrorism Insurance: Status of Coverage Availability for Attacks Involving Nuclear, Biological, Chemical, or Radiological Weapons*, GAO-09-39 (Washington, D.C.: Dec. 12, 2008).

[15] Established by the Dodd-Frank Wall Street Reform and Consumer Protection Act, Treasury's Federal Insurance Office monitors the insurance sector and advises on important national and international insurance matters. According to Treasury officials, as of June 2011, the Federal Insurance Office started assisting the Treasury Secretary in administering the Terrorism Risk Insurance Program.

[16] Treasury issued the majority of the regulations for TRIA's implementation in 2003.

[17] PWG comprises the Secretary of the Treasury and the Chairs of the Board of Governors of the Federal Reserve System, Securities and Exchange Commission, and the Commodity Futures Trading Commission (or their respective designees). The Secretary of the Treasury (or a designee) serves as PWG chair.

[18] GAO, *Terrorism Insurance: Status of Coverage Availability for Attacks Involving Nuclear, Biological, Chemical, or Radiological Weapons*, GAO-09-39 (Washington, D.C.: Dec. 12, 2008); *Terrorism Insurance: Status of Efforts by Policyholders to Obtain Coverage*, GAO-08-1057 (Washington, D.C.: Sept. 15, 2008); and *Terrorism Insurance: Implementation of the Terrorism Risk Insurance Act of 2002*, GAO-04-307 (Washington, D.C.: Apr. 23, 2004).

[19] Department of the Treasury, *Assessment: The Terrorism Risk Insurance Act of 2002* (Washington, D.C.: June 30, 2005).

[20] See President's Working Group on Financial Markets, *Terrorism Risk Insurance* (Washington, D.C.: September 2006); *Market Conditions for Terrorism Risk Insurance* (Washington, D.C.: 2010); and *The Long-Term Availability and Affordability of Insurance for Terrorism Risk* (Washington, D.C.: April 2014).

[21] The federal government retains the authority to regulate insurance, but has given primary responsibility for insurance regulation to the states in accordance with the McCarran-Ferguson Act of 1945. See Pub. L. No. 79-5, ch. 20, 59 Stat. 33 (1945) codified as amended at 15 U.S.C. §§ 1011-1015. See also GAO, *Ultimate Effects of McCarran-Ferguson Federal Antitrust Exemption on Insurer Activity Are Unclear*, GAO-05-816R (Washington, D.C.: July 28, 2005). Nevertheless, the federal government is involved in many areas relating to the insurance sector, including operation of the National Flood Insurance Program, and crop and terrorism insurance programs. In addition, the Board of Governors of the Federal Reserve System supervises insurers designated by the Financial Stability Oversight Council.

[22] For purposes of this report, market data also refer to take-up rates (percentage of businesses buying coverage), information on policyholder surplus, industrywide capacity, insurers with NBCR exposures, and insurers purchasing reinsurance for terrorism risks.

[23] According to NAIC representatives, the NAIC has license agreements with the states, and would, therefore, need permission from those states that use the system to access filing information.

[24] ISO is a leading source of information about property and casualty insurance risk. For a broad spectrum of personal and commercial lines of insurance, the company provides statistical, actuarial, and claims information; standardized policy language; information about specific locations; fraud-identification tools; and technical services. ISO representatives told us they collect data on losses and premiums, and that their data for commercial lines of insurance represent approximately two-thirds of the U.S. domestic industry's premium volume. This represents the majority of property and casualty lines (except workers' compensation) and primarily includes business written in the admitted market (that is, insurance policies or products purchased from companies or agents admitted or licensed to sell in a state). The main purpose of ISO's terrorism data collection is to enable the data to be excluded from ratemaking for standard coverages. Coding was not

intended to provide a detailed analysis of the terrorism exposure. A.M. Best provides news, credit ratings and financial data products and other services for the insurance industry. According to A.M. Best representatives, the company captures premium information through its annual supplemental rating questionnaire. A.M. Best representatives told us that although they do not know exactly what proportion of the market the estimated premiums charged for terrorism coverage equal, they believe the information encompasses the vast majority of the market.

[25] PWG also relied on data submitted by brokers. While the information that brokers compile is not anecdotal, it is also not representative of the entire insurance industry, as previously discussed.

[26] In general, a premium is the total amount paid by a policyholder to an insurer for a given amount of insurance coverage. A premium rate is the price per unit of coverage, such as the price per $1,000 of coverage. Premium rates are based on the insurer's expectation of losses associated with a particular class of risk, and may be regulated by state insurance offices.

[27] Treasury last directly surveyed insurers in 2005 for a report to Congress. See Department of the Treasury, *Assessment: The Terrorism Risk Insurance Act of 2002* (Washington, D.C.: June 30, 2005). To draft this 2005 report, Treasury contracted with a research firm to survey policyholders and insurers. Treasury also consulted with NAIC, a range of experts in the insurance industry, policyholders, and others. PWG reports list the sources of information on which Treasury relied.

[28] TRIA's data compilation requirement for Treasury could be termed "pre-event." In contrast, Treasury has regulatory authority to compile data following a terrorist event. For example, Treasury may issue a data call to insurers for insurer deductible and insured loss information by program year for purposes of determining initial or recalculated recoupment amounts (that is, the amounts Treasury would collect from insurers as repayment of the federal assistance provided under TRIA). Treasury also may issue a data call for insured loss information to determine an initial or recalculated pro-rata loss percentage. Other TRIA and regulatory provisions discuss how companies must maintain records, including information on premiums, and when they must provide them to Treasury.

[29] See GAO, *Standards for Internal Control in the Federal Government*, GAO/AIMD-00-21.3.1 (Washington, D.C.: November 1999).

[30] See GAO, *Fiscal Exposures: Improving the Budgetary Focus on Long-Term Costs and Uncertainties*, GAO-03-213 (Washington, D.C.: Jan. 24, 2003).

[31] See GAO, *Fiscal Exposures: Improving Cost Recognition in the Federal Budget*, GAO-14-28 (Washington, D.C.: Oct. 29, 2013).

[32] For example, ISO was asked to review projections of initial federal share as a percentage of total losses presented in another study, and advise whether the set of relationships derived by Treasury from that study were reasonable for budget projection purposes.

[33] As we previously reported, for programs in which the time between incurring a cost and the resulting payment is relatively short, the budget often provides sufficient information on and control over the government's spending commitments. However, for some programs in which the government legally obligated itself to make future payments or incur losses if an event occurs, the generally cash-based measures used in the budget do not reflect the magnitude of the government's legal commitment of future resources at the time decisions are made. See GAO-14-28.

[34] Treasury made certain assumptions for the scenario, including the amount of direct earned premiums, the number of insurers affected, and the amount of insured losses.

[35] Additionally, according to Treasury officials, insurers vary greatly in size and smaller insurers will more likely trigger the program because larger insurers' deductibles far exceed the program trigger. Similar to the example provided above, if smaller insurers trigger the program, the government's share of losses is likely to be triggered at an amount less than the aggregated industry deductible.

[36] See GAO/AIMD-00-21.31.

[37] See GAO-14-28.

[38] All estimates of future spending introduce some degree of additional uncertainty into the budget and the ease of implementation differs. Some measures already may be used widely in other forms of reporting, whereas others are relatively new concepts for federal budget reporting and may involve developing new models and technical skills. Despite any implementation challenges, approximate estimates of the full cost to government may be preferable to some current measures that are incomplete or potentially misleading. Furthermore, a requirement to produce estimates for budget reporting may help improve the quality of estimates by drawing more attention to them. Although using estimates may introduce uncertainty in primary budget data, it would result in earlier cost recognition in the budget. This would help reinforce up-front controls in the budget process. See GAO-14-28.

[39] Representatives of a risk modeling firm with whom we spoke reported advances in terrorism risk insurance modeling over the past decade, including more information (such as information about U.S. intelligence agencies and counter-terrorism efforts), a better understanding of terrorist activity, and more data on the number of terrorist plots. We determined that because these advances make it possible for industry participants to better quantify the cost of potential terrorist attacks with specific estimated circumstances, these industry

best practices were also relevant for assessing the impact on the insurance industry, and the potential magnitude of fiscal exposure to the government of specific scenarios of potential terrorist attacks.

[40] Wharton Risk Management and Decision Processes Center, The Wharton School, University of Pennsylvania, *TRIA and Beyond: Terrorism Risk Financing in the U.S.* (Philadelphia, Penn.: 2005).

[41] Although these data may not reflect the entire market, they are the best available data because insurers are not required to report terrorism insurance premiums to Treasury or NAIC. In 2004, A.M. Best began collecting data on premiums charged for terrorism coverage as a part of its annual survey of insurers (specifically, the Supplemental Rating Questionnaire for U.S property and casualty). A.M. Best collects these data for insurance rating units that provide commercial lines on a primary basis, in which the commercial lines make up more than 10 percent of the rating units' direct written premiums. A.M. Best does not know exactly what proportion of the market the estimated premiums charged for terrorism coverage equal, but company representatives believe the information encompasses the vast majority of the terrorism insurance market.

[42] According to A.M. Best representatives, data for 2013 will not be available until June 2014.

[43] For many insurers, direct exposure to the financial crisis, the U.S. mortgage market, and related securities appeared to have been limited. But the financial crisis nonetheless had an impact on the insurance industry, primarily on their investment portfolios.

[44] We calculated this number ($1.7 billion) based on each insurer's response to our questionnaire about the percentage of overall commercial property and casualty premiums that terrorism coverage constitutes and multiplied those responses by each insurer's entire commercial property and casualty premiums in 2012 (according to SNL Financial insurance data). The $1.7 billion matches A.M. Best's estimate for terrorism insurance premiums discussed earlier in this report. Both A.M. Best's estimate for terrorism insurance premiums and our calculation of terrorism insurance premiums from the questionnaire data are minimum estimates because neither is representative of the entire market.

[45] For the purposes of this report section and table 3, "insurers" means insurance groups— A.M. Best and SNL Financial report data by groups. For example, SNL Financial analysts review ownership structure as a basis for the SNL insurance groups.

[46] Federal Insurance Office, Department of the Treasury, *Annual Report on the Insurance Industry* (Washington, D.C.: June 2013).

[47] Using SNL Financial insurance data for 2012, we compiled company-level data for direct earned premiums for the insurance lines subject to TRIA (see table 1).

[48] Per risk capacity is a measure used for estimating market capacity that aggregates the maximum amount of coverage an insurer is willing to provide to any one insured.

[49] The stand-alone terrorism market has additional capacity. According to an Aon report, in 2013, from $750 million to $2 billion per risk was available. Stand-alone policies can provide excess coverage above all-risk policies or fill gaps in coverage; for example, by covering losses from noncertified acts of terrorism. In general, coverage purchased in the stand-alone terrorism market is not subject to TRIA.

[50] See GAO-08-1057.

[51] Rates are calculated by dividing the premium by the total insured value of a property.

[52] The pricing data are for Marsh clients that purchased terrorism coverage as part of a property policy. The data do not include pricing for terrorism coverage purchased as part of a liability or workers' compensation policy. For this reason and because Marsh's data solely represent its clients, the data are not representative of the entire market. However, we found Marsh's data the most readily available data on pricing.

[53] Marsh, *Market Update 2013 Terrorism Risk Insurance Report,* May 2013.

[54] According to the Marsh data, in 2012, businesses paid about 5 percent of their total property premium for terrorism coverage. As previously reported, according to our questionnaire of 15 insurers, terrorism insurance premiums made up approximately 2 percent of overall premiums, in 2012. Marsh's data solely consists of property policies, while our questionnaire data includes property policies, as well as other policies that may include terrorism coverage, such as liability or workers' compensation policies.

[55] For example, Marsh does not collect data for the percentage of businesses buying terrorism coverage as part of commercial liability policies.

[56] See Marsh, *Market Update 2013 Terrorism Risk Insurance Report,* May 2013.

[57] This does not include workers' compensation, which as previously stated has a 100 percent take-up rate. We did not further analyze take-up rate data obtained as part of our questionnaire because of data reliability concerns (how each insurer obtained and reported the information to us). Because terrorism coverage is typically included in an all-risk property policy that covers several insurance lines, the information reported to us varied significantly. A multiperil policy refers to a policy that may contain a few named perils and exclude others.

[58] Nationwide take-up rates increased from 27 percent in 2003 to 62 percent in 2013; while terrorism insurance median rates per million dollars of coverage declined from $56 in 2003 to $27 in 2013.

[59] Reinsurance is insurance for insurers. Insurance-linked securities are financial instruments, with values driven by insurance loss events. The most common type of insurance-linked security is a catastrophe bond, which we discuss later in this report.

[60] Congressional Budget Office, *Federal Reinsurance for Terrorism Risk: Issues in Reauthorization* (Washington, D.C.: August 2007).

[61] J. Eric Smith, *The Terrorism Risk Insurance Act of 2002.* Swiss Re Americas. Sep. 19, 2013.

[62] Rather than insuring each type of exposure individually, a multiperil policy, or treaty, combines coverage for various types of exposures into a single contract. Other types of reinsurance contracts include automatic treaties, quota share treaties, and surplus treaties. With automatic treaties the reinsurer agrees in advance to accept a portion of the insurance line of the writing company or a portion of certain risks. Quota share treaties are an arrangement where the writing company and the reinsurance company agree to share the amount of each risk on some percentage basis. Surplus treaties are arrangements where the reinsurer agrees to accept some amount of insurance on each risk in excess of a specified net retention. See Emmett J. Vaughan and Therese M. Vaughan, *Fundamentals of Risk and Insurance* (New York: John Wiley & Sons; 2003).

[63] According to the 2010 PWG report, the reduction in the supply of reinsurance and significant price rises following the September 11 attacks were a typical industry response to a catastrophic loss shock. President's Working Group on Financial Markets, *Market Conditions for Terrorism Risk Insurance*.

[64] President's Working Group on Financial Markets, *Market Conditions for Terrorism Risk Insurance*.

[65] House Committee on Financial Services, *The Future of Terrorism Insurance: Fostering Private Market Innovation to Limit Taxpayer Exposure*, 113th Cong., 1st sess.; testimony of John Seo, Fermat Capital Management (Nov. 13, 2013).

[66] See GAO, *Catastrophe Insurance Risks: The Role of Risk-Linked Securities and Factors Affecting Their Use*, GAO-02-941 (Washington, D.C.: Sept. 24, 2002) and *Catastrophe Insurance Risks: Status of Efforts to Securitize Natural Catastrophe and Terrorism Risk,* GAO-03-1033 (Washington D.C.: Sept. 24, 2003).

[67] One bond was developed by the Fédération Internationale de Football Association, the world football [soccer] governing body, to protect its investment in organizing the 2006 World Cup in Germany. The security, rated investment-grade (A3) by Moody's, covered natural and terrorist catastrophic events that would result in the cancellation of World Cup games. Catastrophic mortality transactions were the basis for the second bond related to terrorism risk. It covered significant increases in population mortality for any reason. Rating agencies and investors have become comfortable with these transactions, because the main source of risk is a pandemic or natural catastrophe with higher expected loss value than a terrorist attack, so that terrorism risk contributes only a small portion of the expected loss.

[68] Ginger Turner, *Terrorism Risk Insurance Act: The Economic Case for Public-Private Partnership* (Swiss Re: September 2013).

[69] Aon, response to the President's Working Group on Financial Markets, Sept. 16, 2013.

[70] American Academy of Actuaries, response to President's Working Group on Financial Markets, Sept. 16, 2013.

[71] Reinsurance Association of America, response to President's Working Group on Financial Markets on the long-term availability and affordability of insurance for terrorism risk, September 16, 2013.

[72] The insurer said that the exclusions would not apply to workers' compensation policies.

[73] Congressional Budget Office, *Federal Reinsurance for Terrorism Risks: Issues in Reauthorization* (Washington, D.C.: August 2007).

[74] By surplus, we mean policyholder surplus, which is an important measure of an insurer's ability to pay claims and represents the extent to which an insurer's assets exceed its liabilities. See GAO-14-136. Treasury officials noted that, among others, the reliability of modeling and potential for unlimited losses in concentrated geographic locations are additional factors that can influence the amount of insurance and reinsurance written.

[75] Department of the Treasury, *Assessment: The Terrorism Risk Insurance Act of 2002* (Washington, D.C.: June 30, 2005).

[76] State funds are insurers of last resort for employers that otherwise cannot find workers' compensation insurance in their respective states. See GAO, *Terrorism Insurance: Measuring and Predicting Losses from Unconventional Weapons Is Difficult, but Some Industry Exposure Exists*, GAO-06-1081 (Washington, D.C.: Sept. 25, 2006).

[77] See GAO, *September 11: Overview of Federal Disaster Assistance to the New York City Area*, GAO-04-72 (Washington, D.C.: Oct. 31, 2003).

[78] See GAO, *Disaster Recovery: Experiences from Past Disasters Offer Insights for Effective Collaboration After Catastrophic Events*, GAO-09-811 (Washington, D.C.: July 31, 2009).

[79] GAO, *Homeowners Insurance: Multiple Challenges Make Expanding Private Coverage Difficult*, GAO-14-179 (Washington, D.C.: Jan. 30, 2014).

[80] In January 2013, Congress passed and the President signed the Disaster Relief Appropriations Act of 2013 and the Sandy Recovery Improvement Act of 2013 providing this assistance.

[81] Four insurers wanted the trigger to stay the same.

[82] A.M. Best, *Future of TRIPRA Remains Uncertain, Rating Pressure Intensifies* (Oldwick, NJ: Oct. 9, 2013). According to A.M. Best, the 34 insurers provided action plans or corrected information and therefore would not be subject to rating action. See A.M. Best, *No Rating Actions Taken on Insurers with Terrorism Exposure Despite Uncertain Future of TRIPRA* (Oldwick, NJ: Dec. 19, 2013).

[83] By surplus, we mean policyholder surplus, which is an important measure of an insurer's ability to pay claims and represents the extent to which an insurer's assets exceed its liabilities. See GAO-14-136.

[84] We calculated the industry-wide deductible as a percentage of policy holder surplus by taking the industry-wide deductible in 2012 ($37 billion) and dividing it by the A.M. Best estimate for policyholder surplus of insurers potentially exposed to terrorism risk ($221 billion). A.M. Best's estimate takes total surplus for the U.S. property and casualty industry ($612 billion) and deducts surplus related to insurers not subject to TRIA, such as those that are predominantly writing personal lines, medical professional liability, reinsurance, fidelity, surety, and commercial automobile.

[85] Using SNL Financial insurance data from 2012, for the 10 largest insurers, we calculated their deductible amounts based on 20 percent and divided them by estimates for each insurer's surplus. For the small insurers (all other insurers other than the 10 largest) we calculated the deductible amount based on 20 percent and then divided it by 40 percent of A.M. Best's estimate for the surplus of insurers potentially exposed to terrorism. (In 2012, A.M. Best's estimate was $221 billion.) According to A.M. Best, the 10 largest insurers held roughly 60 percent of the estimated surplus and therefore all other insurers accounted for roughly 40 percent.

[86] The act refers to this program parameter as the insurance marketplace aggregate retention amount.

[87] The remaining three insurers did not to respond to this question.

[88] On the basis of 2012 SNL Financial data, 20 percent of direct earned premiums in TRIA-eligible lines equaled $37 billion.

[89] According to a report by the Federal Office of Insurance, the property and casualty sector reported $529 billion and $597 billion in surplus, for 2007 and 2012, respectively; which represented an increase of 13 percent over this period. A 13 percent increase in the retention amount would bring the total to approximately $31 billion.

[90] TRIA also sets limits on discretionary surcharges. For example, the surcharge is based on the policy's overall property and casualty premium charged and instances of discretionary recoupment cannot exceed 3 percent of the overall property and casualty premium. Because of these limitations, theoretically speaking, a loss could be so large that the federal government could not recoup (discretionally) and be fully repaid.

[91] As discussed earlier, the government's legal commitment to pay losses when a certified terrorist event occurs makes the terrorism risk insurance program an explicit exposure. See GAO-14-28.

[92] See appendix I for information on how we developed these examples. We examined the potential effects if different numbers of insurers were affected (10 largest insurers, 20 largest insurers, and all insurers) because losses from an attack are highly unlikely to impact all insurers or be distributed evenly among all insurers. Our illustrative examples also took into account variously sized terrorist attacks—attacks that would result in $25 billion, $50 billion, $75 billion, or $100 billion of insured losses. The illustrative examples are not specific determinations of federal fiscal exposure under TRIA and do not take into account the requirement for Treasury to recoup 133 percent of the payments to insurers under the program. All mandatory recoupment from insurers for all acts of terrorism after January 1, 2012, must be collected by September 30, 2017.

[93] Because of the program's recoupment mechanism, changes to program parameters effectively only could reduce the government's estimated fiscal exposure when attacks resulted in insured losses exceeding the industry aggregate retention amount of $27.5 billion. That is, the federal government must recoup any payments initially made to insurers in instances when the private sector's share of losses is less than $27.5 billion under the current law.

[94] When we examined the potential effects of the 20 largest insurers affected instead of the 10 largest insurers, we did notice a change to federal exposure when the coshare was increased. This is because the federal share of losses is less, as more insurers are affected by an event (that is, suffer losses).

[95] See GAO-06-1081.

[96] "Make Available"; "Property & Casualty Insurance" (Nuclear, Biological & Chemical) / TRIA Sections 102(12) and 103(c) / 31 C.F.R. §§ 50.5.5(l), 50.23., found at http://www.treasury.gov/resource-center/fin-mkts/Pages/letters.aspx.

[97] State workers' compensation laws generally do not permit insurers to exclude NBCR risks.

[98] GAO-09-39.

[99] GAO-06-1081.

[100] Captives are special-purpose insurance companies set up by commercial businesses to self-insure risks arising from the owners' business activities. Captives may be insurers under TRIA and therefore may be eligible for payments for losses related to certified NBCR events. See GAO-06-1081.

[101] Aon, *Response to U.S. Treasury and President's Working Group: Terrorism (Re)insurance*, September 2013.

[102] Guy Carpenter, *Terrorism: Reinsurers Standing By*, June 2010.

[103] As previously discussed: (1) there must be a sufficiently large number of homogeneous units exposed to random losses, both historically and prospectively, to make the future losses reasonably predictable, (2) the loss must be definite and measurable, (3) the loss must be fortuitous or accidental and (4) the loss must not be catastrophic. See GAO-06-1081.

[104] In 31 C.F.R. § 50.9, Treasury provided a procedure for requesting TRIA interpretations and noted that responses by the TRIP office would be made publicly available. See Department of the Treasury, *"Make Available";*

"Property and Casualty Insurance" (Nuclear, Biological, and Chemical) / TRIA Sections 102(12) and 103(c) / 31 C.F.R. §§ 50.5.5(l), 50.23.

[105] GAO-14-28.

[106] Terrorism Risk Insurance Act of 2002 (Pub. L. No. 107-297), the Terrorism Risk Insurance Extension Act of 2005 (Pub. L. No. 109-144), the Terrorism Risk Insurance Program Reauthorization Act of 2007 (Pub. L. No. 110-160), and the Code of Federal Regulations (31 CFR Part 50).

[107] Congressional Research Service, *Terrorism Risk Insurance: Issue Analysis and Overview of Current Program* (Washington, D.C.: May 24, 2013 and March 28, 2014).

[108] See GAO, *Terrorism Insurance: Status of Coverage Availability for Attacks Involving Nuclear, Biological, Chemical, or Radiological Weapons*, GAO-09-39 (Washington, D.C.: Dec. 12, 2008); *Terrorism Insurance: Status of Efforts by Policyholders to Obtain Coverage*, GAO-08-1057 (Washington, D.C.: Sept. 15, 2008); and *Terrorism Insurance: Implementation of the Terrorism Risk Insurance Act of 2002*, GAO-04-307 (Washington, D.C.: Apr. 23, 2004).

[109] See President's Working Group on Financial Markets, *Terrorism Risk Insurance* (Washington, D.C.: September 2006); *Market Conditions for Terrorism Risk Insurance* (Washington, D.C.: 2010); and *The Long-Term Availability and Affordability of Insurance for Terrorism Risk* (Washington, D.C.: April 2014).

[110] SNL Financial, through a partnership with NAIC, provides comprehensive statutory financial data for the insurance industry.

[111] See GAO-14-28, *Fiscal Exposures: Improving Cost Recognition in the Federal Budget*, GAO-14-28 (Washington, D.C.: Oct. 29, 2013); and *Fiscal Exposures: Improving the Budgetary Focus on Long-Term Costs and Uncertainties*, GAO-03-213 (Washington, D.C.: Jan. 24, 2003).

[112] In 2004, A.M. Best began collecting data on premiums charged for terrorism coverage as a part of its annual survey of insurers (the Supplemental Rating Questionnaire for U.S property and casualty). A.M. Best collects these data for insurance rating units that provide commercial lines on a primary basis, in which the commercial lines make up more than 10 percent of the rating units' direct written premiums. A.M. Best defines rating units as a single operating company or several affiliated member companies that have common rating assignments due to common operations, internal pooling, or reinsurance agreements. A.M. Best provided us with aggregated data from the questionnaire and told us that in 2012 they collected information on premiums charged for terrorism coverage for 226 rating units (of a total of 889 rating units). As part of the survey, A.M. Best asks insurers for their total amount of terrorism premium received, including premium received as a separate endorsement or included as a risk load in the policy premium. A.M. Best also asks for the terrorism premium broken down by workers' compensation, commercial property, and all other commercial lines of business.

[113] We chose to present only the $50 billion and $75 billion loss event scenarios in the report because they best illustrated the magnitude of changes to federal fiscal exposure under changes to the program parameters.

Chapter 3

THE LONG-TERM AVAILABILITY AND AFFORDABILITY OF INSURANCE FOR TERRORISM RISK[*]

President's Working Group on Financial Markets

I. EXECUTIVE SUMMARY

The Terrorism Risk Insurance Act of 2002, as amended (TRIA),[1] requires U.S. insurers to make insurance available for losses resulting from acts of terrorism, and provides a federal government backstop for the insurers' resulting financial exposures. TRIA established in the U.S. Department of the Treasury (Treasury) the Terrorism Risk Insurance Program (TRIP), which is responsible for administering the essential components of TRIA.[2]

Section 108(e) of TRIA requires the President's Working Group on Financial Markets (PWG)[3] to conduct, on an ongoing basis, an analysis of the long-term availability and affordability of insurance for terrorism risk, and to report to Congress regarding the PWG's findings.[4] The PWG previously reported to Congress in 2006 and again in 2010 (the 2006 PWG Report and 2010 PWG Report, respectively).[5] The analysis and conclusions in the 2006 PWG Report and the 2010 PWG Report were based on consultations with industry participants and comments responding to Federal Register notices. In addition, Treasury provided an assessment of TRIA to Congress on June 30, 2005.[6] The 2005 Treasury report relied in part on surveys of various stakeholders conducted by an independent research firm under Treasury auspices.

To assist the PWG's analysis in connection with this report (this Report), on July 16, 2013, Treasury published a notice and request for comment (the PWG Notice),[7] in reply to which 29 written comments were submitted. Submissions in reply to the PWG Notice are available at treasury.gov/initiatives/fio.

This Report draws upon the comments received in response to the PWG Notice, as well as from direct engagement by PWG member staff (staff) with a range of stakeholders, including consumer advocates, insurers, reinsurers, industry services firms, state insurance

---

[*] This is an edited, reformatted and augmented version of a report issued April 2014.

regulators, commercial insurance policyholders, the National Association of Insurance Commissioners (NAIC), and industry trade associations. Most comments submitted to the PWG addressed whether and to what extent uncertainty concerning TRIA's scheduled expiration at the end of 2014 affects the affordability and availability of terrorism risk insurance, which is referenced in this Report.

The Long-Term Availability and Affordability of Insurance for Terrorism Risk

Consistent with the 2006 and 2010 PWG reports, this Report draws its data and conclusions from comments submitted in response to the PWG Notice, particularly data provided by two global insurance brokers, as well as from consultations with various stakeholders.

The findings of the PWG in this Report include:

- Insurance for terrorism risk currently is available and affordable. The availability and affordability of insurance for terrorism risk has not changed appreciably since 2010.
- Prices for terrorism risk insurance vary considerably depending upon the policyholder's industry and the location of the risk exposures.
- Such prices have declined since TRIA was enacted and, in the aggregate, currently approximate 3 to 5 percent of commercial property insurance premiums.
- Take-up rates – *i.e.*, the percentage of policyholders that purchase coverage for terrorism risk – have improved since the adoption of TRIA and are roughly stable at 60 percent in the aggregate (as compared to 27 percent in 2003, the first full year TRIA was in effect).
- Information provided to the PWG in response to the PWG Notice indicates that the market currently is tightening in light of uncertainty as to whether TRIA will be renewed.
- The private market does not have the capacity to provide reinsurance for terrorism risk to the extent currently provided by TRIA.
- In the absence of TRIA, terrorism risk insurance likely would be less available. Coverage that would be available likely would be more costly and/or limited in scope.

Overview of the Terrorism Risk Insurance Act

After the September 11th attacks (9/11), insurers and reinsurers largely withdrew from the terrorism risk insurance market.[8] This and other factors contributed to a severe market shortage for terrorism risk insurance, which Congress sought to address through the enactment of TRIA.

In general, TRIA requires each commercial property and casualty (P/C) insurer to participate in TRIP and to make coverage available for losses resulting from certified acts of terrorism. Further, TRIA authorizes the Secretary of the Treasury (the Secretary) to make federal payments to an insurer for a portion of insured losses resulting from a certified act of terrorism that exceed the insurer's deductible. Insurers also co-participate with federal funding with respect to payments for losses above the deductible, and may be required to surcharge policyholders in order to fund recoupment payments made to Treasury. Treasury has never made a payment to any insurer under TRIP.

As enacted, TRIA was originally scheduled to expire on December 31, 2005, but was reauthorized in 2005 and again in 2007.[9] With both reauthorizations, Congress modified elements of TRIP, in part to reduce federal taxpayer exposure under TRIA to insured losses from acts of terrorism. The 2007 reauthorization of TRIA is scheduled to expire on December 31, 2014. House and Senate Committee hearings regarding the question of reauthorization were conducted on September 11, 2012,[10] September 19, 2013,[11] September 25, 2013,[12] November 13, 2013,[13] and February 25, 2014.[14]

Availability and Affordability of Terrorism Risk Insurance

The per-risk capacity – a metric used to measure the amount of available coverage – of the market for terrorism risk insurance increased only modestly since 2010.[15] The aggregate policyholder take-up rate appears to have stabilized at 60 percent.[16] In certain industries, take-up rates may be substantially higher (*e.g.*, 81 percent for the media industry) or lower (*e.g.*, 42 percent for the chemicals industry).[17] Similarly, costs vary broadly, and may be much higher for high risk properties and in certain urban areas, such as Chicago, New York City, San Francisco, and Washington, D.C.[18] Overall, premium rates for terrorism risk coverage have declined by about half since the post-9/11 peak, have been relatively stable over the last several years, and currently represent a small percentage of overall commercial property insurance premiums.[19]

Several factors may affect, and in some instances challenge, the availability and affordability of insurance for terrorism risk, including: (1) the ability of insurers to estimate the frequency and severity of losses resulting from terrorism; (2) the potential for catastrophic losses resulting from terrorism; (3) insurer policyholder surplus levels; (4) insurer credit rating agency considerations; (5) private reinsurance capacity; and (6) uncertainty relating to the reauthorization of TRIP.

After 9/11 and prior to the enactment of TRIA, property owners and developers reported the inability to procure adequate insurance coverage for terrorism risk, or the inability to find coverage at reasonable prices.[20] In 2005 and again in 2007, in each case as then-scheduled expirations of TRIA approached, prices for terrorism risk insurance increased.[21] Similarly, industry sources report concerns that the long-term availability and affordability of insurance for terrorism risk will be adversely affected if TRIA is not renewed before it expires at the end of 2014, and that the market is already tightening in anticipation of the termination of the federal government backstop.[22]

As TRIP has evolved through amendments to TRIA, the U.S. insurance industry has adapted to the resulting increases in net terrorism exposure under commercial policies. However, the U.S. insurance industry remains unprepared to retain the entire exposure to terrorism risk. In fact, 28 of the 29 commenters to the PWG Notice assert, to varying degrees, that pricing for terrorism risk insurance will be adversely affected, and its availability substantially curtailed, should TRIA expire at the end of 2014.[23] In its response to the PWG Notice, Aon plc (Aon), a global insurance and reinsurance broker, concluded from a survey of over 1,200 of its clients that: "If TRIA were to expire in 2014, the vast majority of the existing insurance market for terrorism will disappear."[24] Marsh & McLennan Companies

(Marsh), another global industry services provider, made a similar observation, noting that some insurers it surveyed "have indicated to us that they could be forced to withdraw from geographical areas that have the greatest need for terrorism coverage or they may even exit certain lines of business, such as workers' compensation or commercial property in high profile jurisdictions."[25] Some commenters disagreed with this conclusion. For example, one commenter suggested that the market is sufficiently robust and mature to operate without the government backstop, albeit at higher prices.[26]

Comments to the PWG Notice Regarding Potential Modifications to the Terrorism Risk Insurance Program

In light of the pending expiration and potential reauthorization of TRIA, commenters to the PWG Notice and other interested parties have suggested various modifications to TRIA intended to bring greater certainty to the marketplace, improve the availability and affordability of insurance for terrorism risk, and/or decrease federal taxpayer exposure to insured losses resulting from acts of terrorism. Although an analysis of potential modifications to TRIA is outside the scope of PWG's mandate to report on the long-term availability and affordability of insurance for terrorism risk,[27] such comments are summarized in this Report.

II. OVERVIEW OF THE TERRORISM RISK INSURANCE ACT

This section of the Report provides a brief background regarding the commercial property and casualty insurance sector in general, and then describes the Terrorism Risk Insurance Program, including how it has evolved since TRIA's enactment in 2002.

A. Commercial Property and Casualty Insurance

Commercial lines insurance policies allow businesses to transfer risk exposure to insurers in exchange for premium payments. Just as with personal lines of insurance for homeowners or private passenger auto, commercial lines policies stipulate the causes of loss (*i.e.*, perils) covered, as well as other terms and conditions for the insurance policy to remain in effect. In 2012, commercial P/C insurance policies (including workers' compensation) accounted for $247 billion – or 47 percent – of the approximately $524 billion of premiums written by the U.S. P/C insurance sector (commercial and personal lines).[28]

With the exception of workers' compensation insurance, commercial P/C policies are generally either "all-peril"[29] or "named peril" policies. All-peril policies cover losses arising from perils that are not expressly excluded and typically cover losses arising from fire, smoke, windstorm, hail, civil disobedience, and vandalism, but exclude losses caused by acts of war. Prior to 9/11, losses from acts of terrorism typically were not excluded from all-peril policies. A named peril policy covers only losses arising from perils specified in the policy. Under state laws, workers' compensation insurance must provide compensation for injuries or illnesses to covered individuals that occur in the course of employment, regardless of the peril.[30]

The business of commercial P/C insurance is primarily regulated by state law. Most state insurance regulators are authorized to review and approve policy forms and rates, though the form and rate filing process and the applicable consumer protection standards vary by state. State law may prohibit certain exclusions in commercial P/C policies. For example, twenty-nine states, including New York, Illinois, and California, require an insurer to cover losses from fire following a broad range of events. Of those states, fifteen permit exclusions of fire losses following acts of terrorism, and fourteen states prohibit such exclusions.[31]

Prior to 9/11, commercial all-peril P/C insurance policies generally did not exclude losses arising from acts of terrorism. Following the events of 9/11, which resulted in $32.5 billion of insured losses,[32] insurers and reinsurers moved to reduce the potential for catastrophic insured losses resulting from acts of terrorism. Reinsurance renewals excluded terrorism risk. Due to limited availability of reinsurance coverage for terrorism risk, insurers sought to avoid exposure to catastrophic terrorism losses by excluding coverage of terrorism risk in commercial P/C insurance policies.[33]

By early 2002, insurers were submitting terrorism exclusions for review by state insurance regulators in order to exclude coverage of losses arising from acts of terrorism. Where coverage of losses arising from acts of terrorism could not be excluded, such as for workers' compensation insurance, some insurers declined to renew insurance policies altogether.[34]

The relative unaffordability or outright unavailability of insurance for terrorism risk had far-reaching and adverse effects on the national economy, including the cancellation or delay of construction projects and commercial real estate transactions.[35]

B. Terrorism Risk Insurance Program

TRIA was enacted on November 26, 2002, in recognition that the widespread unavailability of insurance for terrorism risk "could seriously hamper ongoing and planned construction, property acquisition, and other business projects, generate a dramatic increase in rents, and otherwise suppress economic activity."[36] The stated purpose of TRIA is to establish a temporary federal program of shared public and private compensation for insured losses resulting from acts of terrorism, in order to:

- Protect consumers by addressing market disruptions and ensure the continued widespread availability and affordability of property and casualty insurance for terrorism risk; and
- Allow for a transitional period for the private markets to stabilize, resume pricing of such insurance, and build capacity to absorb any future losses, while preserving state insurance regulation and consumer protections.[37]

TRIA established TRIP within Treasury.[38] TRIA authorizes the Secretary to administer TRIP and to pay a federal share of compensation to insurers for insured losses from a certified act of terrorism.[39] TRIA requires insurers of certain commercial lines to participate in TRIP and to make coverage available for losses resulting from certified acts of terrorism.[40] TRIA also defines a process for repayment by the insurance sector of some or all of any federal compensation paid under TRIP.[41]

Subtitle A of Title V of the Dodd-Frank Wall Street Reform and Consumer Protection Act (Dodd-Frank Act)[42] established the Federal Insurance Office (FIO) in Treasury. The statute provides FIO with the authority to assist the Secretary in administering TRIP.

1. Mandating the Availability of Insurance for Terrorism Risk

TRIA requires insurers offering certain lines of commercial P/C insurance, commonly known as "TRIP-eligible lines," to participate in TRIP. Specifically, TRIA requires each entity that meets the definition of an insurer[43] to make available coverage for insured losses resulting from certified acts of terrorism "that does not differ materially from the terms, amounts, and other coverage limitations applicable to losses arising from events other than acts of terrorism" (the "make available" provision).[44]

Subject to exclusions specified in TRIA,[45] TRIP-eligible lines of insurance consist of certain commercial lines of P/C insurance.[46] Under the implementing regulation, such commercial lines of insurance include excess insurance, workers' compensation insurance, directors and officers liability insurance, and commercial insurance within the following lines:[47]

- Fire and allied lines;
- Commercial multiple peril (liability and non-liability portions);
- Ocean marine;
- Inland marine;
- Workers' compensation;
- Other liability;
- Products liability;
- Aircraft (all perils); and
- Boiler and machinery.

The regulation lists the following lines of business as not falling within the scope of TRIP-eligible lines:[48]

- Federal crop insurance issued or reinsured under the Federal Crop Insurance Act (7 U.S.C. § 1501 *et seq.*), or any other type of crop or livestock insurance that is privately issued or reinsured;
- Private mortgage insurance (as defined in section 2 of the Homeowners Protection Act of 1988) (12 U.S.C. § 4901) or title insurance;
- Financial guaranty insurance issued by monoline financial guaranty insurance corporations;
- Insurance for medical malpractice;
- Health or life insurance, including group life insurance;
- Flood insurance provided under the National Flood Insurance Act of 1968 (42 U.S.C. § 4001 *et seq.*) or earthquake insurance;
- Reinsurance or retrocessional reinsurance;
- Commercial automobile insurance;

- Burglary and theft insurance;
- Surety insurance;
- Professional liability insurance;[49] and
- Farmowners multiple peril insurance.

TRIA voided by operation of law any exclusion for acts of terrorism that existed in contracts for TRIP-eligible lines of insurance in force as of November 26, 2002.[50] Additionally, TRIA voided any state approvals of terrorism exclusions for TRIP-eligible lines of insurance that were in force as of that date. An insurer may only exclude coverage for an act of terrorism if the policyholder authorizes the exclusion in writing, or fails to pay the increase in premium attributable to the terrorism risk coverage within 30 days of notification of the premium amount and the policyholder's rights with respect to such coverage.[51]

While TRIA requires insurers to make available insurance for terrorism risk on the same terms as other insurance, the law does not mandate any particular price for such coverage. Premiums charged by insurers remain subject to state regulatory authority, which varies by state in terms of the nature and extent of the regulatory review of rates charged by insurers. TRIA does not require a policyholder to purchase insurance for terrorism risk. If a policyholder declines coverage, an insurer may, but is not required to, "negotiate with the policyholder an option for partial coverage" if permitted by state law.[52]

TRIA requires an insurer to make additional disclosures to policyholders as a condition for federal payment eligibility under TRIP. At the time of offer, purchase, and renewal of a policy, an insurer must provide clear and conspicuous disclosure to the policyholder of the premium charged for the coverage of losses from certified acts of terrorism, and of the federal share of compensation for such losses.[53] In addition, an insurer also must provide to the policyholder a clear and conspicuous notice of the $100 billion Program Cap (described below).[54]

2. Certifying an Act of Terrorism

Only losses from certified acts of terrorism are eligible for federal payments to insurers under TRIP. A certified "act of terrorism" is an act certified by the Secretary, in concurrence with the Secretary of State and the Attorney General:

- to be an act of terrorism;
- to be a violent act or an act that is dangerous to human life, property, or infrastructure;
- to have resulted in damage within the United States; and
- to have been committed by an individual or individuals, as part of an effort to coerce the civilian population of the United States or to influence the policy or affect the conduct of the U.S. government by coercion.[55]

TRIA prohibits the Secretary from certifying an act that was either committed as part of the course of a war declared by Congress,[56] or that does not result in aggregate industry insured losses subject to TRIP exceeding $5 million.[57] TRIA neither prescribes how insured losses should be measured[58] nor what source(s) of insured loss data should be relied upon by the Secretary.[59]

The Terrorism Risk Insurance Program Reauthorization Act of 2007 (TRIPRA) expanded the scope of acts to which TRIA may apply. Prior to TRIPRA, only an act of terrorism committed by individuals "acting on behalf of any foreign person or foreign interest" could have been certified.[60] TRIPRA removed this condition, so that an act committed by any person may be certified.[61]

As of this Report, no event has been certified by the Secretary, in concurrence with the Secretary of State and the Attorney General, as an act of terrorism.

3. *Providing a Federal Share of Compensation for Insured Losses*

Determination of whether and in what amounts insurers are eligible for payments under TRIP and whether and in what amount some or all of such payments may be subject to recoupment involves the interplay of multiple factors, including the $5 million certification requirement, the Program Trigger, individual insurer deductibles, federal and private co-participation percentages, an industry aggregate retention, and the Program Cap. These factors are described below.

a. Federal Payments to Insurers under TRIP

As originally established, the federal share of compensation to an insurer under TRIP for losses from a certified act of terrorism was equal to 90 percent (*i.e.*, the federal share) of the portion of insured losses exceeding that insurer's deductible during a Program Year (*i.e.*, a given calendar year).[62] Individual "insurer deductibles" are determined as a percentage of the insurer's direct earned premium (DEP)[63] for TRIP-eligible lines of insurance during the preceding calendar year. As enacted, TRIA established the insurer deductible at 1 percent of DEP for the period beginning on November 26, 2002, and ending on December 31, 2002, but increased it to 7 percent of DEP for the 2003 Program Year, 10 percent for 2004, and 15 percent for 2005.[64]

The Terrorism Risk Insurance Extension Act of 2005 (TRIEA) decreased the federal share from 90 percent to 85 percent of the portion of insured losses that exceeds an insurer's deductible during a Program Year, beginning with 2007. Put another way, insurers with eligible losses were each subject to a 15 percent co-participation. Separately, TRIEA increased the insurer deductible from 15 percent of DEP to 17.5 percent in 2006 and to 20 percent in 2007 (in each instance DEP is based on the preceding calendar year). The deductible remains at 20 percent through 2014.[65]

Federal payments to insurers under TRIP for losses from a certified act of terrorism are not permitted unless the act of terrorism results in losses exceeding a "Program Trigger."[66] As originally enacted, TRIA included the $5 million certification requirement, but not a separate Program Trigger. TRIEA established a Program Trigger of $50 million for 2006, and increased that threshold to $100 million for 2007 and future years.[67]

The effect of these modifications to the federal share and to the insurer deductible, and the introduction and expansion of the Program Trigger, has been to steadily decrease the amount of federal payments potentially available to a given insurer under TRIP for losses from a certified act of terrorism. To illustrate, if in 2004 an insurer with $1 billion of DEP (as of 2003) incurred $400 million of losses from a certified act of terrorism, that insurer would have been eligible for a federal share of compensation amounting to $270 million.[68] However, if in 2005 an insurer with $1 billion of DEP (as of 2004) incurred $400 million of losses from a certified act of terrorism, that insurer would have been eligible for a lesser federal share of compensation, amounting to $225 million.[69] Similarly, if in 2010 an insurer with $1 billion of DEP (as of 2009) incurred $400 million of losses from a certified act of terrorism, that insurer would have been eligible for a share of federal compensation of only $170 million.[70] Finally, if in 2010 an insurer with DEP (as of 2009) of $2 billion incurred $400 million of losses from a certified act of terrorism, that insurer would not have been eligible for federal payments under TRIP, because its losses would not have exceeded the applicable deductible.[71]

Figure 1 illustrates how the insurer co-participation share and deductible have increased from 2002 to the present.

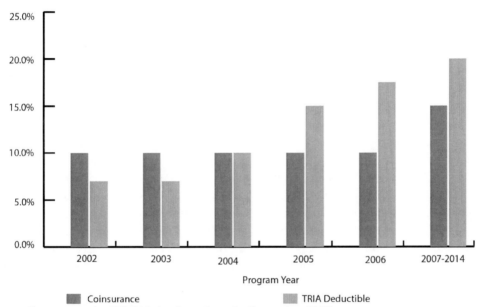

Source: Comment to the PWG Notice from Aon plc (September 2013).

Figure 1. TRIA Coinsurance & TRIA Deductible Increases.

b. Limit on Aggregate Annual Liability

For certified acts of terrorism, TRIA limits the ultimate exposure of insurers under TRIP-eligible lines and of the federal government for payments to insurers under TRIP. Specifically, TRIA prohibits the Secretary from making payments for any portion of aggregate insured losses from acts of terrorism which exceed the "Program Cap" of $100 billion during a Program Year.[72] Moreover, an insurer that meets its insurer deductible under TRIP is not liable for any portion of losses that exceeds the Program Cap.[73] TRIA requires the Secretary to determine the *pro rata* share of insured losses to be paid by each affected insurer and to notify Congress in the event that insured losses under TRIP exceed the Program Cap.[74]

c. Recoupment of Federal Payments under TRIP

In the event that federal payments are made to insurers under TRIP, TRIA authorizes the Secretary to collect "terrorism loss risk-spreading premiums" from insurers.[75] Insurers are required to collect such premiums from policyholders as a surcharge on insurance policies for TRIP-eligible lines of insurance after the Program Year in which federal payments are made, and to remit them to the Secretary.[76] The requirement to collect terrorism loss risk-spreading premiums and remit such amounts collected to Treasury is not limited to insurers that received federal payments under TRIP, but rather applies to all insurers of TRIP-eligible lines.[77]

Collection by the Secretary of such terrorism loss risk-spreading premiums is either mandatory or discretionary, depending on the amount of federal payments made under TRIP and the total insured losses from certified acts of terrorism during a Program Year. If "uncompensated insured losses" (*i.e.*, the total insured losses less federal payments) do not exceed the "insurance marketplace aggregate retention amount" (*i.e.*, a minimum amount of insured losses, depending on the aggregate amount of insured losses, that must ultimately be paid by the private markets), TRIA requires the collection of terrorism loss risk-spreading premiums.

The insurance marketplace aggregate retention under TRIA is equal to the lesser of aggregate insured losses from acts of terrorism during a Program Year and retention amounts established in the law, which have increased over time: $10 billion for 2003; $12.5 billion for 2004; $15 billion for 2005; $25 billion for 2006; and $27.5 billion for 2007 and each Program Year thereafter.[78]

The "mandatory recoupment amount" is the difference between the insurance marketplace aggregate retention amount and uncompensated insured losses.[79] TRIA also authorizes the Secretary to recoup an additional amount of the federal financial assistance above the mandatory recoupment amount.[80] TRIA currently requires the Secretary to collect an amount equal to 133 percent of the mandatory recoupment amount.[81]

Accordingly, the minimum recoupment amount that the Secretary would have been required to collect from insurers after a Program Year has steadily increased over the years since the enactment of TRIA. To illustrate, if insured losses from acts of terrorism had totaled $40 billion in 2005, and if $20 billion of federal payments had been made under TRIP, then mandatory recoupment would not have occurred.[82] Any recoupment of the $20 billion federal payment would have been discretionary. On the other hand, if insured losses from acts of terrorism had totaled $40 billion in 2010, and if $20 billion of federal payments had been made under TRIP, then recoupment of 133 percent of $7.5 billion of the federal payments (*i.e.*, $10 billion) would have been mandatory.[83] Recoupment of any of the remaining $12.5 billion of federal payments would have been discretionary.

d. Summary

Figure 2 summarizes the TRIP coverage mechanism for certified acts of terrorism satisfying the $5 million certification requirement.

In the event of a certified act of terrorism that exceeds the $100 million Program Trigger, TRIA makes available a federal share of compensation to insurers with qualifying losses in excess of applicable deductibles, calculated based on prior year premiums for TRIP-eligible lines. Federal payments to an insurer under TRIP equal 85 percent of the portion of insured losses exceeding the insurer's deductible during a Program Year.

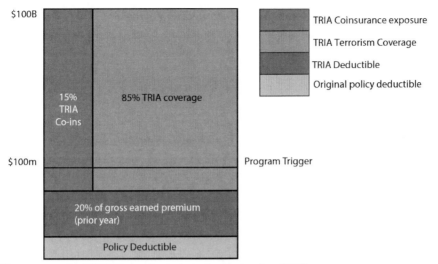

Source: Comment to the PWG Notice from Aon plc (September 2013).

Figure 2. TRIP Summary Illustration.

The Program Cap is $100 billion of aggregate insured losses. TRIA does not permit the Secretary to authorize payments for any portion of losses over that figure, and an insurer that has met its deductible is not liable for any portion of losses exceeding the Program Cap.

The Secretary is required to recoup federal payments made under TRIP which exceed a mandated industry retention through collection of terrorism loss risk-spreading premiums charged by insurers on TRIP-eligible lines. If uncompensated insured losses do not exceed the insurance marketplace aggregate retention amount, the Secretary is required to collect 133 percent of the difference. The insurance marketplace aggregate retention amount is the lesser of total insured losses from certified acts of terrorism or $27.5 billion. Recoupment of federal payments that exceed the mandatory recoupment amount is subject to the discretion of the Secretary. As of this Report, a payment has never been made through TRIP.

III. AVAILABILITY AND AFFORDABILITY OF TERRORISM RISK INSURANCE

For purposes of this Report, the PWG relied on information provided in comments submitted in response to the PWG Notice, including the results provided therein of surveys conducted by two large insurance brokerage firms, as well as on consultations with a range of stakeholders.[84]

In 2005, Treasury issued a report to Congress assessing TRIA, which was based in part on survey data Treasury collected from insurers and policyholders via an independent research firm.[85] Through those surveys, Treasury evaluated the effectiveness of TRIP, evaluated the likely capacity of the P/C industry to offer insurance for terrorism risk after the then-scheduled termination of TRIP, and addressed the availability and affordability of such insurance for various policyholders, including railroads, trucking, and public transit.

In this section, findings from the 2006 PWG Report and the 2010 PWG Report are briefly summarized. Various factors affecting the long-term availability and affordability of insurance for terrorism risk are then discussed, including market indications relating to the scheduled expiration of TRIA in December 2014. Finally, industry metrics with respect to the availability and affordability of insurance for terrorism risk are reviewed.

A. Findings of the PWG's 2006 and 2010 Reports to Congress

The PWG reported the following key findings in 2006:[86]

- The availability and affordability of terrorism risk insurance improved from 2001 to 2006, despite the statutory increases in insurer retentions during that period under TRIA. Insurers allocated additional capacity to terrorism risk, prices declined, and take-up rates increased. Terrorism risk insurance take-up rates grew from 30 percent in 2002 to approximately 60 percent in 2006.
- Improvements in the terrorism risk insurance market were due to several important factors including: better risk measurement and management, improved modeling, greater reinsurance capacity, and the recovery in the financial condition of property and casualty insurers.
- Take-up rates increased as prices fell, but a significant proportion of policyholders still did not purchase terrorism coverage by 2006.
- Further improvements in insurers' ability to model and manage terrorism risk likely would have contributed to the long-term development of the terrorism risk insurance market. The high level of uncertainty associated with predicting the frequency of terrorist attacks and a general unwillingness by a significant number of insurance policyholders to purchase insurance coverage, made any prediction of the potential degree of long-term development of the terrorism risk insurance market difficult.
- Coverage for terrorism risk in group life insurance policies remained generally available and at affordable prices, despite that group life insurance has not been part of TRIP.
- Insurers generally did not provide coverage for losses resulting from nuclear, biological, chemical, and radiological (NBCR) events even before 9/11, and for the most part were not providing NBCR coverage even with a federal backstop in place. Given the general reluctance of insurers to provide coverage for these types of risks, limited capacity, relatively high prices, and policyholder expectations, little potential for future market development appeared to exist. Subsequently, the Government Accountability Office (GAO) found that available capacity for NBCR terrorism risk insurance and reinsurance was limited.[87]

The PWG reported the following key findings in 2010:[88]

- The availability and affordability of terrorism risk insurance provided by the private sector had improved since 2006, and insurers had built capital and increased aggregate capacity.

- Overall, aggregate terrorism risk insurance capacity had increased, and significantly in some forms. Nevertheless, capacity was constrained in some markets (*e.g.*, high-risk geographic locations and properties), and some commercial insurance policyholders in high-risk urban areas had difficulty obtaining coverage with sufficient limits.
- Improvements in the terrorism risk insurance market may have occurred due to improvements in modeling and managing accumulation and concentration of aggregate loss exposure; new market entrants and increased competition; and improved capital positions of the property and casualty insurance and reinsurance industries. The industry was developing a better understanding of aggregate risk for the peril of terrorist attacks, and the increased capacity and competition had resulted in decreases in price generally.
- Take-up rates among commercial insurance policyholders reached approximately 60 percent in 2006, but remained roughly flat through 2010. Among those commercial insurance policyholders taking up terrorism risk insurance, some indications suggested that more coverage, as measured by policy limits, was being purchased.
- Market participants (policyholders, insurers, and reinsurers) remained uncertain about the ability of models to predict the frequency and severity of terrorist attacks. Such views influenced policyholder perception of risk and purchase decisions, as well as insurer and reinsurer capacity allocations to support terrorism risk coverage.

As described in sections III.C and III.D, the availability and affordability of terrorism risk insurance through 2013 are largely comparable to the findings the PWG reported in 2010.

B. Factors Affecting the Long-Term Availability and Affordability of Terrorism Risk Insurance

The availability and affordability of insurance for terrorism risk depends on a variety of factors, and appears to have been substantially influenced by TRIA. Comments submitted in response to the PWG Notice identified several factors affecting availability and affordability, certain of which are discussed below.

1. Ability of Insurers to Estimate Frequency and Severity

According to commenters, a significant challenge to pricing terrorism risk is the lack of credible empirical historical data on which to base loss projections and pricing.[89] When empirical historical data are not available, insurers often rely on commercial catastrophe risk models to price risk (*e.g.*, for other low-frequency, high-severity perils such as earthquakes, floods, and severe storms). These models simulate the frequency and severity of catastrophic events over a period of many years, and estimate the damage and financial effects of such damage on a given set of insured exposures.

Terrorism risk models have become more advanced in the past twelve years, and today consider a spectrum of potential targets and weapons and incorporate expertise from counterterrorism and law enforcement professionals when available. These models offer insurers additional tools to evaluate accumulations of exposures and probable maximum losses within areas affected by potential attacks.[90] Nonetheless, commenters report that such models are still of relatively limited utility, particularly in terms of developing pricing for the risk of large-scale attacks with a sufficient degree of confidence.[91]

Aon describes modeling of terrorism risk as "a means for underwriters to measure how much limit [an insurer has] at risk in a given geographic area – nothing more, nothing less."[92] Among others, the following impediments to more robust modeling of terrorism risk have been identified to the PWG:[93]

- Lack of sufficient experience and historical information by which to validate a model (frequency);
- Unique nature of terrorism risk;
- Geographic concentration of terrorism risk (proximity of insured assets to perceived "targets");
- Diversity of potential weapons scenarios;
- Number of potential targets; and
- Insufficient exposure data.

2. Potential for Catastrophic Losses

Insurers have exhibited reluctance to offer coverage for terrorism risk if the associated losses cannot be predicted and may be unlimited. TRIP limits an insurer's exposure by sharing the risk of insured losses that could exceed the insurer deductible and capping the aggregate liability of insurers and the federal government at $100 billion.

An essential objective for any insurer is to limit the possibility that a single event could result in insured losses that threaten its solvency or otherwise bear on its ability to pay future claims and write new business. Thus, an insurer estimates and takes action to limit its probable maximum loss (PML) relating to any single event. An insurer may reduce its exposure to an unacceptable PML by canceling insurance policies for some exposures, particularly if sufficiently reliable loss estimates cannot be made.

The American Academy of Actuaries has developed several estimates of insured losses from large-scale NBCR attacks in various U.S. locations, including a $778 billion estimated loss which could result from a potential NBCR terrorist attack in New York City.[94] In certain "Tier 1" urban centers in the United States, such as Manhattan, the potential for catastrophic losses from an act of terrorism could significantly limit the ability of the private market to make insurance for terrorism risk available in the absence of a federal program such as TRIP.

3. Insurer Policyholder Surplus

An insurer's policyholder surplus is the excess of its assets over its liabilities, as measured on an accounting basis prescribed by state insurance regulators. The relevant state insurance regulator and credit rating agencies (CRAs) monitor the surplus level of an insurer relative to its portfolio of risks as a principal indicator of its solvency. Greater surplus allows an insurer to absorb unexpectedly large insured losses or to write additional business. Aggregate policyholder surplus is one indicator of the amount of coverage that the insurance industry can make available.

The aggregate policyholder surplus of the U.S. P/C insurance industry increased from $295 billion in 2002 to $597 billion in 2012.[95] The aggregate premium-to-surplus ratio declined from 1.38 in 2002 to 0.88 in 2012,[96] meaning the industry decreased its leverage. Some commenters argue that the substantial growth in aggregate surplus is evidence that the private market is now positioned to insure terrorism risk.[97] Further reauthorization of TRIP, such commenters conclude, would amount to unnecessary federal assistance to a financially sound insurance industry.[98]

Notwithstanding the growth in aggregate industry surplus, insurance industry commenters argue that current insurer exposures to terrorism risk are significant, relative to individual insurer surplus levels.[99] These commenters report that, for many insurers, exposure to terrorism risk would be too large, relative to surplus, in the absence of reinsurance through private markets or support through TRIP.[100] Notably, exposure to terrorism risk is not a factor in the state regulatory method of measuring the minimum amount of required capital for insurers.

Seventy-three of the approximately 900 insurers reporting DEP for TRIP-eligible lines have surplus levels that exceed $1 billion. These 73 insurers account for approximately 76 percent of the market for TRIP-eligible lines of insurance in terms of premium volume. One hundred fifteen insurers (approximately 83 percent of the market by DEP for TRIP-eligible insurance) have surplus levels that exceed $500 million, and 282 insurers (approximately 93 percent of the market) have surplus levels that exceed $100 million. The remaining insurers, accounting for approximately 7 percent of the market, have surplus levels of less than $100 million.[101]

To some degree, growth in aggregate industry surplus is countered by the increase in the industry's exposure to unreimbursed losses from acts of terrorism as TRIA has evolved. As described above, the insurer deductible has increased from 7 percent in 2003 to 20 percent today.

Among the approximately 900 insurers with DEP for TRIP-eligible lines, the median insurer deductible represented as a percent of surplus is approximately 8 percent. However, 179 insurers, accounting for approximately 21 percent of the market by premium volume, have TRIA deductibles that exceed 20 percent of surplus.

In addition, the federal share of compensation to insurers for losses exceeding the deductible was lowered from 90 percent to 85 percent in the 2005 reauthorization, effective January 1, 2007. Insurers estimate that the potential insured losses that would not be compensated by federal payments average between 8 and 12 percent of policyholder surplus.[102] Insurers expect that exposure to terrorism risk of many insurers would "double or triple and leave exposures in excess of 20 percent of total surplus" if TRIP is not reauthorized.[103]

4. Credit Rating Agency Considerations

CRAs rate insurers based on quantitative and qualitative assessments, including exposure to losses from natural catastrophes or acts of terrorism. A.M. Best, for example, considers an insurer's aggregate exposure, number of insured locations, and concentration of exposures within certain locations.[104] Given these factors, A.M. Best evaluates an insurer's exposure to losses from a terrorist attack, the effect such losses would have on the insurer's surplus, and the ability the insurer would have to pay additional, expected claims after such losses. A.M. Best reports that insurers "with more concentrations – that are in excess of 20 [percent] of surplus prior to any recoveries from a federal backstop – are at a greater risk than [insurers] with fewer insured concentrations."[105]

Commercial viability of insurers is influenced by credit ratings. Policies offered by a lower rated insurer may be less viable or attractive in the marketplace, and therefore, insurers prefer to achieve higher ratings. CRAs are taking steps that may lead to downgrades of insurers if and when TRIA expires; this may have adverse implications for the availability and affordability of terrorism risk insurance.

For example, in 2013, A.M. Best assessed insurers' exposures to terrorism risk in the absence of TRIP, and asked some insurers to present action plans "detailing the steps they will take to reduce concentration of exposure to terrorism risk, should [TRIA] protection change materially."[106] Any such insurer that did not present a sufficient plan likely would have been subjected to negative rating pressure by A.M. Best.[107] In December 2013, A.M. Best reported that all such insurers presented action plans to sufficiently reduce exposure to terrorism risk in the event that TRIA is not renewed, and that, therefore, negative rating actions were not taken.[108] Subsequent to this exercise A.M. Best remains concerned with TRIA's potential expiration, and notes that it will continue to monitor insurers' exposures to terrorism risk and "will be prepared to take appropriate rating actions where necessary."[109]

5. Private Reinsurance Capacity

Reinsurance is a mechanism by which insurers transfer, or "cede," portions of risk exposures to other insurers (reinsurers) in exchange for a premium. Reinsurance serves a number of functions for a primary insurer, including allowing it to offer coverage for large exposures, protect policyholder surplus, and stabilize loss experience. Reinsurance increases the capacity of the primary insurance market (*i.e.*, the amount of coverage that insurers can make available) by providing access to additional capital.

The availability of reinsurance is particularly important to primary insurers covering terrorism risk because of the potential for catastrophic losses. The unwillingness of reinsurers to offer affordable coverage for terrorism risk in the aftermath of 9/11 contributed to the unavailability of coverage for terrorism risk in the primary insurance market. Currently, and in the absence of reinsurance or other sources of funding for terrorism risk in the private sector, TRIP provides a level of protection to primary insurers, which preserves the availability of private capital for terrorism risk insurance on affordable terms.

Although a private reinsurance market for terrorism risk exists, the market is supported by limited capital and coverage has not been available in amounts approaching that afforded under TRIP. According to some industry estimates, as little as $6 to $8 billion of global reinsurance coverage is available for terrorism risk in the United States.[110] Moreover, the scope of coverage available from the private reinsurance market has been narrower in comparison to coverage available through TRIP. For example, private reinsurance may not cover losses caused by NBCR attacks, even though such losses may not be excluded from insurers' workers' compensation policies.[111] Private market reinsurance for terrorism risk has typically limited coverage to acts carried out by foreign persons, whereas a certified act of terrorism under TRIA is not subject to that limitation.[112]

Figure 3, which was submitted with testimony before the House Committee on Financial Services by Marsh,[113] shows estimated North American reinsurance dedicated capital of $100 billion; however only a fraction of this is presently available to support terrorism risk.

The Long-Term Availability and Affordability of Insurance for Terrorism Risk   81

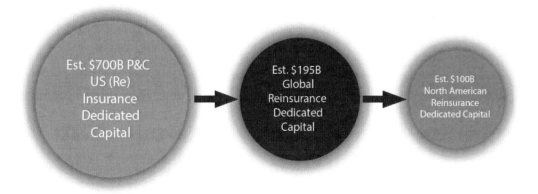

Figure 3. Analysis of Dedicated Insurance and Reinsurance Capital.

In connection with Figure 3, Marsh commented to the Committee:

> It is important to note, however, that not all capital is dedicated to or capable of writing terrorism coverage. While alternative, or "capital markets," providers have brought substantial reinsurance capacity into the industry, most have little to no appetite for the peril. Some are forced to decline on the basis of legal obligations made to their investors, whereas others simply avoid the exposure on the grounds of correlations with financial markets risk.[114]

Marsh estimates that $1 to $2 billion of capacity for terrorism coverage is currently available from private reinsurance markets, and that capacity is likely smaller in major metropolitan areas due to concentration of risk;[115] the amount of coverage available is also more limited if NBCR coverage is not excluded.[116] The cost of standalone terrorism reinsurance may be 1 to 4 percent of the limits purchased in "non-target, lightly populated regions," but in "target cites and/or densely populated commercial centers," the cost may be 15 percent of the reinsurance limit or more.[117]

The largest modeled conventional terrorist attack (involving a truck bomb detonation in Manhattan) produced an estimated insured loss of approximately $38 billion, while a nuclear detonation in Manhattan could produce a loss approaching $950 billion.[118] To the extent covered by insurance, commenters note that such losses would overwhelm the industry in the absence of federal support.[119]

As mentioned by Marsh, recent capital market developments have added a new dynamic to the private reinsurance market with minimal impact in the terrorism risk insurance sector. Investment capital, including from hedge funds and pension funds, has added new reinsurance capacity, including through insurance linked securities (ILS) such as catastrophe bonds. Although this development in ILS markets has made P/C reinsurance more available and affordable, insurers report that ILS transactions have not offered coverage for terrorism risk.[120]

6. Market Uncertainty Relating to the Reauthorization of TRIP

In the timeframe leading up to the previous scheduled TRIA expirations, pricing for terrorism risk insurance spiked. This can be seen on Figure 6 in section D.1 below. Figure 6 also shows a recent upward pricing trend.[121] Aon's comment to the PWG Notice states:

It is expected that pricing volatility will increase throughout the balance of 2013 and will become particularly acute in [the fourth quarter of 2013], as major insurance contracts come up for renewal in 2014 with a portion of the contract extending beyond the end of 2014, and TRIA's scheduled expiration on 12/31/2014.[122]

Aon's view, supported by others, is that "the insurance market has repeatedly signaled that it will not offer the same level of terrorism coverage"[123] mandated by TRIA if its government backstop is not in place. Proponents of a long-term reauthorization argue that insurance for terrorism risk would not be available or affordable in the absence of TRIP. These proponents include a broad range of stakeholders, including insurers, reinsurers, insurance agents and brokers, policyholders, state legislators and regulators, some insurance consumer advocates, and academics. Insurers, reinsurers, and agents and brokers acknowledge the developments in the market from 2002 to 2013, but warn that insurers would again exclude coverage of losses from acts of terrorism if TRIP is not reauthorized. State insurance regulators echo industry views and also expect that an availability crisis would result.[124] State legislators express concern regarding the adverse effects that such unavailability would have on state economies.[125]

Despite the adverse effects of uncertainty regarding the potential reauthorization of TRIP on the availability and affordability of terrorism risk insurance, as expressed by a range of stakeholders, support for a long-term reauthorization of TRIP is not unanimous. Some public policy organizations, including the Cato Institute, Taxpayers for Common Sense, and certain insurance consumer representatives, such as the Consumer Federation of America, comment that TRIA should expire.[126] These commenters assert that insurance for terrorism risk would still be available and affordable in the absence of a federal program that mandates coverage and limits insurer exposure. One commenter argues that insurers would have a strong incentive to offer insurance for terrorism risk in the absence of a federal backstop because failing to do so would risk losing policyholders (*i.e.*, to other insurers that are willing to make coverage available).[127] Another commenter argues that TRIP "crowds out" what would otherwise be a vibrant private reinsurance market for terrorism risk by offering coverage at no cost.[128]

C. Availability of Terrorism Risk Insurance

The availability of insurance for terrorism risk refers to whether insurers offer coverage for losses arising from an act of terrorism. Availability of insurance for terrorism risk typically is evaluated by measuring the available capacity in the private insurance market. Capacity refers to the maximum amount of coverage (*i.e.*, the limit) that an insurer is willing to make available, and often is measured in terms of limit per insured risk exposure (*i.e.*, per-risk). A common practice in analyzing the capacity available in the private insurance market is to aggregate the per-risk limits that insurers are willing to offer. This approach may overestimate the amount of actual capacity available in the market, but it serves as a useful benchmark when considering year-over-year trends.

Insureds most commonly purchase terrorism risk insurance by accepting the offer, required of insurers by TRIA, in insurance contracts for TRIP-eligible lines. This market for terrorism risk insurance is called the "embedded" market because the coverage for terrorism risk is included in a broader policy. The foundation of the embedded market, therefore, is TRIA itself. Embedded terrorism coverage is offered on terms that do not differ materially from those of other coverages, in accordance with TRIA. A relatively small market also exists for specialized "standalone" insurance policies covering terrorism risk, which is described below.

1. Embedded Market

Policyholders of insurance for terrorism risk overwhelmingly purchase coverage that is "embedded" in TRIP-eligible commercial P/C insurance policies. Marsh and Aon report that 95 percent[129] and 80 percent[130] of clients that purchased some form of terrorism risk insurance protection for property risks, respectively, did so through the embedded market. The standalone market, discussed below, is an important complement to the embedded market.

Aggregate DEP for TRIP-eligible lines – for which TRIA requires insurers to make coverage of terrorism risk available – was approximately $184 billion in 2012.[131] Of the approximately 900 insurers that reported DEP for TRIP-eligible lines in 2012, fourteen insurers accounted for 50 percent of the market DEP; 58 insurers accounted for 80 percent of the market DEP; and 376 insurers constituted 99 percent of the market DEP.[132]

Estimates of the capacity in the embedded market are approximately $14 billion of coverage on a per-risk basis, a moderate increase from the $13.5 billion estimate provided in the 2010 PWG Report.[133] Less capacity may be available in areas prone to natural catastrophe perils.[134] For example, terrorism risk insurance capacity for policyholders also requiring protection from catastrophic perils such as hurricanes, earthquakes, and floods may drop to between $2 and $4 billion.[135]

2. Standalone Market

For some insureds, the embedded market is not sufficient to meet coverage needs for terrorism risk. For insureds with the highest risk profiles in particular, "standalone" insurance policies can provide additional or alternative terrorism risk insurance coverage. Such coverage generally is written on customized terms, and is outside the scope of TRIA's coverage mandate and provisions for a government share of loss exposure.[136] For example, standalone policies may provide coverage of non-certified acts of terrorism, or coverage limits that are higher than those available in embedded policies. Standalone terrorism risk insurance typically is sold to policyholders with large or complex exposures that may be perceived as being more susceptible to losses from acts of terrorism.

The cost of standalone terrorism risk insurance can be as much as five to ten times that of embedded (TRIP-eligible) coverage.[137] Even with the ability to charge higher rates, insurers continue to limit available coverage, particularly in high-risk locations.[138] The tables in Figures 4 and 5 indicate the capacity that may be available from insurers writing standalone terrorism risk insurance.

The amount of coverage for terrorism risk offered by the standalone market is influenced by a number of factors and can decrease to $750 million or less in high-risk locations.[139] Bermuda and European insurers (or U.S. subsidiaries), including Lloyd's of London, contribute significantly to standalone terrorism risk insurance capacity in the United States.[140]

Underwriter	Normal ($) maximum Line	Absolute ($) maximum Line
Various Syndicates at Lloyd's	925,000,000	1,195,000,000
AIG / Lexington	100,000,000	250,000,000
Arch Insurance Company (Europe) Ltd	5,000,000	5,000,000
Ace European	50,000,000	50,000,000
Axis Specialty	150,000,000	200,000,000
Hannover Rückversicherungs-Aktiengesellschaft	15,000,000	50,000,000
Hiscox USA	100,000,000	100,000,000
Lancashire Insurance Company UK Ltd	100,000,000	200,000,000
Montpelier Re	50,000,000	50,000,000
Validus/Talbot US	100,000,000	100,000,000
Total	1,595,000,000	2,200,000,000
National Indemnity Company	500,000,000	1,000,000,000
Total incl Berkshire	2,095,000,000	3,200,000,000

Source: Comment to the PWG Notice from Aon plc (September 2013)

Figure 4. Standalone Terrorism Insurance Market Capacity.

INSURER/REINSURER	CAPACITY
Chartis	$1,500
Berkshire Hathaway	$1,000
Lloyd's	$900
Lancashire Insurance Group	$200
AXIS Specialty	$150
Hiscox USA	$100
Validus	$100
Western Re	$85
ACE Global Markets	$50
Montpelier Re	$50
Transatlantic Re	$50
Beazley US	$50
Torus	$40
IRI/Westport	$40
Aspen Re	$30
Inter Hannover	$25

Source: Marsh 2013 Report (May 2013)

Figure 5. Standalone Terrorism Insurance Market Capacity (in $Millions).

The standalone terrorism risk insurance market has grown following 9/11 and the passage of TRIA. The market's current per-risk capacity is more than twice the 2006 capacity of $685 million per-risk.[141] Per-risk capacity has increased for several reasons, including the availability of new capital to the market, and the profitability of the standalone terrorism risk insurance in light of the absence of material terrorist attacks in the United States.[142]

3. Workers' Compensation Market

Workers' compensation insurance provides wage replacement and medical benefits to employees who are injured in the scope of employment, as well as death benefits to surviving spouses and dependents. Workers' compensation is a statutorily-mandated product; under state law, employers must provide it, and insurers may not exclude or limit liability for losses that result from certain perils. Workers' compensation insurance often receives special attention in discussion of terrorism risk insurance because by state law the coverage cannot exclude losses resulting from acts of terrorism (including NBCR). A workers' compensation insurer wishing to avoid terrorism exposures in a given jurisdiction would have to cease writing such business altogether. Thus, the availability of commercial workers' compensation insurance in some localities may wholly depend upon the existence of TRIA and its coverage mandate, federal backstop, and Program Cap.

Aon's submission in response to the PWG Notice, for example, states: "We are confident that without TRIA (or similar reinsurance capital) the cost of workers' compensation insurance will be significantly higher, if available at all."[143] Marsh offered similar observations in its comments: "Without [TRIA], some insurers have indicated to us that they could be forced to withdraw from geographical areas that have the greatest need for terrorism coverage or they may even exit certain lines of business, such as workers' compensation or commercial property in high profile jurisdictions in the event that they are unable to limit their exposure to terrorism."[144] In January 2014, Marsh reported that in light of the pending expiration of TRIA, insurers have begun endorsing workers' compensation renewals to advise policyholders that the premium may change at December 31, 2014, and that some insurers are setting policy expirations at that date.[145]

D. Affordability of Terrorism Risk Insurance

Affordability of insurance for terrorism risk refers to the ability of policyholders to purchase coverage when it is offered. Policyholders able to afford terrorism risk insurance may nonetheless decline coverage for reasons unrelated to the price (*e.g.*, a policyholder has a high risk tolerance or a low perceived risk from acts of terrorism). Nonetheless, the insurance sector generally references the following terrorism risk insurance affordability metrics: (1) terrorism risk premium as a percentage of property insurance premiums; (2) terrorism risk premium as a percentage of total insured value (TIV);[146] and (3) the percentage of policyholders purchasing terrorism risk coverage, known as the take-up rate. Such metrics are applicable to the embedded market.

Terrorism risk insurance affordability data have been collected by both Aon and Marsh,[147] and both indicate that terrorism risk insurance premiums, viewed in the aggregate, constitute between 3 and 5 percent of overall property insurance premiums. Pricing appears to have remained consistent, or even to have declined slightly, over the past several years. Recent trends, however, indicate that prices are increasing in anticipation of a potential expiration of TRIA. Finally, both Aon and Marsh report that, in the aggregate, approximately 60 percent of policyholders elect to purchase coverage of terrorism risk, a figure which also has been relatively stable for several years.

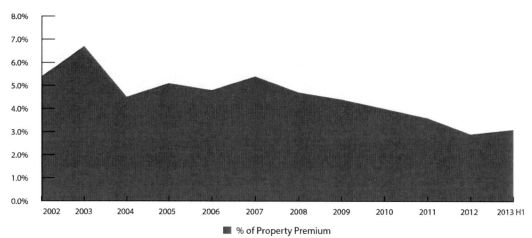

Source: Comment to the PWG Notice from Aon plc (September 2013).

Figure 6. Median Terrorism Premium as a Percentage of Median Property Premium.

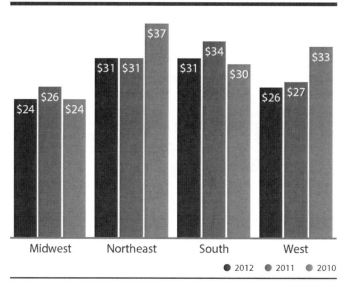

Source: Marsh 2013 Report (May 2013).

Figure 7. Terrorism Insurance Pricing – Median Rates by Region (Rates per $1 Million of Coverage).

1. Pricing Data and Illustrations

Overall, the price for terrorism risk insurance, viewed as a percentage of median property premiums, has declined by half from its 2002 peak. Aon's data, illustrated in Figure 6, show that the figure has declined from nearly 7 percent to approximately 3 percent, with the lowest point being in early 2012.

Pricing of insurance for terrorism risk can vary on a regional basis. For example, an initial (*i.e.*, after the enactment of TRIA) Insurance Services Office (ISO)[148] grouping of U.S. cities into "tiers" according to expected commercial property loss potential from acts of terrorism included the cities of Chicago, New York, San Francisco, and Washington, D.C. in "Tier 1" (*i.e.*, the group with the highest expected loss potential), and the cities of Boston,

The Long-Term Availability and Affordability of Insurance for Terrorism Risk   87

Houston, Los Angeles, Philadelphia, and Seattle in "Tier 2" (*i.e.*, the group with the second-highest expected loss potential).[149] Insurers may reflect ISO's assessment of expected loss potential by charging higher premiums for exposures located in high-risk tiers than for exposures in low-risk tiers.

Marsh supplied Figure 7, which shows that terrorism risk insurance pricing generally is lower in the Midwest and higher in the Northeast. For 2012, median premiums ranged from $24 per million of coverage in the Midwest to $31 per million in the South and the Northeast.

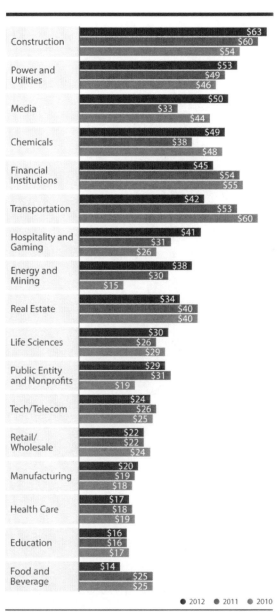

Source: Marsh Global Analytics.

Figure 8. Median Rates by Industry (Rates per $1 Million of Coverage).

Terrorism risk pricing data are also available on an industry basis. Certain industries attract higher prices due to perceived risk exposure to terrorism.[150] Construction, transportation and financial industries face the highest rate per million, with education, healthcare, retail/wholesale, and telecom industries at the lower end of the scale. Considered as a percentage of overall property premiums, however, the construction industry is at the low end, in the 2 to 3 percent range, with transportation, hospitality, and health care at the higher end on a percentage basis. Figures 8 and 9, based on data collected by Marsh, show pricing differences by industry, displayed both as cost per million dollars of coverage, and as percentage of premium by industry.

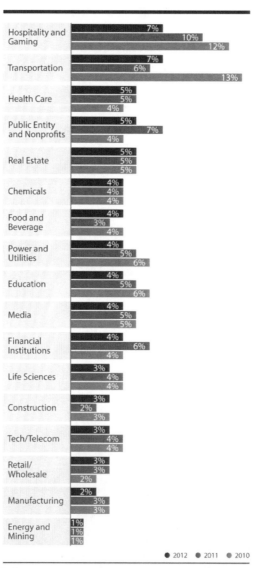

Source: Marsh Global Analytics.

Figure 9. Pricing as a Percentage of Property Premium by Industry.

The Long-Term Availability and Affordability of Insurance for Terrorism Risk 89

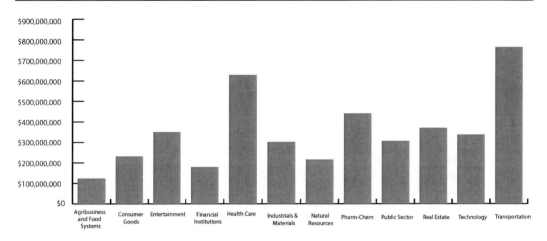

Figure 10. Average Terrorism Limit by Industry Twelve Months Ending 6/30/13.

When benchmarking total terrorism risk insurance premiums divided by TIV, Aon reports (as of June 2013) a general trend toward increasing prices on renewal across most industry subsectors.[151] Terrorism risk pricing in general moves with the overall rates for property insurance. Natural catastrophe exposure (whether by industry or geography) and associated premium trends will similarly influence terrorism risk insurance premiums in order to maintain the same relative premium allocation. Thus, for example, the record natural catastrophe insured losses experienced since 2011 pushed up terrorism risk insurance pricing to some extent.[152] Independent of such influences, however, commenters report upward price trends for terrorism risk insurance "as markets have begun to respond to the prospect of TRIA expiring at the end of 2014."[153]

Marsh reports that median property terrorism risk insurance premium rates decreased for some industries in 2012, notably financial products and services, food and beverage, and transportation, while rates increased most significantly for the media industry, and less so for the chemicals, hospitality, energy, life sciences, and manufacturing industries.[154]

Figure 10 shows that policyholders in the transportation and health care industries purchase the highest limits – approximately $800 and $600 million, respectively.

Figures 11 and 12, from Marsh, show terrorism risk insurance pricing as a function of TIV – displayed as cost per million, and as a percentage of property premium.

Figures 11 and 12 show that property terrorism rates tend to be relatively lower as the size of the insured risk increases. Median rates for smaller companies have declined somewhat in the last few years, but remain more than twice that of larger firms. Considered as a percentage of overall property premiums, the rates vary far less appreciably by TIV – ranging from 4 to 5 percent.

2. Take-Up Rate Data and Illustrations

The overall take-up rate for terrorism risk insurance is approximately 60 percent. Figure 13 shows that the aggregate take-up rate for U.S. terrorism risk insurance has not varied appreciably in nearly a decade.

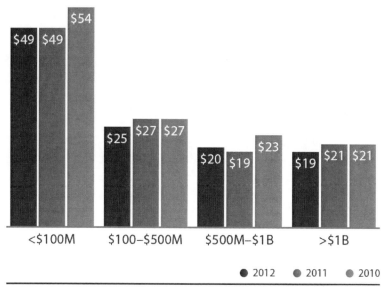

Source: Marsh 2013 Report (May 2013).

Figure 11. Terrorism Insurance Pricing – Median Rates by TIV (Rate per Million).

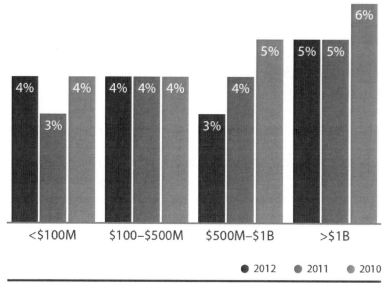

Source: Marsh 2013 Report (May 2013).

Figure 12. Terrorism Insurance Pricing as Percentage of Property Premium by TIV.

Take-up rates are not uniform across industries, however. Figure 14 illustrates both take-up rate and annualized premium on an industry-by-industry basis for terrorism risk coverage, based on data collected by Aon. The real estate and entertainment industries have the highest take-up rates of approximately 80 to 90 percent. The take-up rate for the transportation industry is much lower, at roughly 50 percent.

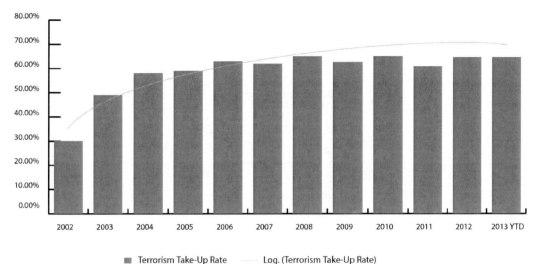

Source: Comment to the PWG Notice from Aon plc (September 2013).

Figure 13. Property Terrorism Insurance Take-Up Rate by Year.

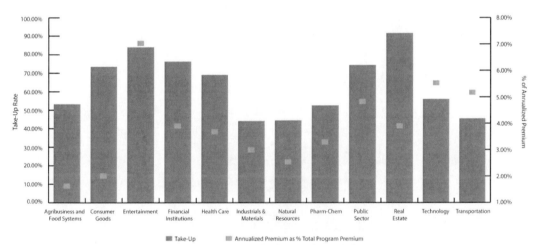

Source: Comment to the PWG Notice from Aon plc (September 2013).

Figure 14. Property Terrorism Insurance Take-Up and Pricing by Industry Twelve Months Ending 6/30/13.

Marsh also reports terrorism risk insurance take-up rates by industry and region. As shown in Figure 15, of seventeen industries defined by Marsh, the media, education, and financial institution industries had the highest take-up rates in 2012 at 81 percent, 75 percent, and 75 percent, respectively. The industries with the lowest take-up rates in 2012 were the chemical, energy and mining, and manufacturing sectors at 42 percent, 43 percent, and 48 percent, respectively.

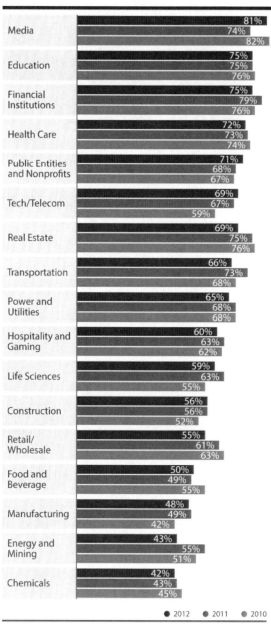

Source: Marsh 2013 Report (May 2013).

Figure 15. Terrorism Insurance Take-Up Rate by Industry.

Figure 16 shows that, considered by region, policyholders in the Northeast had a take-up rate of 77 percent in 2012, while firms in the rest of the country had take-up rates between 53 and 63 percent. These observations are consistent with general risk perceptions, *i.e.*, Tier 1 exposures in the Northeast.

Marsh also analyzed take-up data against TIV. The highest take-up rates (60 to 70 percent) correspond to TIV of $500 million or more, while the lowest take-up rates (60 percent) correspond to TIV of less than $100 million.[155]

The Long-Term Availability and Affordability of Insurance for Terrorism Risk   93

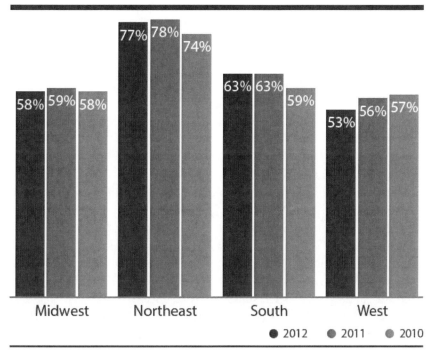

Source: Marsh 2013 Report (May 2013).

Figure 16. Terrorism Insurance Take-Up Rate by Region.

3. Standalone Market

Aon commented in 2013 that "many [insurers] have begun to scale back capacity for terrorism risk."[156] Both Aon and Marsh have stated that pricing volatility in the standalone market had been expected to increase substantially during 2013 in view of uncertainty regarding whether TRIA will expire. According to Aon and Marsh, renewal pricing increases in the standalone market may be an early indicator of substantial decreases in capacity should the embedded category cease to exist, *i.e.*, in the absence of TRIA.[157]

IV. COMMENTS TO THE PWG NOTICE REGARDING MODIFICATIONS TO THE TERRORISM RISK INSURANCE PROGRAM

TRIA is scheduled to expire at the end of 2014, and Congress is considering whether and in what form TRIP may be reauthorized. In anticipation of its possible reauthorization, some commenters to the PWG Notice and other interested parties have offered views on potential modifications to TRIP, including modifications that could reduce federal taxpayer exposure under TRIP, clarify the scope of TRIP regarding losses from NBCR and cyber attacks, and enhance the process for certifying an event as an act of terrorism. Although an analysis of potential modifications to TRIP is outside the scope of PWG's mandate to report on the long-term availability and affordability of insurance for terrorism risk,[158] this section of the Report identifies issues commenters raised regarding those matters.

A. Reducing Federal Taxpayer Exposure

Prior modifications to TRIP generally reduced federal taxpayer exposure. Some stakeholders argue that if TRIA is not allowed to expire, further reductions to federal taxpayer exposure are appropriate, including modifications to the insurer deductible, the federal share of insured losses above the deductible, or the Program Trigger, or the establishment of *ex ante* premium payments.[159] However, most commenters favor a long-term reauthorization of TRIP without further material changes to the program.[160]

1. Modifications to the Deductible and/or the Federal Share

The insurer deductible and the federal share of losses that exceed the deductible determine the amount of federal payments potentially made to insurers under TRIP. Supporters of further reductions to federal taxpayer exposure under TRIP express the view that private markets could support greater exposure, in part because of the P/C sector's record-high aggregate surplus level and ability to insure against large-scale losses from natural catastrophes.[161] Conversely, P/C sector representatives take the view that federal taxpayer exposure already has been substantially reduced,[162] and that insurers are not positioned to bear additional increases to the deductible or co-share levels.[163]

2. Modifications to the Program Trigger

TRIA prohibits federal payments to insurers under TRIP unless aggregate insured losses from a certified act of terrorism exceed the Program Trigger. As originally enacted, TRIA did not include a Program Trigger. TRIEA implemented a Program Trigger of $50 million in 2006, which increased to $100 million in 2007. The Program Trigger remains at $100 million today.

Some commenters argue that because the P/C sector has demonstrated that it can support losses much larger than $100 million, the current Program Trigger should be increased substantially.[164] Conversely, at least one commenter argues that evaluating the Program Trigger relative to aggregate industry surplus is misleading, and that increasing the Program Trigger would drive small or mid-size insurers from the market and "expose the federal government to greater costs in the form of post-disaster assistance."[165]

3. Introduction of Ex Ante Premiums

Unlike conventional private sector insurance and reinsurance programs, TRIP does not require an up-front premium for the coverage provided.[166] Commenters favoring *ex ante* premiums argue that TRIP is subsidizing the insurance industry and that *ex ante* premiums would reduce any subsidy to insurers and provide a pool of funds that could be available for future federal payments under TRIP.[167]

B. Clarifying Coverage for NBCR and Cyber Attacks

TRIA requires an insurer to make available coverage for losses from acts of terrorism "that does not differ materially from the terms, amounts, and other coverage limitations applicable to losses arising from events other than acts of terrorism,"[168] but does not explicitly address coverage for losses from NBCR or cyber attacks.

Commercial lines insurance policies generally exclude coverage for losses resulting from NBCR attacks. In 2008, the GAO found that insurers limit NBCR coverage through "long-standing exclusions for nuclear and pollution risks, which already have been approved by state regulators," and concluded that NBCR coverage was generally unavailable.[169] TRIA is silent as to the presence or absence of an NBCR exclusion in an insurer's P/C policy.[170]

Insurance for cyber security risk is an emerging line of insurance that is gaining increasing attention. Premium volume in the U.S. cyber insurance market is estimated to be approximately $1 billion – a fraction of the $247 billion of direct premiums written for the total U.S. commercial lines insurance market in 2012.[171] One commenter representing insurers argued that clarity is needed regarding the application of TRIA to losses from NBCR and cyber attacks.[172] Another commenter, representing commercial insurance policyholders, argued that coverage of NBCR attacks should be mandatory under TRIA.[173]

C. Enhancing Transparency of the Certification Process

Commenters also advocate enhancing transparency of the certification process under TRIP. Commenters suggest that increased clarity regarding how an event is certified as an act of terrorism could increase certainty for insurance markets and policyholders.[174]

TRIA does not impose a time frame on the process for determining whether an event should be certified as an act of terrorism, and Treasury declined to introduce such a time frame through regulation in 2003.[175] Some insurers comment that the Secretary should be required to determine whether to certify an event as an act of terrorism within a certain time frame, because certification may affect an insurer's assessment regarding whether losses caused by the event are covered under the terms of insurance policies.[176] Moreover, state insurance laws or regulations may require an insurer to settle claims within specified time frames.[177] One commenter notes that an insurer could be required to pay certain claims before ascertaining whether such claims reasonably may have been excluded as losses resulting from acts of terrorism.[178]

CONCLUSION

The factors examined in this Report regarding the long-term availability and affordability of terrorism risk insurance center around indicators of private market per-risk capacity (*i.e.*, the amount of coverage insurers can make available) and demand for coverage. In summary, private market per-risk capacity for terrorism risk insurance coverage has increased only moderately since 2010. Policyholder take-up rates have remained stable overall, and prices of terrorism risk insurance have been fairly steady, although the market appears to be tightening in anticipation of a potential expiration of TRIA. Policyholders who wish to obtain terrorism risk insurance evidently are able to do so, although some in higher risk industries and some in key urban locations pay relatively higher prices.

Challenges continue to exist regarding the ability of the private market to provide terrorism risk insurance without a federal backstop, particularly with respect to the ability of insurers to model the frequency and severity of losses that could arise from acts of terrorism. Also, reinsurers and the capital markets appear reluctant to provide further support to the terrorism risk insurance market.

Private reinsurance does not appear to be a sufficient substitute for the market certainty provided by TRIA. Despite the 2007 reauthorization of TRIA, private property reinsurance generally continued to exclude acts of terrorism committed by those who are "domestic" agents, as well as all losses caused by NBCR attacks. This suggests that the private terrorism risk insurance market would be different in the absence of TRIA. Comments submitted to the PWG state that insurers would offer significantly less coverage or exit the market altogether without the "make available" requirement and a viable means to cede risk and limit exposure. The existence of only a relatively small standalone terrorism risk insurance market is consistent with this view. Absent TRIA, terrorism risk insurance, particularly for high-value exposures, may become a smaller, specialty market if such coverage remains available at all.

Data and comments provided to the PWG highlight market uncertainty surrounding whether TRIA will be renewed in any form before it expires at the end of 2014. For example, Marsh – whose submission in response to the PWG Notice provided much of the data cited in this Report – published a briefing in January 2014, which states:

> Coupled with increasing claims costs, historical unprofitability, and a continued weak interest rate environment, the uncertainty around [TRIA's] future is leading to less availability of workers' compensation capacity and rate increases for risks located in major urban areas.[179]

Most commenters generally describe TRIP as an appropriate public-private shared risk model that: (1) ensures that terrorism risk coverage is available to all commercial P/C insurance buyers; (2) makes $100 billion of aggregate private and federal capital available to fund the recovery costs of a potential terrorist attack; (3) provides an overall limit on industry exposure; and (4) includes a recoupment mechanism in the event Treasury makes any payments.

Relatively few comments in response to the PWG Notice argued against TRIA on grounds of public policy or efficiency. Comments from insurers and policyholders generally shared the view that, in the absence of TRIA, terrorism risk insurance would be less available and/or less affordable due to insurers' reluctance to maintain exposure to terrorism risk in the face of potentially unlimited losses and unpredictable loss scenarios.[180] Nevertheless, the industry share of exposure to terrorism risks has steadily increased since enactment of TRIA without significant adverse effects on price or availability. Further gradual increases to the industry share appear unlikely to cause significant market disruptions assuming some level of a federal government backstop is maintained.

GLOSSARY OF ACRONYMS AND ABBREVIATIONS

Program Year	Calendar year, as defined by TRIA § 102(11)
Program Cap	Cap on annual liability, as provided by TRIA § 103(e)(2)
CRAs	Credit rating agencies

Treasury	Department of the Treasury
DEP	Direct earned premium
Dodd-Frank Act	Dodd-Frank Wall Street Reform and Consumer Protection Act of 2010
FIO	Federal Insurance Office
PWG Notice	Federal Register notice published July 16, 2013 (78 Fed. Reg. 42,588)
GAO	Government Accountability Office
ILS	Insurance Linked Security
ISO	Insurance Services Office.
TRIP-eligible lines	Lines of insurance for which federal payments may be made under TRIA
NAIC	National Association of Insurance Commissioners
NBCR	Nuclear, biological, chemical, or radiological
PWG	President's Working Group on Financial Markets
PML	Probable Maximum Loss
P/C	Property and casualty
Secretary	Secretary of the Treasury.
TRIA	Terrorism Risk Insurance Act of 2002, as amended
TRIEA	Terrorism Risk Insurance Extension Act of 2005
TRIP	Terrorism Risk Insurance Program
TRIPRA	Terrorism Risk Insurance Program Reauthorization Act of 2007
9/11	The terrorist attacks of September 11, 2001
Program Trigger	Threshold for federal payments, as provided by TRIA § 103(e)(1)(B)
TIV	Total Insured Value

End Notes

[1] 15 U.S.C. § 6701 note. Citations herein to TRIA, as amended, refer to the relevant section(s) of the statute.

[2] For purposes of this report, TRIA refers to the statute, as amended, and TRIP refers to the program, as it is administered.

[3] The PWG is composed of the Secretary of the Treasury, the Chairman of the Board of Governors of the Federal Reserve System, the Chair of the Securities and Exchange Commission, and the Chairman of the Commodity Futures Trading Commission (or their respective designees). The Secretary of the Treasury, or his designee, is the Chairman of the PWG. Exec. Order No. 12,631; 53 Fed. Reg. 9,421 (Mar. 18, 1988).

[4] The PWG must submit the reports to the Committee on Banking, Housing, & Urban Affairs of the Senate and the Committee on Financial Services of the House of Representatives. TRIA § 108(e).

[5] PRESIDENT'S WORKING GROUP ON FINANCIAL MARKETS, *Terrorism Risk Insurance* (September 2006), *available at* http:// www.treasury.gov/resource-center/fin-mkts/Documents/report.pdf (hereinafter *PWG 2006 Report*); PRESIDENT'S WORKING GROUP ON FINANCIAL MARKETS, *Market Conditions for Terrorism Risk Insurance* (2010), *available at* http://www.treasury.gov/resource-center/fin-mkts/Documents/PWG%20Report%20Final%20January%2013.pdf (hereinafter *PWG 2010 Report*).

[6] U.S. DEPARTMENT OF THE TREASURY, *Assessment: The Terrorism Risk Insurance Act of 2002* (June 30, 2005), *available at* http://www.treasury.gov/resource-center/fin-mkts/Documents/tria_studyby_treas.pdf (hereinafter *Treasury 2005 Report*). In 2008, the GAO submitted a report to Congress addressing the availability of coverage for attacks involving NBCR weapons. U.S. Government Accountability Office, *Terrorism Insurance, Status of Coverage Availability for Attacks Involving Nuclear, Biological, Chemical, or Radiological Weapons*, GAO-09-39 (December 2008), *available at* http:// www.gao.gov/new.items/d0939.pdf (hereinafter *GAO 2008 Report*).

[7] 78 Fed. Reg. 42,588.

[8] *See, e.g.*, GENERAL ACCOUNTING OFFICE (currently known as the Government Accountability Office), *Terrorism Insurance, Rising Uninsured Exposure to Attacks Heightens Potential Economic Vulnerabilities*, 3-7 (February 27, 2002) (hereinafter *GAO 2002 Report*); Comment to the PWG Notice from the Risk Management Society, 2 (September 2013) (characterizing the potential unavailability and unaffordability of insurance for terrorism risk as an economic problem).

[9] The Terrorism Risk Insurance Extension Act of 2005 (TRIEA) was enacted on December 22, 2005. 119 Stat. 2660-2662. TRIEA reauthorized TRIP for two years, through December 31, 2007. The Terrorism Risk Insurance Program Reauthorization Act of 2007 (TRIPRA) was enacted on December 26, 2007. 121 Stat. 1839-1841. TRIPRA reauthorized TRIP for seven years, through December 31, 2014.

[10] *TRIA at Ten Years: The Future of the Terrorism Risk Insurance Program: Hearing before the H. Comm. on Financial Services Subcommittee on Housing and Insurance*, 112th Cong. (September 11, 2012), *available at* http://financialservices.house.gov/ calendar/eventsingle.aspx?EventID=307443.

[11] *The Terrorism Risk Insurance Act of 2002: Hearing before the H. Comm. on Financial Services*, 113th Cong. (September 19, 2013), *available at* http://financialservices.house.gov/calendar/eventsingle.aspx?EventID =349518.

[12] *Reauthorizing TRIA: The State of the Terrorism Risk Insurance Market, Hearing before the S. Comm. on Banking, Housing, & Urban Affairs*, 113th Cong. (September 25, 2013), *available at* http://www.banking.senate.gov/public/index.cfm?FuseAction=Hearings.Hearing&Hearing_ID=b9077dbb-2ae2-425a-89dd-793fcb049190.

[13] *The Future of Terrorism Insurance: Fostering Private Market Innovation to Limit Taxpayer Exposure: Hearing before the H. Comm. on Financial Services Subcommittee on Housing and Insurance*, 113th Cong. (November 13, 2013), *available at* http:// financialservices.house.gov/calendar/eventsingle.aspx?EventID=360497.

[14] *Reauthorizing TRIA: The State of the Terrorism Risk Insurance Market, Part II, Hearing before the S. Comm. On Banking, Housing, & Urban Affairs*, 113th Cong. (February 25, 2014), *available at* http://www.banking.senate.gov/public/index. cfm?FuseAction=Hearings.Hearing&Hearing_ID=08e1735c-d2be-4260-a1dc-12975ab9397f.

[15] *See* section III.C.1.

[16] Marsh and McLennan Companies, 2013 *Terrorism Risk Insurance Report*, 8 (May 2013) (hereinafter *Marsh 2013 Report*).

[17] *Id*. at 9.

[18] *Id*. at 10.

[19] *Id*. at 11-14; Comment to the PWG Notice from Aon plc, 6-7 (September 2013).

[20] *See, e.g., GAO 2002 Report* at 10-11.

[21] *See* Comment to the PWG Notice from Aon plc, 6 (September 2013) (showing median terrorism risk insurance premiums as a percentage of median property insurance premiums from 2002 through 2013).

[22] *See, e.g. Marsh 2013 Report*. at 19-21; Comment to the PWG Notice from Aon plc, 12, 18-21 (September 2013).

[23] One commenter, the Cato Institute, expressed a contrary view. Specifically, the Cato Institute argued that the private market is capable of insuring terrorism risk and that TRIA should be allowed to expire at the end of 2014. Comment to the PWG Notice from the Cato Institute, 1 (September 2013).

[24] Comment to the PWG Notice from Aon plc, 3 (September 2013). Aon reported to the PWG that the clients included in its survey resemble businesses of the size and complexity similar to those in the Fortune 2000. Data from the Aon survey reflect the twelve-month period ending June 30, 2013.

[25] *See Marsh 2013 Report* at 1-2.

[26] Comment to the PWG Notice from the Cato Institute, 16 (September 2013).

[27] *See* TRIA § 108(e).

[28] SNL Financial LC, U.S. Insurance Statutory, P/C Industry Briefing Books – Income Statement (September 2013).

[29] All-peril policies may also be referred to as special peril policies.

[30] With the exception of Texas, states require employers to provide workers' compensation benefits to employees.

[31] *See Marsh 2013 Report* at 19.

[32] In 2001 dollars.

[33] *See, e.g., GAO 2002 Report* at 3-7.

[34] *See, e.g.*, Comment to the PWG Notice from the National Council on Compensation Insurance, 6-7 (September 2013).

[35] *See, e.g., GAO 2002 Report* at 13-14.

[36] TRIA § 101(a)(5).

[37] TRIA § 101(b).

[38] TRIA § 103(a)(1).

[39] TRIA § 103(a)(2).

[40] TRIA §§ 103(a)(3), (c).

[41] TRIA § 103(e)(7).

[42] Pub. L. 111-203, 124 Stat. 1589.

[43] An insurer is any entity, including any affiliate thereof, which receives direct earned premiums for TRIP-eligible lines of insurance and is: licensed or admitted to engage in the business of insurance in any state; an eligible surplus lines carrier; a federally-approved maritime, energy, or aviation insurer; a state residual market or workers' compensation fund; or, to the extent provided in rules issued by the Secretary, a captive insurer or a self-insurance arrangement. TRIA § 102(6).

[44] TRIA § 103(c).

[45] TRIA § 102(12)(B).

[46] TRIA § 102(12)(A).

[47] 31 C.F.R. § 50.5(u)(1).

[48] Id.

[49] TRIEA added "directors and officers liability insurance" to the scope of TRIP-eligible insurance. TRIEA § 3(b)(2), 119 Stat. 2661.

[50] TRIA § 105(a).

[51] TRIA § 105(c).

[52] 31 C.F.R. § 50.21(d). "Partial coverage" means "coverage that is on different terms, amounts, or coverage limitations, as long as such an offer does not violate any applicable State law requirements." 31 C.F.R. § 50.24(a).

[53] TRIA § 103(b)(2); 31 C.F.R. § 50.10.

[54] TRIA § 103(b)(3); 31 C.F.R. § 50.15.

[55] TRIA § 102(1). TRIA also provides that an act may occur outside the United States in the case of certain air carriers or vessels, or the premises of an U.S. mission. TRIA § 102(1)(A)(iii)(I)-(II).

[56] This limiting clause does not apply with respect to coverage for workers' compensation insurance. TRIA § 102(1)(B)(i).

[57] TRIA § 102(1)(B)(ii).

[58] For example, paid losses measure losses already paid to claimants, but may develop slowly and therefore underrepresent actual losses that will develop in the months following an insured event. Incurred losses may develop more quickly, but typically include estimates of unpaid losses, which will vary based on an insurer's reserving practices and view of loss development.

[59] *See, e.g.*, Comment to the PWG Notice from the Property Casualty Insurers Association of America, 8 (September 2013).

[60] TRIA § 102(1)(A)(iv).

[61] TRIPRA § 3(a).

[62] TRIA § 103(e)(1)(A).

[63] Direct earned premium represents the amount of premium exposed to loss during a given period. Earned premium for a calendar year is equal to written premium plus the unearned premium reserve at the start of the year less the unearned premium reserve at the end of the year.

[64] TRIA § 102(7).

[65] TRIEA § 3(c).

[66] TRIA § 103(e)(1)(B)(ii).

[67] Id.

[68] Insurer deductible was 10% of DEP, or $100 million. The federal share in 2004 was 90 percent of losses exceeding the insurer deductible (0.90 * [$400 million – $100 million] = $270 million).

[69] Insurer deductible was 15% of DEP, or $150 million. The federal share in 2005 was 90 percent of losses exceeding the insurer deductible (0.90 * [$400 million – $150 million] = $225 million).

[70] Insurer deductible was 20% of DEP, or $200 million. The federal share in 2010 was 85 percent of losses exceeding the insurer deductible (0.85 * [$400 million – $200 million] = $170 million).

[71] Insurer deductible was 20% of DEP, or $400 million. The federal share in 2010 was 85 percent of losses exceeding the insurer deductible (0.85 * [$400 million – $400 million] = 0).

[72] TRIA § 103(e)(2)(A).

[73] Id.

[74] TRIA §§ 103(e)(2)-(3).

[75] TRIA § 103(e)(7).

[76] TRIA § 103(e)(8)(A), (B).

[77] Id.

[78] TRIA § 103(e)(6).

[79] TRIA § 103(e)(7).

[80] TRIA § 103(e)(7)(D).

[81] TRIA § 103(e)(7)(C).

[82] Twenty billion dollars of uncompensated insured losses would have exceeded the insurance marketplace aggregate retention amount for 2005 (the lesser of $15 billion or total insured losses of $40 billion).

[83] The mandatory recoupment amount of $7.5 billion equals the insurance marketplace aggregate retention amount for 2010 (the lesser of $27.5 billion or total insured losses of $40 billion) less the uncompensated insured

losses ($20 billion). Under TRIPRA the Secretary would have been required to collect 133 percent of the mandatory recoupment amount (1.33 * $7.5 billion = $10 billion).

[84] Among others, staff consulted with representatives from the insurance regulatory departments of Massachusetts, New York, and California, as well as from the NAIC. Staff also consulted with various consumer advocates, insurers, reinsurers, commercial insurance policyholders, trade associations, and industry services providers.

[85] *Treasury 2005 Report.*

[86] *PWG 2006 Report.*

[87] *GAO 2008 Report* at 14.

[88] *PWG 2010 Report.*

[89] Comment to the PWG Notice from the American Insurance Association, 5 (September 2013) (distinguishing the data that are available to insurers for pricing terrorism risk from the data that are available for pricing natural catastrophe risk); *Reauthorizing TRIA: The State of the Terrorism Risk Insurance Market, Hearing before the S. Comm. on Banking, Housing, & Urban Affairs*, 113th Cong. (September 25, 2013) (statement from Robert P. Hartwig, Ph.D., CPCU, Insurance Information Institute, at 19), *available at* http://www.banking.senate.gov/public/index.cfm?FuseAction=Hearings. Testimony&Hearing_ID=b9077dbb-2ae2-425a-89dd-793fcb049190&Witness_ID=8f726a39-e80f-412f-9672-7afb49e64fb7 (explaining that insurers do not have data with which to estimate the frequency of terrorist attacks).

[90] *See The Terrorism Risk Insurance Act of 2002: Hearing before the H. Comm. on Financial Services*, 113th Cong. (September 19, 2013) (statement from Dr. Gordon Woo, Catastrophist, Risk Management Solutions Inc., at 1), *available at* http:// financialservices.house.gov/uploadedfiles/hhrg-113-ba00-wstate-gwoo-20130919.pdf (explaining that catastrophe insurance modeling addresses the need of insurers to quantify risk).

[91] *See, e.g.*, Comment to the PWG Notice from Liberty Mutual Insurance, 3 (September 2013); Comment to the PWG Notice from the American Insurance Association, 5 (September 2013); Comment to the PWG Notice from the National Association of Mutual Insurance Companies, 6 (September 2013); Comment to the PWG Notice from the Property Casualty Insurers Association of America, 1 (September 2013); *Reauthorizing TRIA: The State of the Terrorism Risk Insurance Market, Hearing before the S. Comm. on Banking, Housing, & Urban Affairs*, 113th Cong. (September 25, 2013) (statement from Robert P. Hartwig, Ph.D., CPCU, Insurance Information Institute, at 19), *available at* http://www.banking.senate.gov/ public/index.cfm?FuseAction=Hearings.Testimony&Hearing_ID=b9077dbb-2ae2-425a-89dd-793fcb049190&Witness_ ID=8f726a39-e80f-412f-9672-7afb49e64fb7 (stating that terrorism risk models can predict the severity but not the frequency of insured losses from acts of terrorism); *but see The Terrorism Risk Insurance Act of 2002: Hearing before the H. Comm. on Financial Services*, 113th Cong. (September 19, 2013) (statement from Dr. Gordon Woo, Catastrophist, Risk Management Solutions Inc., at 1), *available at* http://financialservices.house.gov/uploadedfiles/hhrg-113-ba00-wstate-gwoo-20130919.pdf (stating that "terrorism insurance risk modeling has attained a level of capability").

[92] Comment to the PWG Notice from Aon plc, 16 (September 2013).

[93] *Id.*

[94] Comment to the PWG Notice from the American Academy of Actuaries, 2-3 (September 2013). *See also* Comment to the PWG Notice from Liberty Mutual Insurance, 2-3 (September 2013) (referencing modeled terrorist events that exceed $750 billion of insured losses, including modeled anthrax attacks that exceed $900 billion of insured losses).

[95] SNL Financial, U.S. Insurance Statutory, P/C Industry Briefing Books – Balance Sheet (September 2013).

[96] Aggregate property and casualty sector premium was $407 billion in 2002, relative to $295 billion of aggregate surplus. Aggregate premiums were $524 billion in 2012, relative to $597 billion of aggregate surplus. SNL Financial, U.S. Insurance Statutory, P/C Industry Briefing Books – Balance Sheet, Income Statement (September 2013).

[97] *See, e.g.*, Comment to the PWG Notice from the Cato Institute, 12-13 (September 2013).

[98] *Id.* at 14.

[99] *See, e.g.*, Comment to the PWG Notice from the American Insurance Association, 14-15 (September 2013).

[100] *Id.*

[101] SNL Financial LC (November 2013) (aggregating DEP for TRIP-eligible lines of insurance, in addition to Policyholder Surplus, as reported for 2012). "Insurers" in this case are identified at the "SNL Groups" level (*i.e.*, insurance groups, as opposed to legal entities).

[102] Comment to the PWG Notice from the American Insurance Association, 14 (September 2013).

[103] *Id.* at 15.

[104] A.M. Best Methodology, *The Treatment of Terrorism Risk In the Rating Evaluation*, 1 (November 27, 2013), *available at* http://www3.ambest.com/ambv/ratingmethodology/OpenPDF.aspx?rc=197680.

[105] *Id.* at 5.

[106] A.M. Best, *Future of TRIPRA Remains Uncertain, Rating Pressure Intensifies*, 1 (October 9, 2013), *available at* http://www3.ambest.com/DisplayBinary/DisplayBinary.aspx?TY=P&record_code=217533&URatingId=2421524. A.M. Best's assessment included a stress test of insurers' balance sheets, which simulated the result of a

conventional terrorist attack "similar to a five- or six-ton TNT truck bomb." Those insurers that failed the stress test, under the assumption that TRIP did not exist, were asked to present plans for reducing exposure to terrorism risk in the event that TRIA expires.

[107] *Id.*

[108] A.M. Best, *No Rating Actions Taken on Insurers with Terrorism Exposure Despite Uncertain Future of TRIPRA* (December 19, 2013), *available at* http://www3.ambest.com/frames/frameserver.asp?site=press&tab=1&altsrc=14&altnum=&refnum=65504648775446506655.

[109] *Id.* A.M. Best also noted that its stress test "was not meant to be a worst-case scenario." *Id.*

[110] Comment to the PWG Notice from the Reinsurance Association of America, 3 (September 2013); *TRIA at Ten Years: The Future of the Terrorism Risk Insurance Program, Hearing before the H. Comm. on Financial Services Subcommittee on Housing and Insurance*, 112th Cong. (September 11, 2012) (statement of Edward B. Ryan, Aon Benfield, at 3), *available at* http://financialservices.house.gov/uploadedfiles/hhrg-112-ba04-wstate-eryan-20120911.pdf.

[111] *See* Comment to the PWG Notice from Marsh, 8 (September 2013) ("the industry is not adequately capitalized to support such exposure").

[112] Comment to the PWG Notice from Aon plc, 30 (September 2013).

[113] *The Terrorism Risk Insurance Act of 2002: Hearing before the H. Comm. on Financial Services*, 113th Cong. (September 19, 2013) (statement from Peter J. Beshar, Executive Vice President and General Counsel, Marsh & McLennan Companies, at 5), *available at* http://financialservices.house.gov/uploadedfiles/hhrg-113-ba00-wstate-pbeshar-20130919.pdf.

[114] *Id.* at 6.

[115] Comment to the PWG Notice from Marsh, 9 (September 2013).

[116] Comment to the PWG Notice from Aon plc, 30-31. Aon also reports that "[r]einsurers have grown slightly more comfortable with the exposure, and capacity has increased.... Nevertheless, the inability to assign frequencies to the occurrence of terrorism events makes the value proposition for buyers difficult to assess." *Id.* at 31.

[117] Comment to the PWG Notice from Marsh, 10 (September 2013).

[118] *Id.* As indicated above, the American Academy of Actuaries also has reported several estimates of insured losses, including a $778 billion estimated loss resulting from a potential NBCR terrorist attack in New York City. Comment to the PWG Notice from the American Academy of Actuaries, 2-3 (September 2013). *See also* Comment to the PWG Notice from Liberty Mutual Insurance, 2-3 (September 2013).

[119] *See, e.g.*, Comment to the PWG Notice from Liberty Mutual Insurance, 2-3 (September 2013); Comment to the PWG Notice from the Reinsurance Association of America, 3 (September 2013); *TRIA at Ten Years: The Future of the Terrorism Risk Insurance Program, Hearing before the H. Comm. on Financial Services Subcommittee on Housing and Insurance*, 112th Cong. (September 11, 2012) (statement of Edward B. Ryan, Aon Benfield, at 3).

[120] Comment to the PWG Notice from the American Insurance Association, 20 (September 2013). Capital markets-linked reinsurance vehicles have been primarily dedicated to weather risks and to date represent approximately $45 billion of capacity worldwide. Aon Benfield, *Reinsurance Market Outlook: Post Convergence – The Next USD100 Billion* (September 2013).

[121] The graph shows in part "insurance markets beginning to adjust their portfolios of risk to manage the potential expiration of TRIA." Comment to the PWG Notice from Aon plc, 6 (September 2013).

[122] *Id.* at 7.

[123] *Id.* at 6.

[124] Comment to the PWG Notice from the New York Department of Financial Services (September 2013); Comment to the PWG Notice from the National Association of Insurance Commissioners (September 2013).

[125] Comment to the PWG Notice from the National Council of Insurance Legislators (September 2013).

[126] *See* Comment to the PWG Notice from the Cato Institute (September 2013); *The Terrorism Risk Insurance Act of 2002: Hearing before the H. Comm. on Financial Services*, 113th Cong. (September 19, 2013) (statement from Steve Ellis, Vice President, Taxpayers for Common Sense), *available at* http://financialservices.house.gov/uploadedfiles/hhrg-113-ba00-wstate-sellis-20130919.pdf. Staff consulted with the Consumer Federation of America (CFA) regarding TRIA. Although the CFA did not submit a comment in response to the PWG Notice, the PWG understands that its views are consistent today with its earlier reports advocating TRIA's expiration. *See, e.g.*, Consumer Federation of America, *Weaning the Insurance Industry and Large Commercial Policyholders from Taxpayer Subsidies under the Terrorism Risk Insurance Act* (July 26, 2005), *available at* http://www.consumerfed.org/elements/www.consumerfed.org/file/finance/TRIA_Report_072605.pdf.

[127] Comment to the PWG Notice from the Cato Institute, 13 (September 2013).

[128] *See, e.g., Hearing before the H. Comm. on Financial Services*, 113th Cong. (September 19, 2013) (statement from Steve Ellis, Vice President, Taxpayers for Common Sense, at 3-4), *available at* http://financialservices.house.gov/uploadedfiles/hhrg-113-ba00-wstate-sellis-20130919.pdf.

[129] *Marsh 2013 Report* at 10.

[130] Comment to the PWG Notice from Aon plc, 9 (September 2013).

[131] SNL Financial LC (November 2013).

[132] SNL Financial LC (November 2013) (aggregating DEP for TRIP-eligible lines of insurance, as reported for 2012). "Insurers" in this case are identified at the "SNL Groups" level (*i.e.*, insurance groups, as opposed to legal entities).

[133] Comment to the PWG Notice from Aon plc, 8 (September 2013); *PWG 2010 Report* at 15.

[134] Comment to the PWG Notice from Aon plc, 8 (September 2013).

[135] *Id.*

[136] Standalone coverage may also be accessed via reinsurance. *See* Comment to the PWG Notice from Aon plc, 6 (September 2013).

[137] *Marsh 2013 Report* at 19.

[138] *Id*

[139] *Id.*

[140] *See id.* at 11.

[141] *See id.* at 9.

[142] *See id.* at 10.

[143] Comment to the PWG Notice from Aon plc, 27 (September 2013). Aon expressed further that the cost impact would affect all companies, not just those that present particularly high terrorism risk exposure. *Id.*

[144] Comment to the PWG Notice from Marsh, 1 (September 2013).

[145] Marsh Risk Management Research, *Pending TRIPRA Expiration Impacts Workers' Compensation Industry* (January 21, 2014), *available at* http://usa.marsh.com/NewsInsights/MarshRiskManagementResearch/ID/34179/Pending-TRIPRA-Expiration-Impacts-Workers-Compensation-Industry.aspx.

[146] Total Insured Value (TIV) is the total in dollars of covered property and associated insured interests. As used by Aon, TIV means insured physical assets and business interruption values.

[147] Aon reported to staff that its survey relied on data collected from over 1,200 of its clients that resemble businesses of the size and complexity similar to those in the Fortune 2000. The Aon report reflects the twelve-month period ending on June 30, 2013, and is included with its comment to the PWG Notice. Comment to the PWG Notice from Aon plc (September 2013). The Marsh report was based on data relating to 2,558 of its clients with a median total insured value of $165 million. The Marsh data reflect the 2012 calendar year. *Marsh 2013 Report* at 27.

[148] ISO aggregates industry data and develops advisory prospective loss costs (projections of future claim costs and loss adjustment expenses), among other services, on behalf of its participating insurers. *See* About ISO, http://www.iso.com/About-ISO/Overview/About-ISO.html.

[149] ISO has since revised its terrorism risk insurance rating tiers, generally through refinements within tiers. Other service providers and individual insurers may assess risk tiers differently than ISO, based on proprietary models. *See, e.g.*, Comment to the PWG Notice from Aon plc, 11 (September 2013).

[150] Comment to the PWG Notice from Aon plc, 21 (September 2013).

[151] *Id.* at 19.

[152] *Id.* at 21.

[153] *Id.*

[154] *Marsh 2013 Report* at 13.

[155] *Marsh 2013 Report* at 9.

[156] Comment to the PWG Notice from Aon plc, 6 (September 2013).

[157] *Id.* at 6-7; *Marsh 2013 Report* at 19.

[158] *See* TRIA § 108(e).

[159] See Comment to the PWG Notice from the Cato Institute, (September 2013); *The Future of Terrorism Insurance: Fostering Private Market Innovation to Limit Taxpayer Exposure: Hearing before the H. Comm. on Financial Services Subcommittee on Housing and Insurance*, 113th Cong. (November 13, 2013) (statement of Ernest N. Csiszar, Associate Fellow, R Street Institute, at 9), *available at* http://financialservices.house.gov/uploadedfiles/hhrg-113-ba04-wstate-ecsiszar-20131113.pdf.

[160] Twenty-eight of the 29 comments to the PWG Notice support a long-term reauthorization of TRIP.

[161] *See, e.g.*, Comment to the PWG Notice from the Cato Institute, 7-8, 12-13 (September 2013); *The Future of Terrorism Insurance: Fostering Private Market Innovation to Limit Taxpayer Exposure: Hearing before the H. Comm. on Financial Services Subcommittee on Housing and Insurance*, 113th Cong. (November 13, 2013) (statement of Ernest N. Csiszar, Associate Fellow, R Street Institute, at 9), *available at* http://financialservices.house.gov/uploadedfiles/hhrg-113-ba04-wstate-ecsiszar-20131113.pdf.

[162] *See* Comment to the PWG Notice from the American Insurance Association, 6, 14 (September 2013) (arguing that the current balance of public and private exposure under TRIP provides for complete private market coverage of potential losses from conventional terrorist attacks, and that the industry manages a significant level of exposure under the current parameters of TRIP).

[163] *See, e.g., id.* at 2, 14; Comment to the PWG Notice from the Property Casualty Insurers Association of America, 2 (September 2013) (arguing that the current insurer deductible and co-share levels are close to a "tipping

point at which further increases will begin to threaten insurer solvency"); Comment to the PWG Notice from the National Association of Mutual Insurance Companies, 4 (September 2013) (warning that further increases to the insurer deductible or co-share amounts would force small- to medium-sized insurers out of the market for terrorism risk); Comment to the PWG Notice from the Coalition to Insure Against Terrorism, 8-9 (citing an Aon 2009 report as evidence that, if TRIA were allowed to expire or were materially altered, property owners would be largely unable to satisfy insurance coverage requirements).

[164] *See, e.g.,* Comment to the PWG Notice from the Cato Institute, 16 (September 2013); *The Future of Terrorism Insurance: Fostering Private Market Innovation to Limit Taxpayer Exposure: Hearing before the H. Comm. on Financial Services Subcommittee on Housing and Insurance*, 113th Cong. (November 13, 2013) (statement of Ernest N. Csiszar, Associate Fellow, R Street Institute, at 9), *available at* http://financialservices.house.gov/uploadedfiles/hhrg-113-ba04-wstate-ecsiszar-20131113.pdf.

[165] Comment to the PWG Notice from the National Association of Mutual Insurance Companies, 5 (September 2013).

[166] TRIA § 103(e)(7).

[167] *See* Comment to the PWG Notice from the Cato Institute, 16 (September 2013). Congress considered and rejected insurer premiums for TRIP coverage when it passed TRIA in 2002, in part because of the perception that *ex ante* funding would lead to a permanent program. *See, e.g., Terrorist Risk Insurance: Hearing before the S. Comm. on Banking, Housing, & Urban Affairs,* 107th Cong. 17 (2001) (statement of Sheila Bair, Assistant Secretary for Financial Markets, U.S. Department of the Treasury); *id.* at 76-77 (prepared statement of Paul H. O'Neill, Secretary, U.S. Department of the Treasury).

[168] TRIA § 103(c).

[169] *GAO 2008 Report* at 14.

[170] Importantly, however, states generally prohibit NBCR exclusions in workers' compensation insurance, and some states require "fire following" coverage consistent with the New York Standard Fire Policy.

[171] DEPARTMENT OF THE TREASURY, *Report to the President on Cybersecurity Incentives Pursuant to Executive Order 13636*, 24 (2013), *available at* http://www.treasury.gov/press-center/Documents/Supporting%20Analysis%20Treasury%20Report%20to%20the%20President%20on%20Cybersecurity%20Incentives_FINAL.pdf (citing The Betterley Report, *Cyber/ Privacy Insurance Market Survey* (June 2012) for the premium volume of the U.S. market for cybersecurity insurance).

[172] Comment to the PWG Notice from the Property Casualty Insurers Association of America, 12 (September 2013) (arguing for greater certainty regarding TRIA's application to losses resulting from cyber terrorist attacks).

[173] Comment to the PWG Notice from the Risk Management Society, 5-6 (September 2013) (arguing for the inclusion of NBCR coverage in TRIP).

[174] *See, e.g.,* Comment to the PWG Notice from the Property Casualty Insurers Association of America, 7-8 (September 2013) (arguing for increased transparency in the certification process and increased objectivity in the definition of an act of terrorism); *Reauthorizing TRIA: The State of the Terrorism Risk Insurance Market, Hearing before the S. Comm. on Banking, Housing, & Urban Affairs,* 113th Cong. (September 25, 2013) (statement from Robert P. Hartwig, Ph.D., CPCU, Insurance Information Institute, at 21), *available at* http://www.banking.senate.gov/public/index.cfm?FuseAction=Hearings.Testimony&Hearing_ID=b9077dbb-2ae2-425a-89dd-793fcb049190&Witness_ID=8f726a39-e80f-412f-9672-7afb49e64fb7 (arguing for a timeframe under which a certification of an event as an act of terrorism must be made).

[175] Treasury previously offered the following view of a pre-determined time frame for certification (68 Fed. Reg. 41,252 (Jul. 11, 2003)):

T[]here is no way to predict future events and ascertain a time frame that would be appropriate for all potential situations. Facts could be immediately available and, after consultation, present a clear basis for a quick determination by the Secretary; conversely, a determination could require more time to gather information and conduct an analysis of the act. Given this inherent uncertainty and the significance of an act of terrorism determination to all aspects of the Program, Treasury does not believe that it would be in the public interest to establish in advance a regulatory time frame that may later prove to be inappropriate or unattainable.

[176] *See, e.g.,* Comment to the PWG Notice from the Property Casualty Insurers Association of America, 7-8 (September 2013) (arguing for increased transparency in the certification process and increased objectivity in the definition of an act of terrorism); Comment to the PWG Notice from the National Association of Mutual Insurance Companies, 5 (September 2013); *Reauthorizing TRIA: The State of the Terrorism Risk Insurance Market, Hearing before the S. Comm. on Banking, Housing, & Urban Affairs,* 113th Cong. (September 25, 2013) (statement from Robert P. Hartwig, Ph. D., CPCU, Insurance Information Institute, at 21), *available at* http://www.banking.senate.gov/public/index.cfm?FuseAction=Hearings.Testimony&Hearing_ID=b9077dbb-2ae2-425a-89dd-793fcb049190&Witness_ ID=8f726a39-e80f-412f-9672-7afb49e64fb7.

[177] *See* Comment to the PWG Notice from the Property Casualty Insurers Association of America, 8 (September 2013).

[178] *Id.* Some commercial insurance contracts may use policy forms developed by ISO which provide that a policyholder declining the mandatory offer of coverage for terrorism risk may retain coverage for an act of terrorism that is not certified.

[179] Marsh Risk Management Research, *Pending TRIPRA Expiration Impacts Workers' Compensation Industry* (January 21, 2014), *available at* http://usa.marsh.com/NewsInsights/MarshRiskManagementResearch/ID/34179/Pending-TRIPRA-Expiration-Impacts-Workers-Compensation-Industry.aspx. The Marsh article emphasizes that employers should "review and consider the potential impact on workers' compensation pricing and capacity" when making decisions regarding real estate plans in major metropolitan areas.

[180] *See* Comment to the PWG Notice from Marsh, 1 (September 2013) ("Although there has been relative stability in this segment of the market in recent years, this has largely been due to (a) the lack of large subsequent events following September 2001, and (b) the presence of government support through" TRIA); *Id.* at 10 ("Without some form of backstop to manage the uncertainty of extreme terrorist attacks, our conversation with our (re)insurance suppliers and clients suggest that the current supply of terrorism capacity will contract, the cost ... will increase, and certain geographic zones most in need of the protection may not be able to find adequate supply").

In: Terrorism Risk Insurance Act
Editor: Ernie L. Duke

ISBN: 978-1-63463-128-0
© 2014 Nova Science Publishers, Inc.

Chapter 4

MEMORANDUM FOR THE HEARING ON "THE FUTURE OF TERRORISM INSURANCE: FOSTERING PRIVATE MARKET INNOVATION TO LIMIT TAXPAYER EXPOSURE"[*]

To:	Members of the Committee on Financial Services
From:	FSC Majority Staff
Date:	November 8, 2013
Subject:	November 13, 2013, Housing and Insurance Subcommittee Hearing entitled "The Future of Terrorism Insurance: Fostering Private Market Innovation to Limit Taxpayer Exposure"

The Subcommittee on Housing and Insurance will hold a hearing entitled "The Future of Terrorism Insurance: Fostering Private Market Innovation to Limit Taxpayer Exposure" at 10:00 a.m., on Wednesday, November 13, 2013, in Room 2128 of the Rayburn House Office Building. This hearing will examine the Terrorism Risk Insurance Act of 2002, as amended (TRIA), with a specific focus on whether the program created by that act can leverage private sector capital and innovation to limit taxpayer exposure.

This will be a one-panel hearing with the following witnesses:

- Mr. Sean McGovern, Director, Risk Management & General Counsel, Lloyd's of London
- Mr. Kean Driscoll, Chief Executive Officer, Validus Reinsurance, Ltd.
- Mr. Ernest N. Csiszar, Former Director of Insurance, State of South Carolina
- Dr. John Seo, Co-Founder and Managing Principal, Fermat Capital Management, LLC
- Dr. Robert P. Hartwig, Pres. & Economist, Insurance Information Institute

---

[*] This is an edited, reformatted and augmented version of a memorandum to committee members announcing the hearing held on November 13, 2013 before the House Committee on Financial Services, Subcommittee on Housing and Insurance.

BACKGROUND

Before the terrorist attacks of September 11, 2001, insurers generally covered losses resulting from terrorist acts as part of commercial property and casualty insurance policies. As a result of the 9-11 attacks, insurance companies paid $31.6 billion (around $40 billion in current dollars, adjusted for inflation) in terrorism-related claims. The September 11 attacks led reinsurance and insurance companies to recognize potential terrorism losses as a new and significant kind of risk that they could not sufficiently model at that time, making such insurance either unavailable or unaffordable. Reinsurance and insurance companies thus began excluding terrorism coverage from their insurance policies.

According to some industry observers, these exclusions created a void in the insurance market, making terrorism coverage unavailable for businesses and employers, some of whom were contractually obliged to obtain terrorism coverage as a condition for financing. This inability to obtain terrorism coverage thus jeopardized economic development, particularly in large urban areas. To fill this void, some industry participants and analysts called for the creation of a temporary federal government backstop—a form of federal reinsurance—that would allow insurers to offer policyholders coverage for terrorism-related losses. Proponents argued that a temporary government backstop would give the insurance industry the time and opportunity to develop methods of calculating risk, assess capacity, and build accurate models so that appropriately priced, privately-backed coverage could again be made available. Opponents argued that a temporary government backstop would inhibit the development of a functioning reinsurance marketplace by crowding out private insurers.

In response to these calls for a temporary government backstop, Congress enacted TRIA (P.L. 107-297), which established a Terrorism Risk Insurance Program, to be administered by the Treasury Department, the purpose of which was to make terrorism insurance coverage more widely available. Under the program, which was to sunset after three years, the federal government shared the risk of loss from future terrorist attacks with the insurance industry. TRIA mandated that insurers participate in the program and required that insurers make terrorism coverage available in all commercial property and casualty insurance policies. TRIA did not, however, require that businesses purchase terrorism coverage.

Congress designed TRIA as a temporary, transitional federal backstop, with the expectation that the industry would eventually model and price for terrorism risk. While the initial TRIA may have helped address an economic need, the private market did not recover as quickly as many had hoped. As a result, in late 2005, Congress passed the Terrorism Risk Insurance Extension Act (P.L. 109-144) (TRIEA). TRIEA extended TRIA for two more years, until December 31, 2007. The extension left much of the original TRIA program intact, but raised industry retention levels and pared back the insurance lines covered. TRIA now requires $100 million in aggregate industry losses and an individual insurer deductible of 20 percent of premiums before the federal government shares 85 percent of the insured losses.

Despite this extension—or as some critics have argued, because of it—a private market for terrorism insurance has failed to develop. In 2007, with TRIA scheduled to expire for a second time, the 110th Congress again considered legislation to extend TRIA. The House and the Senate initially passed competing bills to significantly expand and extend TRIA:

the House bill would have extended TRIA for 15 years, and the Senate bill for 7 years. Ultimately, Congress enacted H.R. 2761, the Terrorism Risk Insurance Program Reauthorization Act of 2007 (P.L. 110-160). The bill extended the TRIA program for seven years (through December 31, 2014), added domestic terrorism coverage to TRIA, modified TRIA's annual liability cap so that insurers are not responsible for losses exceeding $100 billion, and made other changes to insurers' mandatory surcharge and recoupment amounts.

While the backstop has never been used because there have been no terrorist attacks since 9-11 that met TRIA's loss-sharing criteria, opponents of extending the program beyond 2014 argue that it exposes taxpayers to potentially billions of dollars in losses that the private sector should, some 13 years after 9-11, be prepared to bear on its own. Critics of the program also claim that the existence of a government-provided backstop under TRIA has inhibited the return of private-sector terrorism insurance.

In 2010, the Dodd-Frank Wall Street Reform and Consumer Protection Act (P.L. 111-203) established a Federal Insurance Office at the Treasury Department, headed by a Director. Among other things, the Director of the Federal Insurance Office is charged with assisting the Treasury Secretary in administering TRIA.

LEGISLATIVE PROPOSALS FOR THE 113TH CONGRESS

Three bills have been introduced in this Congress to extend or modify TRIA:

- Rep. Michael Grimm has introduced H.R. 508, the Terrorism Risk Insurance Act of 2002 Reauthorization Act of 2013, which would extend TRIA through December 31, 2019, and require the Treasury Secretary to collect all mandatory premiums for any act of terrorism that occurs on or after January 1, 2012, by September 30, 2024.
- Rep. Michael Capuano has introduced H.R. 2146, the Terrorism Risk Insurance Program Reauthorization Act of 2013, which extends TRIA through December 31, 2024, and requires the Treasury Secretary to collect all mandatory premiums for any act of terrorism occurring on or after January 1, 2012, by September 30, 2027. H.R. 2146 would also require the President's Working Group on Financial Markets to report in 2017, 2020, and 2023 on its findings regarding the long-term availability and affordability of terrorism risk insurance.
- Rep. Bennie Thompson has introduced H.R. 1945, the Fostering Resilience to Terrorism Act of 2013, which extends TRIA through December 31, 2024, and revises the definition of an "act of terrorism" to mean any act certified by the Secretary of Homeland Security in concurrence with the Secretary of the Treasury as meeting the criteria for such an act, among other changes to TRIA.

Chapter 5

TESTIMONY OF SEAN MCGOVERN, DIRECTOR, RISK MANAGEMENT AND GENERAL COUNSEL, LLOYD'S OF LONDON. HEARING ON "THE FUTURE OF TERRORISM INSURANCE: FOSTERING PRIVATE MARKET INNOVATION TO LIMIT TAXPAYER EXPOSURE"[*]

INTRODUCTION

Thank you Chairman Neugebauer, Ranking Member Capuano, and members of the Subcommittee for the opportunity to testify today. My name is Sean McGovern. I have responsibility for Risk Management at Lloyd's and am also General Counsel. It is a privilege to share our views on the Terrorism Risk Insurance Act, which we believe has been an extremely successful program.

From its beginnings in Edward Lloyd's coffee house in the late 17th Century, Lloyd's has been at the forefront of insuring unusual and specialized risks.

Lloyd's has long been a large participant in the US insurance market, through both direct insurance and reinsurance. Our specialism is catastrophe coverage and we have been there to support the US economy in the face of many tragedies over hundreds of years, cementing our reputation with our response to the 1906 San Francisco earthquake and more recently in the very substantial claims arising from Katrina, Rita and Wilma in 2005. We know how to underwrite catastrophic risk and we have an appetite to take risk that others will not - it is our business.

I would like to begin by noting some of the experience on which our views on terrorism risk in general, and on TRIA in particular, are founded.

- Lloyd's paid more claims than any other insurer or reinsurer following the tragic events of September 11th – almost $8 billion.

---

[*] This is an edited, reformatted and augmented version of testimony presented November 13, 2013 before the House Committee on Financial Services, Subcommittee on Housing and Insurance.

- Lloyd's is a major provider of standalone terrorism coverage globally. We most recently incurred over $70 million of claims following the September 2013 Westgate Mall attack in Kenya.
- Lloyd's led the development of the standalone terrorism market in the US in the days following 9/11- a point acknowledged by Congresswoman Maloney at the full Committee hearing in September.[1]
- Lloyd's is generally wary of Government intervention and believes in free markets and private market solutions whenever possible.
- Lloyd's market has specialist providers of property and casualty insurance and reinsurance and also a growing standalone terrorism market.

Terrorism Risk Is Different to Other Catastrophe Risk

Notwithstanding all of the above, the nature of terrorism risk is simply different from other perils, even natural catastrophe perils. To name just a few of the differences:

- Risk assessment for terrorism is very difficult – frequency and severity are extremely hard to predict.
- Only the Government has access to intelligence information regarding terror threats and it cannot share that information with industry, nor should it.
- As the recent tragic events in Boston demonstrated, the likelihood and the mode of attack are highly variable – which adds to the uncertainty around the potential maximum size of an event.
- Although modeling exists, it has limitations – in particular, due to the infrequency of extreme terror events, there is much less historical data available to draw upon than exists for natural catastrophes.

None of this means that terrorism risk cannot ever be underwritten – we already do so after all. Nevertheless, all these factors act to substantially limit the appetite of the insurance and reinsurance industry to absorb this risk, particularly in major urban areas due to the density and accumulation of asset value.

TRIA Is Still Necessary

Lloyd's supports the renewal of TRIA. The basic market conditions that necessitated TRIA still exist - commercial policyholders need insurance to protect the US economy against terrorism losses. But, as outlined above, the coverage of terrorism risk is different from other risks.

TRIA has been successful in giving the insurance industry the confidence to make terrorism coverage available. The availability and high take-up rates of terrorism risk insurance across all sectors of the economy are already well-documented in the record before the Committee. This availability has had a positive impact on pricing which has encouraged take-up and the result is that the Federal Government and ultimately the tax-payer are insulated from potential losses. Since TRIA, through the recoupment provisions, operates essentially as a post event cost-sharing mechanism, the high threshold for Federal involvement ensures that private capacity will absorb all but the most extreme losses.

Without TRIA however, the aggregation of risk would quickly lead the industry to exclude coverage or withdraw capacity from key economic centres in the US.

There is much talk about the excess capital in the insurance industry and its ability to take on more terrorism risk. Nonetheless, it would be wrong to assume that more capital leads to a dramatic increase in the overall appetite to write US terrorism. Reinsurers need to manage risk aggregation and seek diversification. It is important also to bear in mind that there has so far been no TRIA certified terrorist attack since the program began, let alone one that reached the trigger for Government support. Should such an event occur, it is likely that capacity and risk appetite would be affected – just as with other catastrophe perils.

Lloyd's is likewise skeptical of suggestions that the ILS market could provide sufficient capacity to meet demand for terrorism cover absent TRIA. With 9/11 as the precedent, terrorism correlates more closely with adverse market events than even severe natural catastrophes[2], which would limit appetite from ILS investors who are typically looking for risks that do not correlate with financial market risk. ILS investors also typically seek very tightly modeled risks. Modeling techniques have been developed for terrorism risks, but they are limited by the relative paucity of historical data available regarding extreme terrorism losses. While we do not doubt that there will be some appetite from the ILS market, it is no cure-all.

Further factors that need to be considered include the appetite of the cedents to write the original risks without TRIA's backstop and "make available" requirement. Moreover, total reinsurance capacity does not cater only for terrorism risk – and increasing demand outside the United States offers reinsurers opportunity for portfolio diversification.

More broadly, the United States is by no means the only country confronted with the challenge of ensuring the national economy is protected in the event of a failure of counter-terrorism measures. The UK has lived with the threat of domestic terrorism for many years. Whilst the structure of the co-operation between Government and industry to make terrorism cover available in the UK is different from TRIA, the program ("Pool Re") is covered by an unlimited Government backstop. Similar arrangements exist in the major European economies (see *Appendix A)*, as well as many other industrialised nations – despite none having experienced a terrorist event of the magnitude of 9/11.

Looking Ahead to Future of TRIA

Lloyd's believes the current TRIA structure is the right framework within which to encourage greater private market innovation in meeting the demand for terrorism cover. It ensures private sector involvement from the first dollar. It allows the expertise and innovation that have been developed in the context of the TRIA backdrop to evolve, rather than be discarded.

While current modeling methodologies do give some ability to individual insurers to manage their own exposure to terrorism risk, they do not offer any assurance that sufficient cover will be available to meet overall demand. In that scenario, the consequences can be dramatic – as demonstrated by the economic paralysis we saw in late 2001 and 2002.

We accept the need to assess whether or not TRIA should change – and it may well be that the balance between Government and private market involvement could tilt more towards the private market. But any changes to TRIA to facilitate greater private insurance and reinsurance capacity should not sacrifice the stability TRIA has already achieved.

How changes are made can be just as important as what changes are made. For example, sudden or drastic increases in the retentions or co-shares could prompt some insurers to concentrate their capacity elsewhere.

While Lloyd's recognises and supports the goal of reducing the Government's overall exposure to terrorism risk, the best way to increase private participation and benefit from the expertise that TRIA has enabled the industry to develop, would be through incremental changes over the course of a long-term extension of the program.

Hanging the sword of Damocles over the entire edifice every few years creates instability and damaging uncertainty – for industry (the insurance industry and other impacted industries, such as commercial real estate), policyholders and taxpayers alike. By contrast, well-defined incremental changes over the course of a long-term extension of the program may provide a transparent process of reductions in the risk borne by the taxpayer. This would also be consistent with supporting gradually increasing industry appetite and capacity to underwrite terrorism risk.

Making those step-changes contingent on regular, independent assessments of availability and capacity may give a means to safeguard the steady development of a stable private market for terrorism cover.

However it is important to note that Lloyd's does not envisage the end-point of such a transition being the complete removal of TRIA. For the reasons we have outlined, we believe that TRIA will continue to be needed in some form for the foreseeable future. This is not because of any particular failure of either industry or of government, but as a consequence of sociological and political changes both within and without the United States.

Increasing urbanization combined with growing geo-political tensions has created 'tinderbox' conditions both for the emergence of new terrorist threats and also their capacity to inflict concentrated destruction. While it may be possible to increase private participation in covering terrorism risk, we struggle with the notion that there could be no federal backstop.

Nevertheless, some improvements could also be made to the administrative aspects of TRIA. The Boston Marathon attack revealed a need to clarify the operation of the certification process, due to market effects even where federal compensation is not at issue.

Most commercial insurance policies in the U.S. market cover or exclude terrorism peril by reference to a certified "act of terrorism" under TRIA. The lack of guidance to date on whether the Boston attack constitutes an "act of terrorism" therefore continues to create significant uncertainty for claims adjusters, particularly in relation to various claims-handling obligations (and time lines) that insurers face under State laws.

Where exclusions in property policies turn on certification of an event, the decision of whether or not to certify an event must be made by an independent body not a political one, and either of the insurer or the insured should be able to request a determination.

Some aspects of the program, however, should not change. For example, the design of the program as a retrospective assessment is preferable to pre-event pooling, which is always complex for an extremely low-frequency, but potentially catastrophic loss risk.

Likewise the recoupment mechanism protects taxpayers and essentially means that federal support provides bridge liquidity for those insurers hardest hit by an event.

CONCLUSION

Whatever the future of TRIA, Lloyd's will remain committed to providing the fullest cover it can to its American customers – just as we did immediately after 9/11, before TRIA was enacted.

But our ability to do that will be limited by our need to manage our risk aggregation. The same issue will apply across the industry and we have no confidence that the private sector alone is capable of providing the entirety of the coverage that would be needed should TRIA not be renewed.

TRIA has been and continues to be an effective plan for stabilizing the economy in the wake of uncertain terrorism risk, while also ensuring a smooth economic recovery following a future attack. We believe that it should be renewed.

Avenues for increasing private involvement may exist, but must be explored in such a way that the market is protected should additional private market capacity fail to materialize. We look forward to working with the Subcommittee on finding ways to do this.

Thank you, and I am happy answer any questions.

APPENDIX A – EUROPEAN GOVERNMENT TERRORISM POOLS

COUNTRY	GOVERNMENT POOL	COMPULSORY/ OPTIONAL	LIMITATIONS
Austria	Österreichischer Versicherungspool zur Deckung von Terrorisiken	Optional	Limit €5 million per location
Belgium	No government pool is in place	Compulsory	Since May 2008 it has been mandatory for terrorism insurance to be provided by all Belgian insurers
Denmark	No government pool, however a fund established in June 2008 takes effect when insurers reserves have been exhausted	Optional	Most insurers now exclude terrorism cover from policies so cover has to be purchased separately if required
Finland	No government pool is in place	Optional	Two local insurers provide terrorism buy-back within their standard property policy
France	GAREAT	Compulsory	Terrorism exclusions apply for large risks above a stated limit, being €20 million or 20% of the sum insured, whichever is greater. Cover is 'bought back' via GAREAT
Germany	Extremus	Optional	Cover available via Extremus for risks exceeding €25 million. Terrorism buy-back for sums insured below this value is generally available via the primary Insurer
Italy	No government pool is in place	Optional	The majority of policies exclude terrorism cover where the sum insured exceeds €50 million

Appendix A. (Continued)

Country	Pool	Compulsory/Optional	Details
Netherlands	Nederlandse Herverzekeringsmaatschappij voor Terrorismeschaden (NHT)	Optional	Government pool provides cover for risks up to €75 million per location per annum
Norway	No government pool is in place	Optional	Terrorism cover is generally excluded from commercial risks with a limited writeback. Cover is not readily available in the open market
Portugal	No government pool is in place	Optional	Cover is usually excluded from personal and commercial risks
Spain	Consorcio	Compulsory	Consorcio provides terrorism buy-back cover, subject to an appropriate premium
Sweden	No government pool is in place	Optional	Terrorism normally excluded from Property policies and is not readily available through the local market. Where required this has to be secured through the global insurance market
Switzerland	No government pool is in place	Optional	All primary property policies with a sum insured exceeding CHF 10 million exclude terrorism cover. Commercial and industrial risks also contain a terrorism exclusion for risks below CHF 10 million
United Kingdom	Pool Re	Not compulsory, however if cover is required it must be purchased for all properties of the Insured and the Insured may elect to purchase cover for property and business interruption or property only	Cover is subject to the same limits as the UK property damage/business interruption policy. The Pool Re programme provides for terrorism on an 'all risks' basis, but excludes acts of war

Source: Willis European Terrorism Exposure Bulletin February 2011.

Chapter 6

TESTIMONY OF KEAN DRISCOLL, CHIEF EXECUTIVE OFFICER, VALIDUS RE. HEARING ON "THE FUTURE OF TERRORISM INSURANCE: FOSTERING PRIVATE MARKET INNOVATION TO LIMIT TAXPAYER EXPOSURE"[*]

My name is Kean Driscoll and I am the Chief Executive Officer of Validus Re. I am pleased to appear before you today to provide my company's perspective on possible changes to the Terrorism Risk Insurance Program ("TRIP" or the "Program") that would incent more private market involvement. I commend Chairman Neugebauer for holding this important hearing and welcome the opportunity to address the Subcommittee on Insurance, Housing, and Community Opportunity.

Validus Group ("Validus") is a leader in the global insurance and reinsurance markets, operating principally through Talbot Syndicate 1183 at Lloyd's of London, and Validus Re. Talbot has written direct and facultative terrorism business at Lloyd's for more than 12 years and it is now the largest writer of that business by income. Validus Re is one of the largest standalone property terrorism treaty coverage providers in the world, with an estimated 10% market share, and it evaluates business opportunities on approximately 90% of all direct and facultative terrorism business written throughout the world. Validus' guiding objective, through its operating subsidiaries, is to maximize its return on equity subject to prudent risk constraints on the amount of capital its exposes to any single loss event.

BACKGROUND ON REINSURANCE

Reinsurance is commonly referred to as the insurance of insurance companies. The reinsurance market is global and plays an important role in maintaining the financial health of the insurance marketplace and ensuring the availability of property and casualty insurance in the United States. Reinsurance may be used by insurers for several reasons. One of the most

---

[*] This is an edited, reformatted and augmented version of testimony presented November 13, 2013 before the House Committee on Financial Services, Subcommittee on Housing and Insurance.

common purposes is to transfer risk from the primary insurer for catastrophic events, including hurricanes, earthquakes, and conventional acts of terrorism. Reinsurers have responded financially to virtually every major U.S. catastrophe over the past century. By way of example, 60% of the losses related to the events of September 11th were absorbed by the global reinsurance industry, and in 2005, 61% of Hurricanes Katrina, Rita and Wilma losses were ultimately borne by reinsurers.

BACKGROUND OF THE TERRORISM RISK INSURANCE PROGRAM

TRIP was enacted in response to the September 11, 2001 terrorist attacks, which forced all Americans to confront the previously unforeseen realities associated with a catastrophic terrorist attack on U.S. soil. Although the insurance and reinsurance industry responded in an unwavering manner, the events changed the way the industry views the terrorism risk.

TRIP was created to provide a federal backstop, which allowed the insurance industry to provide terrorism coverage to U.S. businesses. By limiting insurers' exposure to catastrophic terrorism losses, TRIP improved the private market for such coverage. The reinsurance industry strongly supported adoption of the Terrorism Risk Insurance Act in 2002, the 2005 Terrorism Risk Insurance Extension Act (TRIEA) and the 2007 Terrorism Risk Insurance Program Reauthorization Act (TRIPRA).

REINSURERS' ROLE UNDER TRIP

TRIP provides a large amount of reinsurance-like protection for commercial insurance exposures. Individual insurers retain a significant amount of terrorism risk losses through both a company deductible and a co-pay requirement for losses above the retention before TRIP funding is available. The insurance industry has significant financial risk and exposure to acts of terrorism because of the significant retentions under TRIP, the mandatory offer of coverage required under TRIP, state regulatory action related to rates and exclusions, and rating agency scrutiny.

Insurers may seek reinsurance from the private market to reduce the conventional terrorism exposure they face for potential losses between the deductible and loss-sharing provisions of TRIP. A reinsurer's ability to provide this coverage is limited by the amount of conventional terrorism risk it is willing and able to supply based on the amount of capital it allocates to terrorism coverage and its own specific risk evaluation. Because reinsurers are not covered by TRIP, reinsurers view TRIP in the context of the benefits provided to the broader industry as a whole.

THE CURRENT REINSURANCE MARKET

Since 2001, insurers and reinsurers have worked hard to develop a better understanding of conventional terrorism risk. Reinsurers have created task forces, consulted military and intelligence experts, hired specialty risk modeling firms, invested in research and development, and implemented new underwriting standards all with the intention of offering private market solutions for the transfer of conventional terrorism risk. Conventional terrorism can be modeled, priced, and managed on a portfolio basis. The probability or frequency of an event can be estimated, albeit with less certainty than risk classes with a more robust historical record; however, the insurance and reinsurance industries have pioneered risk transfer solutions for many other classes of business that suffer the same shortcomings. To supplement the lack of a rich data set on frequency, we use open source intelligence that helps us estimate both the intent and capability of terror threat agents. This information is consolidated into an event set that helps us estimate the probability of various attack types at different targets.

Once we have established a perspective on frequency, we use well established modeling techniques to quantify hazard severity, vulnerability and financial loss. There is very good data on damageability from various blast sizes with secondary effects.

The question is not whether conventional terrorism risk can be priced, but rather, the precision of the parameters in a pricing model. We can and do currently price conventional terrorism risk, and estimate that approximately $7-8 billion of reinsurance coverage is purchased annually on a stand-alone basis for conventional U.S. terrorism. This excludes coverage that is included as part of general property/casualty, worker's compensation and other specialty lines coverages. We believe presently there is adequate reinsurance capacity to cover the insurance industry's current $27.5 billion retention under TRIP, and if the industry retention for conventional terrorism exposure grew over time, so to would the capacity of the reinsurance industry for conventional terrorism risk.

TRIP RENEWAL

TRIP is valuable to the insurance industry in underwriting conventional terrorism risk but it takes a "one size fits all" approach that could be modified to encourage more private market insurance and reinsurance participation. If the Committee is inclined to make changes to the Program, Validus encourages you to tailor the Program in accordance with the following comments.

1. The Program should continue to cover catastrophic terrorism loss scenarios related to nuclear, biological, chemical and radiological ("NBCR") attacks. The broader industry cannot effectively address these perils as the breadth of potential events is either unknowable or could potentially bankrupt the industry.
2. Cyber terrorism, a peril distinct from cyber liability, should be clearly covered by the Program. The scope, duration, potential damage and economic losses from this risk are also unknowable, and therefore, uninsurable.
3. The Program should clarify the process for certifying a terrorism event, including a defined time for making the certification
4. Validus has the ability and willingness to assume more conventional terrorism risk exposure, and I believe the reinsurance industry also has the ability and willingness to meaningfully expand its capacity for conventional terrorism risk. To reflect the fact that the industry's appetite for writing conventional terrorism risk has grown

since the last extension, the Program could be modified through a variety of ways, including:
   a) Gradually increasing the insurance industry retention and the size of a qualifying terrorism loss under the Program. This reduces the likelihood of having to fund a loss through taxpayer funds and it avoids short-term price and capacity dislocation in the broader industry.
   b) An expansion of the co-participation which would better align the insurance industry with the Program.
5. The insurance industry is a critical facilitator of effective risk management in virtually every industry, and every facet of life. Risky behavior, or highly exposed assets typically result in a higher premium charge. Policyholders can reduce higher premiums through effective risk mitigation techniques. Currently, the Program impedes the ability of the insurance industry to properly price its products, by shifting the risk of a conventional terror attack from the policyholder to the taxpayer. The improper allocation of a risk premium facilitates unintended outcomes. We see this phenomenon playing out in the flood market, as the heavily subsidized National Flood Insurance Program ("NFIP") has produced significant deficits. Congress should encourage a greater private sector risk bearing role and appropriate risk pricing. Insureds and insurers will then have an incentive to mitigate risk and price it appropriately, and Congress can focus on genuinely becoming a "reinsurer" of last resort for conventional terrorism risk.
6. Finally, special consideration should be made for smaller insurers, as well as for the insurance industry generally with respect to workers compensation exposure accumulations in metropolitan areas, which could be disproportionately impacted in the near term by any of the changes to the Program.

Thank you for the opportunity to testify. We look forward to continuing this dialogue as the renewal process moves forward.

Chapter 7

TESTIMONY OF ERNEST N. CSISZAR, FORMER DIRECTOR OF INSURANCE, STATE OF SOUTH CAROLINA. HEARING ON "THE FUTURE OF TERRORISM INSURANCE: FOSTERING PRIVATE MARKET INNOVATION TO LIMIT TAXPAYER EXPOSURE"[*]

My name is Ernest N. Csiszar and I am a former insurance commissioner from the State of South Carolina and former President of the National Association of Insurance Commissioners ("NAIC"). I am currently a Clinical Professor of Insurance at the University of South Carolina's Darla Moore School of Business and I am an Associate Fellow of the R Street Institute, a public policy think tank devoted to a free market economy. I also serve as a Director on the Boards of a number of property and casualty insurance companies, including a specialty company that underwrites Workers' Compensation coverage. I am also a member of the Board of Directors of a large infrastructure development company that purchases significant amounts of terrorism insurance coverage for its projects.

I am pleased to appear before you today so as to share my perspective on two different, albeit related, matters:

(1) Whether or not the Terrorism Risk Insurance Act ("TRIA"), as amended and currently scheduled to sunset at year-end 2014, should be extended or renewed; and
(2) Whether there are any legislative or regulatory measures that could be implemented to make the market for private terrorism insurance more attractive and enhance the growth of insurance-linked securities ("ILS").

I thank and commend Chairman Neugebauer for holding this important hearing and I welcome the privilege to address the Subcommittee on Housing and Insurance.

---

[*] This is an edited, reformatted and augmented version of testimony presented November 13, 2013 before the House Committee on Financial Services, Subcommittee on Housing and Insurance.

(1) THE RENEWAL OR EXTENSION OF TRIA

Let me state at the very outset that I favor the renewal of TRIA, albeit with some significant amendments. There are times when, even as a committed opponent of government intrusion, I must admit that a private market may have failed or may not become fully functional without some intervention by government. Terrorism insurance happens to fall into that category. I do not believe that the insurance and reinsurance industries are ready to bear the entire burden of losses from one or more major terrorism events, particularly those committed by nuclear, biological, chemical, or radioactive means ("NBCR"), or some form of cyber-assault. Nor for that matter are the capital markets immediately ready to stand in place of TRIA for those types of risk. Terrorism continues to provide the most devastating, expensive, and disruptive loss scenarios imaginable and matters such as the current unrest in the Middle East and North Africa have only exacerbated the concerns with underwriting terrorism insurance within the insurance and reinsurance industries.

Nonetheless, genuine progress is being made in developing the private terrorism insurance market. Modeling has improved, underwriting is more nuanced, and there has been an influx of new private capital into the market. Capacity in the private market is up, competition is fierce and prices are down, and a sizable market for private standalone global coverage has developed. I am convinced however that a failure to renew TRIA in the face of the continuing unabated threat of terrorism – thereby eliminating the $100 billion federal backstop as well as the mandate to offer coverage – would lead to severe disruptions in availability, exclusion, and pricing. The risk of that occurring is simply too high. Reinsurers, in particular, can enter and exit a market freely as relatively unregulated entities. The industry tends to react to a shock by withdrawing capacity, exiting entirely from the impacted market, making prices unattractive to buyers, or excluding coverage. Dramatic price increases sometimes follow for other lines of business. And since there is no upper bound for terrorism risk losses[1], one could expect these price increases to be enormous.

Let me provide some additional perspective. TRIA was first put in place in 2002, and then amended in 2005 and extended in 2007. Post September 11, 2001, TRIA succeeded in preventing what would have been a prolonged and wholesale disruption in the market as many insurers and reinsurers were prepared to either withdraw from coverage, exclude coverage or invoke the war exclusion that most policies contained. Other lines of business would also have been impacted via price increases. That did not happen substantially because of TRIA which encouraged reinsurers to continue to back their insurer clients with the risk transfer mechanism needed to make TRIA work. For an insurer to be forced to offer terrorism coverage to its customers – as TRIA requires – the purchase of reinsurance is not an option. It is a necessity. It protects the company from insolvency and allows the company to continue to ply its trade post-event. Without reinsurance, there is no insurance! And it is not just any reinsurance that will do. Insurers need reinsurers who are committed to providing terrorism coverage – reinsurers that are well-capitalized, pay their claims quickly, and stand by their insurer clients without hesitation after a large catastrophic event.

Hence, the issue of whether or not to renew TRIA is first and foremost an issue that impacts reinsurers the most and it is to their potential reaction that this Committee must look if it were to take as dramatic a step as to recommend non-renewal.

So let's focus on reinsurance for a moment. Today, the threat of another major terrorism attack involving NBCR or some forms of cyber-attack continues to be among the most feared and potentially the most costly and devastating disasters faced by reinsurers. I think that I can fairly say that the industry does not treat terrorism as a matter of "if" – rather, a "when" and "how severe" and "how often" and "in how many places". Despite the continuing threat however, reinsurers have succeeded in attracting significant new capital since 2002, and particularly since 2007. And, as is the case after every catastrophic event, the industry has managed time and again to find the capital lost due to catastrophes. The industry now has roughly $510 billion in total capital available and that capital has been increasing at the rate of 1% to 5% each year since 2006. $100 billion in new capital is expected over the next ten years. This, of course, is capital that must support many uses besides terrorism – and in many places other than United States. Terrorism is not the only line of business sustained by that capital. Reinsurers allocate capital to other lines as well whether it is auto, homeowners', liability and commercial. Nor is the United States the only place in which they do business. Reinsurance is a global industry, largely located off-shore. Thus, reinsurance capital allocations tend to move quickly to whatever lines or locations offer the most favorable conditions for returns on capital.

As a result, the reinsurance industry has been able to absorb the huge losses from September 11 and from many a natural catastrophe since then, and yet recapitalize lost capital quickly after an event. New capacity[2] seems to move in quickly after an event supported by expectations of improved pricing and higher profits. Interestingly however, to the benefit of consumers, these expectations rarely seem to materialize for very long as new capital flows in and competition for market share takes its toll. As a result, the industry has evolved to the point where paying for yearly catastrophic losses of as much as $20 billion to $25 billion seems to have become routine. Whether it is catastrophic fires and earthquakes in California and the American West, sinkholes and hurricanes in the Southeast or tornadoes, hail, and winter storms in the Midwest and the Northeast – these catastrophes have become a repetitive, predictable, annual ritual for the industry: it responds by paying for these losses without much of a blip in either availability or pricing. Losses of this size have come to be expected it seems. Specifically, even in the immediate aftermath of Hurricane Sandy, the second most expensive storm in U.S. history, property catastrophe reinsurance costs continued to decrease as a whole and for most reinsurance programs.

As for TRIA, the federal backstop continues to be the mainstay for domestic terrorism coverage in the United States. A sizable market for stand-alone commercial coverage has developed. That market tends to serve clients with broader global needs for terrorism coverage, self-insuring captive company clients, and clients interested in coverage up to the $100 million trigger. Since TRIA covers United States territory only, the commercial market also tends to cater to clients interested in both domestic and international coverage, frequently on a "difference in conditions/difference in limits" ("DIC/DIL") basis[3] grounded in a TRIA-based master policy.

In developing these stand-alone terrorism facilities, reinsurers are benefiting from the currently depressed global yields environment by being able to offer higher yields derived from terrorism coverage. It is worth a reminder though that the higher yields are also a reflection of higher risk for those institutional investors like pension funds, hedge funds, private equity, and specialist funds who invest in these facilities. Nonetheless, it has been reported that as much as $2 billion and more of terrorism coverage per client may be available in the private market, depending on location, accumulation, and concentration. Moreover, such new terrorism facilities in the billions of dollars are also being set up by others including brokers, and, hence not surprisingly, prices for customers with more than $1 billion of total insured value have dropped to median rates of $19 per $1 million, down from double and triple that rate in earlier years[4].

For those of us who ultimately favor private markets, these are clear signs of progress in the private market. Nonetheless, some words of caution are in order:

1) Not renewing TRIA would open $100 billion crater in the industry's capital structure. That's roughly a 20% hit to the industry's entire capital[5] – by any measure, a huge loss of capital that would have to be filled – and filled quickly at a time when forecasts for new capital over the next 10 years indicate $100 billion level.

2) Some potential - and almost unthinkably probable - terrorist attacks could be of such a substantial magnitude as to be beyond the pale of even as significant amount of capital as is currently available to the industry. Think of that nuclear device in the center of Manhattan. This is a particular problem for Workers' Compensation insurance which prevents the exclusion of terrorism coverage, mandates unlimited coverage, and prohibits the exclusion of nuclear, chemical, biological, and radiation ("NCBR") related coverage. This has broader economic implications regarding employment, jobs, and economic development, given that no business can operate without Workers' Compensation insurance.

3) It is difficult to tell whether the new capital that has come into the business is of a long-term nature or whether it is of the "quick in and quick out hot money" type driven by investors out for yield in an otherwise zero interest and nominal yield environment. With competitive forces at work, as new capital has come into the business, reinsurers have had a difficult time maintaining rates while protecting their individual market share and, as another sign, yields on cat bonds, for instance, have been plunging and only time will tell how much of this capital is of a more permanent nature. Will the new capital will "stick" or exit in the face of ever-diminishing returns? That remains an open question.

4) It has also been suggested that a good proportion of this new capital comes from naïve investors who have yet to be tested by any significant losses. Cat bonds, for instance, have only been triggered three times out of 200 issues within that last fifteen years. Investors may lose interest if their capital were to be wiped out by a sufficiently large event.

5) Availability and pricing of insurance and reinsurance for catastrophic events depends heavily on modeling the frequency and severity of potential losses. The severity of terrorist events can be modeled reasonably well. The problem lies with frequency. Mother Nature is reasonably predictable. Human beings are not. The intervention of human agency in terrorist events makes frequency essentially unpredictable[6]. Moreover, it leaves little room for ex ante mitigation measures, given that an event could occur anywhere. The problem is further complicated by the fact that models without good data fall into the category of "garbage in, garbage out". Clearly for good reasons, the best data and information regarding the likelihood and impact of a potential terrorist event lies with the intelligence and law enforcement agencies and

is unavailable to reinsurers7. Unfortunately, that only complicates the modeling process so vital to providing terrorism insurance coverage.
6) Natural catastrophes are "low probability – high severity" events, the proverbial fat-tail events or "black swans". Terrorism is not like other tail risk. It is arguable that terrorism presents the industry with "high probability – high severity" events perhaps on a multiple venue and sequential basis, events that are ultimately uninsurable without some form of government program of last resort. Indeed, most other OECD states have had government-backed terrorism insurance pools for twenty years or more, though with a wide variety of intervention mechanisms.

Based on these thoughts, I make the following suggestions to this Committee:

1) Renew TRIA – renew it for a long enough period to avoid uncertainty in the near-term and long enough for some of these issues to play themselves out, 5 to 10 years perhaps. Private markets, as history has proven, sometimes take as much as a generation or two to develop. But raise the $100 million loss trigger significantly - perhaps to as much as $20 billion or $25 billion– in line with the routine payouts for other types of catastrophic losses. This would also bring the TRIA program in line with loss triggers in the private markets for industry loss warranties ("ILW") [8.] There is simply no good reason to keep the trigger at its current low level.
2) Raise the horizontal deductible from its current 20% to 40% of the past year's direct earned premium for the commercial lines subject to TRIA and raise the quota share cost-sharing arrangement for insurers from 15% to 25% of losses that exceed an insurer's deductible, in recognition of the increase in capacity in the industry since 2002 and in the evolution of a private stand-alone market since then. This might also stimulate additional private mitigation efforts.
3) Charge a risk-based price for providing the backstop. There is no reason for not collecting an actuarially sound premium for the government's willingness to continue to provide the $100 billion federal backstop. Government – taxpayers, that is - should be compensated for the service.
4) Use a portion of the industry's premiums, or other funds available to Treasury, to invest in risk transfer, including reinsurance, catastrophe bonds or other vehicles. This initiative would protect taxpayers and support the growth of the terrorism risk market, encouraging private investment in models, data sets and other capabilities. Also by accessing the private market, the program would facilitate risk validation and third-party views of exposure, the efficacy of mitigation initiatives and the effectiveness of prevention regimes.
5) Each of these suggestions could of course be introduced on staggered basis over all or part of the renewal period.

(2) IMPROVING THE ATTRACTIVENESS OF TERRORISM INSURANCE MARKETS AND ENHANCING GROWTH IN THE ILS MARKETS

Reinsurance is but one market for the transfer of risk for an insurer. Another option lies in the capital markets, with investors assuming the risk via ILS. The two transfer mechanisms operate alongside and complement and supplement each other. Given the liquidity, depth, and resilience of global capital markets, they are by far the most effective means for pooling, transferring and diversifying risks of all kinds, including insurance risks. In the past 25 years, they have played an increasingly more prominent role by innovating new ways to transfer risks.

ILS either securitize insurance risks 9 or transform such risks into derivatives. They are ideally suited for catastrophe financing. ILS include catastrophe bonds, exchange-traded catastrophe futures and options, catastrophe swaps, non-indemnity types of derivatives such as industry loss warranties as well as collateralized reinsurance products written on an indemnity basis and transformed into securities. Some of these instruments are liquid and some are not. Some are private and over the counter, others are exchange-traded. Some ILS provide for up front funding while others pay ex-post with no up front funding. While no ILS specific to terrorism coverage have been issued, increased capacity in the ILS catastrophe market would likely generate a flow-over of additional capital allocations to terrorism insurance.

ILS now make up over 15% of the property catastrophe reinsurance market[10]. From a risk standpoint, the capital markets and rating agencies typically treat them akin to high-yield corporate bonds (e.g., junk bonds). By far the most common and liquid ILS is the catastrophe bond. $40 billion in cat bonds have been issued in the last ten years with about $19 billion currently outstanding. That may not seem like much when you consider the industry's total cat exposure of about $300 billion in potential catastrophe-related claims. Nonetheless, the numbers reflect impressive growth, given that ten years ago that figure was a mere $4 billion. Indeed, a small niche market has become a major supplier of capacity to insurers and reinsurers alike. And if forecasts are correct, today's amount is expected to quadruple again within the next decade. There is also evidence that substantial additional risk is being funded through ILS instruments other than cat bonds[11].

While equity and hedge funds were among the early movers into the ILS market, there has been a recent surge of interest from investors with longer-term time horizons such as pension funds, mutual funds, and wealth managers. Some of these entrants are much larger than reinsurers are and, hence, have a much greater ability to absorb greater volatility and more severe losses. Apart from increased yields derived from larger risk premiums, ILS offers investors access to a largely uncorrelated asset class[12], thereby enhancing the potential for diversification. There is also a relatively healthy secondary market. Reinsurers both participate and compete with ILS. Not surprisingly, between new reinsurance capital and ILS, reinsurance premiums have been forced down by 15% this year alone.

Each ILS requires a bankruptcy-remote Special Purpose Vehicle ("SPV") and, while sponsors and investors are mostly from the United States and Europe, the Cayman Islands have become the domicile of choice for these SPVs[13]. In recent years, the Caymans have passed legislation that makes them more attractive for both SPVs and investors. They have also developed a regulatory environment specific to these types of transactions which recognizes the sophistication and higher risk appetite of customers that operate in these markets. Moreover, these types of transactions are often fully collateralized, and hence the fees are high and the capital requirements are usually low[14]. From a fiscal standpoint, SPVs typically receive pass-through treatment as the investment income accumulated within an SPV is intended to be paid out to future claimants.

The use of off-shore SPVs by U.S. entities can be explained by a number of reasons: (1) restrictive GAAP and statutory accounting treatment, resulting in disparate treatment between ILS and reinsurance; (2) taxation issues; (3) uneven and inhibitive state insurance regulations, especially regarding credit for reinsurance provisions; and (4) reserve treatment. For instance, the NAIC model legislation permits an insurance company to set up an on-shore SPV for an ILS but then, unlike the case for traditional reinsurance, prevents a credit to capital until the bond is triggered and the sponsor is indemnified by the SPV. Traditional indemnity-based reinsurance, on the other hand, reflects the transfer of risk as credit to capital immediately upon signing of a reinsurance contract. To add a further complication, a NAIC model law is nothing more than a recommended law – not every state adopts these models, either uniformly or in their entirety. Hence, regulation from state to state is uneven, a very costly and inefficient route for what is in essence a one-time event for each SPV.

The NAIC has also adopted a Special Purpose Reinsurance Vehicle (SPRV) model law, allowing on-shore special purpose reinsurers to issue insurance-linked debt to back up a reinsurance program. The model law however only applies to cases that employ an indemnity-based trigger. Unfortunately, many transactions employ non-indemnity triggers and these are treated purely as additional debt, without any credit to capital whatsoever.

Regulatory certainty in the U.S. is even more opaque when exchange-traded insurance derivatives are involved where many State regulators have not even addressed to issue. Not surprisingly – and to the detriment of the U.S. -the popularity of going off-shore!

In light of the above, I would suggest the following with a view to facilitating the development of the ILS market:

1) Initiate a review15 of all legal, regulatory, accounting and fiscal treatment of insurance-linked securities and derivatives with a dual aim to develop a soup-to-nuts platform for issuing ILS onshore and provide for appropriate accounting, regulatory, and fiscal treatment based on the risks inherent in the various types of instruments. Issues to be addressed could include a separate licensing facility for SPVs, equal accounting and regulatory treatment between reinsurance and ILS where warranted based on risk characteristics, exemptions from the Frank-Dodd legislation and the Federal Reserve systemic risk provisions; clarifying bankruptcy remoteness; exemptions from consumer protections which are not relevant in this context, and so on.

2) Overall, ILS would also benefit from a uniform, a sensible regulatory framework. NAIC model laws, of course, do not have the force of law in any U.S. jurisdiction. Although many states adopt laws following NAIC models in whole or in part, it always remains to be seen how many states will adopt them eventually and at what pace. Reports at the Spring National Meeting 2013 indicate, for instance, that 11 states have adopted revisions to their credit for reinsurance statutes and/or regulations to implement reduced collateral requirements mandated by the Dodd-

Frank legislation and modeled in the NAIC's amendments to its Credit for Reinsurance Model Law and Regulations ("Amended Credit for Reinsurance Model Act"). Twelve (12) others have indicated their intention to do so, leaving the remainder of the states without any position on the matter at this time. As regards full implementation, only Florida and New York have actually approved any reinsurers for collateral reduction at this time. Moreover, even when the NAIC passes a model law of regulation, states are at liberty to make changes at the local level, thereby replacing intended uniformity with a "hodge podge" of local variations. Some argue that the situation would change if the NAIC were to make model laws a condition of state accreditation, in which case all states almost certainly would adopt them in full and without change. But then again, changes to NAIC accreditation standards generally take four or more years to become effective. Real change in a timely manner at the State level to develop attractive ILS markets is therefore unlikely. Given that ILS are in the nature of capital market instruments, federal legislation may well be appropriate.

3) Pass through taxation treatment[16] - which eliminates taxation at the SPV level and thus avoids double taxation—with favorable implementing requirements could facilitate expanded use of ILS and, as a by-product, increase the flow of private capital into the terrorism market.

As for making reinsurance more attractive:

1) Allow for the use of reserves for catastrophic events. For insurers and reinsurers, a more favorable fiscal treatment of catastrophe (including terrorism) or equalization reserves[17] may increase the availability of traditional insurance/reinsurance. In its 2005 report, the GAO noted some discrepancies between the U.S. and European fiscal treatment of catastrophe reserves[18]. A number of European countries allow insurance companies to establish tax-deductible reserves for potential losses associated with catastrophic events, although each country differs in the way it allows reserves to be set-up and used[19]. In the U.S., on the other hand, catastrophe reserves are not tax-deductible. Tax-deductible reserves would offer several potential benefits: they would provide insurers and reinsurers with financial incentives to increase their capital and expand capacity without endangering solvency or contractual commitments. They would also lower the costs of catastrophic coverage, including terrorism in all likelihood. Opponents have noted that permitting insurers to take *ex ante* tax-free reserves may open the door to deceptive or even fraudulent accounting. At the very least, the issue warrants serious study.

To conclude, I wish to thank Chairman Neugebauer for this opportunity to comment at this hearing and I look forward to working with the members of this Subcommittee towards a resolution of these issues.

Thank you!

End Notes

[1] As noted later in this testimony, Workers' Compensation insurance must be offered under State law without limits. Furthermore, some potential terrorist threats, such as the explosion of a nuclear device in the midst of Manhattan, are estimated to cost over $1 trillion.

[2] New reinsurers tend to enter the market with new capital. Within less than three months after Hurricane Katrina in 2005, for instance, eight new reinsurers with $8 billion in new capital had entered the cat market. Also, reinsurers formed sidecar facilities. $4 billion or more came in through these sidecars. Sidecars are capital facilities that are sponsored by reinsurers. Much like a quota-share reinsurance arrangement, an investor in a sidecar takes on a proportion of the risks for a limited category of policies, typically catastrophe exposures, for a limited period of time.

[3] DIC refers to a policy designed to broaden coverage by providing coverage for perils that are excluded on standard coverage forms or supplementing international policies that are written by admitted insurers in the applicable foreign countries. DIC policies are often used to fill the gaps between the coverage provided by a multinational organization's master insurance policies and coverage provided by policies purchased locally in accordance with each country's insurance requirements so that the organization has uniformity of coverage regardless of location. DIL, on the other hand, refers to a provision contained in a master international insurance program that provides coverage for the difference in limits between the limits of local underlying policies and the limits of the master international policy.

[4] See Marsh's "2013 Terrorism Risk Insurance Report".

[5] The ratio of cat losses to gross surplus is a good indicator of the ability to absorb losses from terrorism.

[6] Although some experts believe that human behavior can eventually be modeled via game theory, mathematical power laws and chaos theory, these scientific efforts remain in their infancy.

[7] The types of attacks that do occur, or are aborted or interdicted, would provide good information pertaining to vulnerability of targets, target selection and potential multiple target attacks, and generally speaking, to the terrorists' modi operandi.

[8] As an indicator of a more realistic trigger, in the private market, for instance, a typical ILW usually triggers at $20 billion in industry-wide losses. Industry loss warranties (ILW) are financial instruments which pay off when the industry-wide losses from a catastrophe exceed a certain industry loss index. While lower triggers of $10 billion and $15 billion are available for purchase, they can be very costly. Hurricane Sandy provides a good example. On March 22, 2013, Property Claim Services (PCS) issued its loss estimate for Sandy, falling just short of the typical ILW trigger of $20 billion in estimated insured losses. The storm was a close call for many ILW with $20 billion triggers. Sandy has actually set in motion a rethink of the entire ILW trigger structure, given that it was no more than a Category 1 storm and, upon reaching land, more like a tropical depression.

[9] Typically, a sponsoring insurance or reinsurance company – or it could be a corporation (e.g., Disneyland and Universal Studios transactions) or a state (e.g., Mexico's earthquake issue) – enters into a financial arrangement with a Special Purpose Vehicle (SPV) and, in exchange for a transfer of premiums to the SPV, the SPV assumes the payment of claims. The SPV invests these premiums in high quality instruments and, in turn, issues notes to investors who receive a stream of payments based on risk and use of funds.

[10] See PwC's 2013 "Expanding the potential of ILS" report.

[11] Given that most of these are private, over the counter transactions, the evidence is anecdotal.

[12] Unrelated to the more traditional fixed income and equity instruments that is.

[13] Cayman is the domicile of choice for over 90% of all catastrophe bond related SPVs.

[14] Capital can be as low as $500, though regulators typically adjust that based on the specifics of the bond issue.

[15] See the GAO's 2002 report entitled "Catastrophe Insurance Risks: The role of risk-linked securities and factors affecting their use" and subsequent GAO 2003 report "Catastrophe Insurance Risks: Status of efforts to securitize natural catastrophe and terrorism risk".

[16] Much like the mortgage industry is permitted to do through the use of Real Estate Mortgage Investment Conduits ("REMICs).

[17] These are long-term reserves kept for the purpose of preventing cash-flow depletion in the event of significant unforeseen catastrophes, including terrorism events.

[18] See GAO 2005 report entitled "Catastrophe risk: U.S. and European approaches to insure natural catastrophe and terrorism Risks".

[19] Germany, France, Italy, Spain, Switzerland, and the United Kingdom all allow tax-deductible reserves.

In: Terrorism Risk Insurance Act
Editor: Ernie L. Duke

ISBN: 978-1-63463-128-0
© 2014 Nova Science Publishers, Inc.

Chapter 8

TESTIMONY OF DR. JOHN S. SEO, CO-FOUNDER & MANAGING PRINCIPAL, FERMAT CAPITAL MANAGEMENT, LLC. HEARING ON "THE FUTURE OF TERRORISM INSURANCE: FOSTERING PRIVATE MARKET INNOVATION TO LIMIT TAXPAYER EXPOSURE"[*]

1. INTRODUCTION

I thank the Subcommittee on Housing and Insurance for inviting me to testify at this hearing on the potential role of the so-called Insurance-Linked Securities (ILS) market to privatize a greater part of the terrorism insurance market in the United States. The most commonly known part of the ILS market is the catastrophe bond (cat bond) market. The other, less-well known part of the ILS market is broadly termed collateralized reinsurance, which encompasses a broad array of reinsurance activity. What collateralized reinsurance has in common with cat bonds is that risk capital from outside the traditional insurance and reinsurance market are used to back up promises to pay for insured catastrophe losses. In my testimony today, I will speak broadly about the ILS market, with details and evidence taken largely from the cat bond market.

My name is John Seo. I am a co-founder and managing principal along with my brother, Nelson Seo, of Fermat Capital Management, LLC, which is believed to be the largest investment manager of cat bonds worldwide. Fermat Capital today has $4.5 billion of assets under management, all of it in ILS with a majority in cat bonds. Over the last 15 years, in addition to my "day job" of being a cat bond portfolio manager, I have also been privileged to serve as a state-appointed advisor to the Florida Hurricane Catastrophe Fund and as a bank-appointed advisor to The World Bank's Global Facility for Disaster Reduction and Recovery. In these additional roles, I was asked to help explore mechanisms to privatize catastrophe risks held directly or indirectly by the State of Florida and The World Bank.

---

[*] This is an edited, reformatted and augmented version of testimony presented November 13, 2013 before the House Committee on Financial Services, Subcommittee on Housing and Insurance.

I have been asked by the Subcommittee to testify on the current state and outlook of the ILS market, to discuss common misunderstandings about the ILS market appetite for terrorism risk, and to discuss ways to increase the efficiency of ILS coverage for terrorism risk. Before I get to that, I am afraid I must give a brief history of the ILS market because this market is still so new and its role in insurance markets is still not widely understood. I also think the Subcommittee will find the history of the ILS market relevant to the current situation in terrorism insurance.

2. A Brief History of the ILS Market

The ILS market had its beginning in the mid-to-late 1990s in the aftermath of Hurricane Andrew in 1992 and the Northridge Earthquake in 1994. These two events brought about insured losses of approximately $15 billion each. While such losses unto themselves were somewhat manageable by the insurance market, they were approximately 10 times larger than expected. This had two implications for the insurance market in the mid-1990s.

The first implication was that, as things stood, insurance companies were potentially "broke", in the sense that they likely did not have enough capital to weather worst-case loss scenarios — they were potentially under-reserved by up to 10 times for the "Big One" in hurricane and earthquake. The second implication was that insurance companies were potentially "blind", in the sense that their traditional actuarial methods provided no reasonable indication of worst-case loss scenarios. Not surprisingly, being potentially broke and blind in regard to hurricane and earthquake, the insurance market for these risks collapsed in the mid-to-late 1990s, and state governments had to step in. Although significant progress has been made since then to bring private markets back into the U.S. hurricane and earthquake insurance markets, that progress has been the greatest on the commercial side of the market. Even today, almost 20 years later, in Florida the state owns over 70 percent of homeowners' hurricane risk on the beach; and in California the state owns over 70 percent of homeowners' earthquake risk on the fault-line.

In response to this dire situation in the mid-to-late 1990s, a relative handful of enterprising professionals on Wall Street created the ILS market. Two key visions drove the early formation of the ILS market.

The first vision is the most well known: that capital markets had the potential to easily absorb the worst-case losses of hurricanes and earthquakes. Vast as it is, the insurance market only has a capital base that, depending on how you measure it, is 50 to 100 times smaller than the capital base that backs ILS markets. With an appropriately sized capital base, ILS markets were expected one day to restore the insurability condition to hurricane and earthquake risks and create a "win-win" situation, between insurers, on one hand, and reinsurers and ILS investors, on the other. Note ILS investors are alongside reinsurers because they both perform similar roles, each in a complementary way. ILS and traditional reinsurance help insurers shoulder their greatest risk burdens. ILS does this with global capital diversification; reinsurance, with global risk diversification.

The second vision driving the early formation of the ILS market is less well known: capital markets would make cutting-edge catastrophe models ("cat models") more mainstream in commercial usage. Though in much wider use today, cat models were only being used by a small handful of pioneering insurance and reinsurance companies 20 years ago. By putting the promise of vast amounts of risk capital behind the latest technologies for risk estimation, it was believed that ILS markets could accelerate insurance industry adoption of modern cat modeling techniques. This would eventually make catastrophe insurance markets more transparent, which would increase the efficiency of catastrophe risk financing in all forms.

These two elements, the promise of a huge capital base and the adoption of cutting-edge cat models, were together intended to solve the "broke and blind" problem that afflicted the insurance industry in the aftermath of Hurricane Andrew and the Northridge Earthquake. The jury is still out on whether these two visions of the ILS market will ultimately materialize, but progress to date has been excellent by most anyone's measure.

While investment activity on the non-cat bond side of the ILS market bears a close resemblance to traditional reinsurance activity, the cat bond side of the ILS market has become a distinct and well-accepted sub-sector of the corporate bond market. Just like corporate bonds, cat bonds are typically rated, listed with public exchanges, and are actively traded in the over-the-counter market. Unlike traditional corporate bonds, however, cat bonds collectively provide explicit coverage for hurricane, earthquake, tornado, hail, wildfire, disease, flood, terrorism risk and potentially any other quantifiable risks that would be called a catastrophe by the insurance market. In return for bearing these risks, cat bond investors receive a high coupon, higher typically than those of comparably rated corporate bonds. This high coupon acts as a kind of insurance premium for ILS investors.

3. CURRENT STATE AND OUTLOOK OF THE INSURANCE-LINKED SECURITIES (ILS) MARKET

From its beginnings in the mid-to-late 1990s, the ILS market has grown to $45 billion this year, with $20 billion of that coming from the cat bond market. The non-cat bond side of the ILS market is typically a "buy and hold" market with annually renewed contracts, while the cat bond side of the ILS market is actively traded on a daily basis. The cat bond market is expected to see over $7 billion in secondary market trading volume this year. ILS investors are found on every habitable continent in the world and range from high net-worth individuals, family offices, foundations, endowments, insurance companies, private banks, hedge funds, specialty ILS managers, money managers, mutual funds, pension funds and sovereign wealth funds. Specialty ILS managers collectively have several hundred distinct investors from among all the investor classes just mentioned, who pool their money in ILS fund vehicles, some of which are onshore, listed, and regulated in the UK, Europe, or Australia. New ILS investment vehicles are announced every month now.

As has always been the case, high levels of innovation continue to characterize the ILS market. It is not unusual for a risk to be considered "a bridge too far" in one year, then commonplace a few years later. For example, a cat bond covering the New York Metropolitan Transportation Authority (MTA) for flood risk was successfully placed in the market this year in July. ILS professionals now believe the MTA cat bond to be the first of many such flood bonds that will be issued in coming years; yet, even a few years ago, many of those same ILS professionals considered a burgeoning market for flood bonds to be improbable. This is not an unusual experience in the ILS market.

Regarding the coverage of terrorism risk specifically, I report to the Subcommittee that the cat bond market alone currently covers only $1.4 billion in terrorism risk. If we extrapolate that to the non-cat bond side of the ILS market, we could reasonably estimate that the ILS market in total covers roughly $3 billion in insured terrorism risk today.

From its current base, some market observers expect the ILS market to triple in size over the next five years and create $150 to 200 billion in total risk capacity before the end of this decade. Using only simple extrapolation from our current state, this expected growth trend would take ILS capacity for terrorism risk to $9 to $12 billion by the end of this decade. If the ILS market should more widely adopt coverage of terrorism risk, the ILS market capacity for terrorism risk could easily rise to $20 to $30 billion by the end of the decade. There are the usual caveats that must surround this rosier projection, but it is definitely not out of the realm of future possibility.

4. COMMON MISUNDERSTANDINGS ABOUT THE ILS MARKET APPETITE FOR TERRORISM RISK

Unless a particular part of the ILS market is growing by leaps and bounds, it is common for misunderstanding to arise around the market appetite for the risk or risks in question. Some of these misunderstandings stem from a lack of information, and some of these misunderstandings come from mixing and confusing the preferences expressed among different investor classes. I would like to address one of each kind of misunderstanding now.

The first common misunderstanding is that ILS markets have shown no appetite for terrorism risk to date. I assume that such a view is largely due to a lack of information, so I will simply lay out the numbers on this issue now. The ILS market for terrorism risk began with Golden Goal Finance, Ltd., a $250 million cat bond deal brought to market in October 2013. Golden Goal provided terrorism cancellation coverage to FIFA for the 2006 World Cup. At the time, merely two years after 9/11, Golden Goal was 7 percent of the outstanding cat bond market, quite large for a single cat bond issue. As such, Golden Goal at the time of issuance was the third largest cat bond issue in the market out of 25 outstanding issues. In the ten years since the issuance of Golden Goal, terrorism risk has remained at 7 percent of the cat bond market, growing from $250 million to $1.4 billion in cat bond coverage over the last 10 years, which comes out to a 19 percent compound annual growth rate. Admittedly, these figures do not indicate an overwhelming trend of historical growth, but they certainly do not support the conclusion that ILS markets have exhibited no appetite for terrorism risk to date. Given the proper information, it seems clear that ILS markets to date have kept an open mind on terrorism risk—nothing more and nothing less.

Another common misunderstanding is that ILS investors strictly avoid correlation risk. This very common misperception about ILS investors deserves careful discussion. Confusion around this issue is understandable.

Without getting into too much detail here, ILS markets are supported by a mixture of so-called fast and slow money. Fast money typically comes from hedge funds; slow money, from pension funds. According to the latest figures from Swiss Re Capital Markets, hedge funds make up less than 5 percent of the ILS market. Pension funds are more difficult to track directly because they tend to invest through specialty ILS managers. As one such manager myself, I would gauge pension fund participation in the ILS market to be 60 percent.

Fast money is the most vocal about correlation risk in ILS. Part of this concern is sincere. Fast money often runs highly leveraged positions, in long-short pairing as well. Even a relatively small and brief departure from correlation assumptions can cause big trouble for fast money. This makes fast money naturally sensitized to the possibility of minute flaws in correlation assumptions. Nonetheless, part of the concern expressed around ILS correlation by fast money is a codified way of asking for a higher yield. Fast money reasons that slow money, which I will discuss soon, keeps ILS yields low on the assumption of non-correlation. Fast money goes on to reason that any potential correlation is uncompensated; and, therefore, greater than normal yield is required for ILS with any potential correlation issues. By the way, this concern applies to most earthquake bonds as much as it would to terrorism bonds.

Armed with this kind of reasoning, which borders on militancy at times, fast money can stay on the sidelines for years at a time, waiting for what it perceives as distressed yields before entering a particular part of the ILS market. Perhaps the incorrect view that all ILS investors are hypersensitive to correlation risk comes from the fast money side of the market, but fast money, as already noted, is only a small part of the overall ILS market capacity.

Slow money is clearly enamored with the general low correlation of ILS to stocks and bonds. Perhaps this, too, could mislead a market observer. By incorrectly combining slow money declarations of love for the low correlation of ILS with the non-correlation militancy of fast money, it is possible to come up with the false, composite picture that all ILS investors are a tough bunch when it comes to ILS correlation risk. Yet, this is simply not true.

Slow money likes ILS and believes ILS offer returns that have a low correlation to stock and bond returns. There is no doubt about this, but the sentiment is more declarative than prescriptive. First of all, slow money defines correlation on a much longer time scale than does fast money—years as opposed to days, weeks or months. Does a prolonged economic recession increase the risk of an insured loss event? Does an insured loss event increase the risk of a prolonged recession? Measured on such long time scales, to my knowledge, no significant correlation between ILS and traditional markets has ever been found. Low correlation with traditional investments is desired by slow money, but the insistence is not so strict that zero correlation is required. Furthermore, the long time scale used to gauge correlation washes out most short-term effects usually associated with, or defined as, correlation.

Perhaps just as important as the long time scales on which slow money operates, slow money is also thoughtful about its approach to alternatives markets like ILS. Even if there were some possibility that an insured loss event might cause longer term damage to stock and bond returns, slow money would ask: is that risk, already borne by stock and bond investors, better compensated in ILS than in stocks and bonds? The answer to that question is almost universally: "ILS pays better for the risk." This is because stock and bond investors are almost never compensated for bearing extreme event risk, whereas ILS investors are almost always paid for the extreme event risks they cover. As you might hope and expect, with slow money, any lack of correlation with stock and bond returns is icing on the cake, but fair compensation for the risk is of the greatest importance in the end.

5. WAYS TO INCREASE THE EFFICIENCY OF ILS COVERAGE FOR TERRORISM RISK

I would like to end my testimony by briefly describing two ways to increase the efficiency of ILS coverage for terrorism risk, which could help the ILS market get to a higher adoption of terrorism risk coverage than might be expected at the current pace of progress.

Greater efficiency of ILS coverage is generally achieved by bundling of coverage with risks that are better understood or exclusion of risks that are less well understood or both. Let me explain while being more specific.

ILS coverage for terrorism risk in the cat bond market has never occurred on a pure, standalone basis. ILS coverage for terrorism risk in the cat bond market is typically bundled with so-called extreme mortality risk, which includes mass threats to human life from disease and earthquake.

This bundling is natural and unsurprising, but the bundling of terrorism risk with other risks likely occurs because risk coverage generally becomes more efficient the more risks are put together in a single contract. I am leaving out a great deal of technical details, but the intuition here is simple: risk bundling reduces the negative effects of transaction costs and economic rents for capital. Ideally, the new risks that are being brought into the bundle are better understood, improving the average quality of the risk bundle. Sometimes, other competing market inefficiencies can come into play to counter the benefits of risk bundling, so this is not always a cure all. Nonetheless, if terrorism risk were bundled with natural catastrophe risks such as hurricane and earthquake, the efficiency of ILS coverage for terrorism risk could potentially be improved.

Finally, ILS coverage for terrorism risk in the cat bond market currently includes nuclear, biological, chemical, and radiological (NBCR) causes of loss. Cat models attempt to take into account both conventional and NBCR sources of terrorism losses, but the ILS market believes that NBCR risks are much less well understood than conventional terrorism risks. If NBCR were excluded from ILS coverage, the efficiency of ILS coverage for the remaining conventional terrorism risk would be improved greatly.

6. CLOSING

Thank you for this opportunity to testify to the Subcommittee today. I look forward to answering any questions you may have.

Chapter 9

TESTIMONY OF ROBERT P. HARTWIG, PRESIDENT AND ECONOMIST, INSURANCE INFORMATION INSTITUTE. HEARING ON "THE FUTURE OF TERRORISM INSURANCE: FOSTERING PRIVATE MARKET INNOVATION TO LIMIT TAXPAYER EXPOSURE"[*]

Thank you, Representative Neugebauer, Ranking Member Capuano and members of the Committee.

Good morning. My name is Robert Hartwig and I am President and Economist for the Insurance Information Institute, an international property/casualty insurance trade association based in New York City.[1] I am also a Chartered Property Casualty Underwriter (CPCU) and have worked on a wide variety of insurance issues during my 20 years in the property/casualty insurance and reinsurance industries, including many related to the industry's exposure to catastrophic loss, including acts or terrorism.[2] The Institute's members account for nearly 70 percent of all property/casualty insurance premiums written in the United States. Its primary mission is to improve understanding of the insurance industry and the key role it plays in the U.S. and global economy.

I have been asked by the Committee to provide testimony on the current state the Terrorism Risk Insurance Program and the market for terrorism insurance in the United States. For the purposes of my testimony, I will address the following issues:

(i) The immediate impacts of the September 11, 2001 attacks on insurance and reinsurance markets;
(ii) The essential role that TRIA plays with the nation's national security infrastructure and its benefits to consumers, businesses and communities;
(iii) Taxpayer protection features of TRIA;
(iv) Private sector insurer and reinsurer involvement in terrorism insurance markets since 9/11;

---

[*] This is an edited, reformatted and augmented version of testimony presented November 13, 2013 before the House Committee on Financial Services, Subcommittee on Housing and Insurance.

(v) The unique nature of terrorism risk and the limits of private sector involvement in terrorism insurance markets;
(vi) Changes in the terrorism threat landscape since the enactment of the original TRIA legislation in 2002 and the impacts on terrorism insurance;
(vii) Potential economic, ratings agency and insurance market impacts if TRIA is not extended;
(viii) Obstacles to insuring and reinsuring losses arising from acts of terrorism;
(ix) Cyber terrorism and certification timelines.

IMPACTS OF THE SEPTEMBER 11, 2001 TERRORIST ATTACK ON INSURANCE MARKETS

The terrorist attacks of September 11, 2001, produced insured losses larger than any natural or man-made event in history. Claims paid by insurers to their policyholders eventually totaled some $32.5 billion dollars—$42.1 billion in 2012 dollars (Exhibit 1) and to this day remains the second most costly insurance event in United States history (Exhibit 2).[3] The insured losses arising from the events of that fateful day were unprecedented in virtually every respect, producing catastrophic losses not only in property coverages, but also for the first time in the workers compensation line. The sheer enormity of the loss—coming from an entirely unforeseen peril for which no premium had been collected—combined with the possibility of future attacks, produced financial shockwaves that shook insurance markets worldwide and provoked an extraordinarily swift and severe underwriting and pricing reaction by insurers and reinsurers.

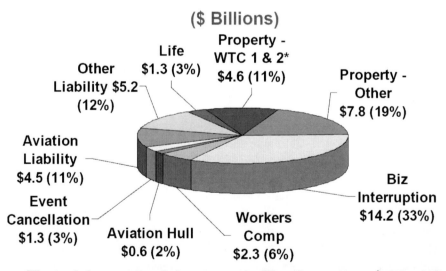

Total Insured Losses Estimate: $42.1B

* Loss total does not include March 2010 New York City settlement of up to $657.5 million to compensate approximately 10,000 Ground Zero workers or any subsequent settlements.
Source: Insurance Information Institute.

Exhibit 1. Loss Distribution by Type of Insurance from Sept. 11 Terrorist Attack ($ 2012).

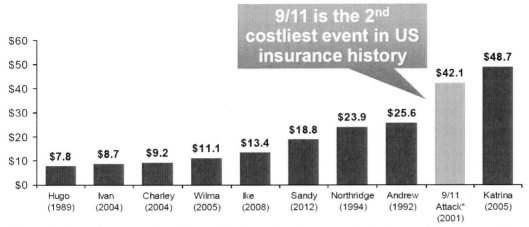

* Insured loss estimate for Sep. 11 terrorist attack includes property, business interruption, workers comp, aviation hull, liability, event cancellation and life insurance losses.
Sources: PCS; Insurance Information Institute inflation adjustments to 2012 dollars using the CPI.

Exhibit 2. Top 10 Most Costly Disasters in U.S. History.

Terrorism Exclusions and Price Shocks in the Wake of the 9/11 Attack

The shock of the September 11 attack led insurers and reinsurers to exclude coverage arising from acts of terrorism from virtually all commercial property and liability policies. Before 9/11 terrorism exclusions were virtually nonexistent in commercial insurance contracts sold in the United States. The economic consequences of such exclusions were quick to manifest themselves. Major commercial property construction projects around the country, unable to secure coverage against the now very real risk of terrorist attack, were in jeopardy of being tabled, hurting job growth at a time of rapidly rising unemployment and when much of the country was in recession. Banks, in turn, threatened to choke off lending to businesses if borrowers failed to secure coverage against terrorist acts. The problem was not confined to high profile "trophy" properties located in major metropolitan areas. Shopping malls, office complexes, factories, sports stadiums, hotels, utilities, airports, port facilities and other critical infrastructure all across the United States were impacted. In short, the macroeconomic consequences associated with the lack of terrorism coverage were beginning to exact a severe toll on businesses and workers alike. *[Note: The potential macroeconomic implications of allowing TRIA to expire in 2014 are discussed in greater detail in the next section of this paper].*

Even as exclusions proliferated, prices soared. The average rate increase for a business seeking to renew coverage in the fourth quarter of 2001 was nearly 30 percent. Reinsurance prices rose sharply as well. Very little private sector coverage for terrorism entered the market as a general consensus emerged that terrorism risk is fundamentally not insurable. Insurers, who are regulated by the states, therefore took the unprecedented step of seeking to establish a risk sharing plan with the federal government in the event of future attacks. Only when the Terrorism Risk Insurance Act (TRIA) was enacted by Congress in November 2002—fourteen months after the attack—did stability finally return to the market and coverage for terrorist attacks resume. In the eleven years since enactment, stability remains a hallmark of this market primarily due to the continued existence of TRIA. That said, the market for terrorism insurance today—in late 2013—is already showing signs of stress associated with uncertainty over the future of TRIA. Already a number of major commercial insurers have stated that policyholders will soon be notified that coverage for certain terrorist acts could be altered or discontinued if TRIA is allowed to expire.[4]

TRIA, NATIONAL SECURITY AND PROTECTION OF THE NATION'S CRITICAL FINANCIAL INFRASTRUCTURE

The war on terror is far from over, as the recent Boston Marathon bombings attest, but TRIA by all objective measures is now a proven and unqualified success. The program not only succeeded in restoring stability to the country's vital insurance and reinsurance markets in the years immediately following 9/11, but it continues more than a decade later to deliver substantive, direct benefits to millions of businesses, workers, consumers and the overall economy—all at essentially no cost to taxpayers.

Upwards of 60 percent of businesses purchased terrorism coverage nationally in 2012, up from 27 percent in 2003, the first full year of the program (Exhibit 3). Industries responsible for much of the country's critical infrastructure such as power and utilities, telecommunications and health care, along with financial institutions and local government have take-up rates that approach or exceed 70 percent. Moreover, the take-up rate for workers compensation is effectively 100 percent, meaning that every worker in America is protected against injuries suffered as the result of a terrorist attack.

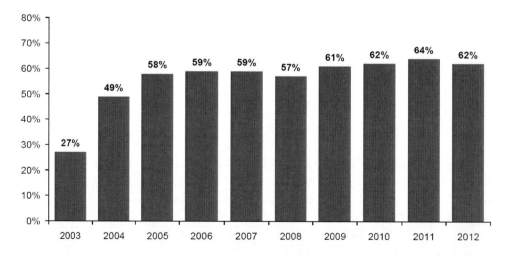

Source: Marsh Global Analytics, *2013 Terrorism Risk Insurance Report,* May 2013.

Exhibit 3. Terrorism Insurance Take-up Rates, by Year, 2003-2012.

The unambiguous success of TRIA demonstrates that the Act has become an invaluable component of the country's national security infrastructure. The continued operation of the nation's financial institutions—including its insurers—during and throughout the aftermath of a major terrorist attack—is absolutely essential to ensure a smooth and expedited recovery from the massive economic and operational shocks of the sort that occurred after the 9/11 attacks and that are certain to accompany future such events, irrespective of where in the country they occur. Failure to institutionalize a permanent plan to protect the nation's financial infrastructure leaves the country unnecessarily vulnerable to economic instability and risk of recession.

Macroeconomic Impacts of the TRIA Expiration

A 2004 study co-authored by R. Glenn Hubbard, Columbia University's Business School Dean and a former chairman of the U.S. Council of Economic Advisors, quantified the potential macroeconomic impacts of a failure to extend TRIA.[5] The study concluded that within three years of the expiration of TRIA (in the absence of a major terrorist attack), GDP could fall by 0.4 percent, household net worth by 0.9 percent and employment by 0.2 percent. Applying the findings of that study to the current period suggests that expiration of the current Act could lead to a meaningful drag on economic growth, reducing real GDP by an estimated $69 billion by 2017, depressing household net worth by an estimated $798 billion and remove 290,000 jobs from the economy.[6]

As Table 1 demonstrates, terrorism remains a threat to the country's national economic security, especially in the context of the still fragile economic recovery. Consequently, maintaining a Terrorism Risk Insurance Program as a component of the country's comprehensive national security plan and infrastructure is both reasonable and prudent. It is also imminently affordable. Indeed, the cost to American taxpayers is effectively zero.

TAXPAYER PROTECTION FEATURES OF THE TERRORISM RISK INSURANCE ACT

TRIA from its inception was designed as a terrorism risk sharing mechanism between the public and private sector—with an overwhelming share of the risk being borne by private insurers, a share which has increased steadily over time. Today, all but the very largest (and least likely) terrorist attacks would be financed entirely within the private sector. In the event of a truly catastrophic attack, TRIA provides the government with the ability to fully recoup any and all federal monies paid. In other words, there would be *no* cost to the taxpayer.

As a point of fact, from the date of TRIA's enactment in November 2002 through today, a span of almost exactly 11 years, the federal government and therefore taxpayers have paid nothing (apart from negligible administrative expenses) under the program. The recent Boston Marathon bombings provide an illustrative example. All of the 207 property/casualty claims filed in the wake of that event were handled by private insurers who have made payments to policyholders totaling at least $1.18 million.[7] Not one taxpayer dollar was used to pay any of these claims.

Table 1. Potential Macroeconomic Impacts Associated with the Expiration of TRIA

Macroeconomic Factor	Estimated Impact within 3 Years of Terrorism Program Expiration
Real GDP	-$69 Billion
Household Net Worth	-$798 Billion
Jobs	-290,000

TRIA's structure actually provides at least eight distinct layers of taxpayer protection as displayed schematically in Exhibit 4's Pyramid of Taxpayer Protection. Each of those layers is discussed in turn below.

SUMMARY OF 8 KEY TAXPAYER PROTECTION FEATURES UNDER TRIA

1. **Certification Definition:** *Criteria Must be Met*[8]
   - **Definition of a Certified Act of Terrorism:** The 2007 extension of TRIA, likes its predecessors, requires that a detailed set of criteria be met before an act of terror can be "certified." Specifically, the term "act of terrorism" refers only to an act that is certified by the [Treasury] Secretary, in concurrence with the Secretary of State and the Attorney General of the United States:
     i. to be an act of terrorism;
     ii. to be a violent act or an act that is dangerous to human life, property or infrastructure;
     iii. to have resulted in damage within the United States, or outside of the United States in the case US air carriers, vessels and/or missions;
     iv. to have been committed by and individuals as part of an effort to coerce the civilian population of the United States or to influence the policy or affect the conduct of the US government by coercion.
2. **Certification Threshold (TRIGGER):** *$5 Million*
   - **$5 Million Minimum:** Under the 2007 reauthorization of TRIA, no act shall be certified by the Secretary as an act of terrorism if property and casualty losses, in the aggregate, do not exceed $5 million.
   - **Acts of War Exclusion:** TRIA further stipulates that no act may be certified as an act of terrorism if the act is committed as part of the course of a war declared by Congress (this provision does not apply to workers compensation).
3. **Triggering Event Threshold:** *$100 Million*
   - Under the 2007 reauthorization of TRIA the triggering event threshold was set at $100 million, up from $5 million in the original act and $50 million in 2006. This means that Federal funds will be paid out *only* in the event of a terrorist act that produces total insurance industry losses above this threshold (even if the event is certified by the Treasury Secretary as a terrorist act).

Exhibit 4. Pyramid of Taxpayer Protection: Strong, Stable, Sound and Secure.

4. **Individual Insurer Deductibles:** *20% of Premiums*
   - The amount of terrorism losses that an individual insurer must pay before federal assistance becomes available. The level rose to 20 percent of an insurer's direct earned premiums for commercial property/casualty insurance in 2007 where it currently remains (up from 17.5% in 2006, 15 percent in 2005, 10% in 2004 and 7% in 2003).

5. **Insurer Co-Payment in Excess of Retention:** *15% of Loss*
   - The share of losses that insurers pay above their individual retentions rose to 15 percent in 2007 where it remains today, up from 10 percent in 2006 and prior years.

6. **Industry Aggregate Retention:** *$27.5 Billion*
   - Under the 2007 reauthorization, the industry as a whole must ultimately cover a total of $27.5 billion of the losses through deductibles and copayments (assuming an event of $27.5 billion or greater). This amount was increased to $27.5 billion in 2007, up from $25 billion in 2006, $15 billion in 2005, $12.5 billion 2004 and $10 billion in 2003 *(Figure 7)*. Government expenditure above this amount can be recouped.

7. **Government Recoupment:** *Full Taxpayer Protection*
   - **Mandatory Recoupment:** TRIA mandates that the government recoup *133 percent* of the difference between the actual amount it has paid and the required retention. This recoupment comes via a surcharge on commercial insurance policyholders not to exceed 3 percent of premium for insurance coverages that fall under the program.
   - **Discretionary Recoupment:** If the insured loss exceeds the $27.5 billion threshold, federal expenditures may be recouped for amounts in excess of the threshold at the discretion of the Secretary of the Treasury.

8. **HARD CAP:** *$100 Billion*
   - **Program Limit:** Losses within a program year are capped at $100 billion, inclusive of both insurer and government participation. Neither the government nor insurers would be required to pay losses for certified acts beyond this amount.

ADDITIONAL TAXPAYER PROTECTION FEATURES OF TRIA

Several other features of TRIA serve as additional protections to taxpayers.

Commercial Lines Only: Only claims occurring in certain property/casualty commercial lines of insurance are included in the calculations of insured losses under TRIA (auto and homeowners insurance, life insurance and health insurance have always been excluded). In addition, the number of lines covered under TRIA has been narrowed over time. At TRIA's inception in 2002 approximately 44 percent of property/casualty insurance industry premiums were covered under the Act. By 2012 that figure had dropped to approximately 35 percent. Excluded commercial lines of coverage under the Act today include: mortgage and title insurance, financial guaranty, medical malpractice, reinsurance, commercial auto, burglary and theft, surety, professional liability (except directors and officers coverage) and farmowners multiperil.

State Guaranty Funds: In the unlikely event that an insurer becomes severely impaired or insolvent as a consequence of a terrorist attack, state insurance regulators will take corrective action. If the insurer's assets are insufficient to meet its liabilities, the resources of the appropriate state guaranty fund(s) could be called upon to satisfy those liabilities. Guaranty associations obtain funds for their operations and payment of claims through assessments against the solvent insurance companies licensed to do business in the state and from the recovery of amounts paid on claims from the insolvent estate.[9] All guaranty fund resources are therefore ultimately derived from the industry itself. *No taxpayer dollars are ever involved.*

Make Available Requirement (Mandatory Offer of Coverage): Commercial insurers are required to offer coverage against terrorist acts and by law, workers compensation must include coverage against such acts. These requirements have led to widespread participation in the program. The take-up rate for terrorism coverage in 2012 was 62 percent according to a recent study by insurance broker Marsh.[10] The take-up rate for workers compensation is effectively 100 percent, meaning that every worker in America is protected against injuries suffered as the result of a terrorist attack.

TRIA WILL REDUCE TAXPAYER FUNDED POST-ATTACK DISASTER AID COSTS

The very fact that terrorism coverage is so widely purchased today and that coverage already extends to every American worker through the workers compensation system means that fewer government (taxpayer) resources will be called upon in the wake of any future terrorist attack. Allowing TRIA to expire will reduce the market penetration of terrorism coverage as prices rise and insurers limit their exposure across all lines of coverage, including workers compensation. Consequently, the uninsured share of losses will rise, increasing the pressure on the government to compensate victims for their uninsured losses. This will impair the ability of individual businesses, affected communities and the overall economy's ability to recover. A sharp spike in business failures, higher unemployment and reduced GDP growth are just a few of the adverse consequences that are certain to follow in the event of a major terrorist attack in the absence of TRIA. In summary, government will be called upon to act in the aftermath of a major terrorist attack. TRIA provides an efficient means for ensuring that most of the costs are financed and administered by the private sector rather than the taxpayer.

USE OF INSURER CLAIM MANAGEMENT INFRASTRUCTURE WILL SAVE TAXPAYER MONEY, IMPROVE POST-ATTACK RESPONSE

Private insurers are today the principal source and conduit for the rapid and direct delivery of recovery funds to victims of terrorist attacks. In the event that TRIA is allowed to expire, the government lacks any formal structure or experience for adjusting, managing and delivering benefits to victims of complex commercial property and liability claims, nor does it have any formal fraud monitoring capability. Maintaining TRIA not only ensures that the costs of future terrorist attacks will be borne primarily by the private sector, it enhances the quality of the outcome. Again, in the absence of TRIA there is no question that the federal government will be called upon to act. TRIA ensures that that much of those costs will be borne and administered by the private insurers.

PRIVATE INSURER AND REINSURANCE PARTICIPATION IN THE MARKET FOR TERRORISM INSURANCE TODAY

One primary goal of TRIA and it successors has been to encourage private sector capacity to enter (and remain) in the marketplace so that an increasing share of losses from future terrorist attacks could be borne in the private sector.

There is no question that billions of dollars in capacity has been attracted to the terrorism risk insurance market. Evidence of the program's success in this respect has been documented by a number of government entities and other organizations. In its latest report on terrorism risk insurance market conditions, the President's Working Group on Financial Markets noted that the program provides an incentive to property/casualty insurers and reinsurers who might not otherwise provide terrorism insurance at current capacity levels or prices.[11] The U.S. Government Accountability Office (GAO), commenting on the availability and affordability of terrorism coverage in large metropolitan areas, reported that with a few exceptions, commercial property terrorism insurance appears to be available nationwide at rates policyholders believe is reasonable, suggesting ample capacity.[12]

Note that this statement is very different from an assessment that such capacity would exist in the absence of a terrorism backstop. Again, it is important to emphasize that the majority of the coverage that exists in the market today exists because of the continued existence of the Terrorism Risk Insurance Program. Insurance broker Aon estimates that 70% to 80% of the market would encounter terrorism exclusions if the program were discontinued. Thus capacity in the market is largely contingent upon the continuation of the program. As detailed earlier in this testimony, policy language that would exclude coverage against terrorist attacks returned to the market each time the expiration of TRIA has loomed.

The so-called market for "standalone" terrorism coverage also provides evidence that in the absence of a Terrorism Risk Insurance Program, coverage capacity (supply) will fall well short of demand. Insurance brokers Marsh and Aon both report that the "theoretical" maximum amount of coverage available per risk in the "standalone" market is approximately $2 billion with larger sums available under some circumstances. This is in contrast with limits of just $150 million or less available in early 2002 before TRIA was enacted. At the time, such coverage also was subject to high deductibles equal to 7 to 10 percent of the stated value of the coverage.[13] While the sums available in the market today may seem large, especially in comparison to 2002, there are many risks for which the coverage is inadequate. Consider, for example, that back in 2001 (prior to the introduction of terrorism exclusions) the twin towers at the World Trade Center site were insured for $3.55 billion—more than what is generally available in the market today. Multibillion dollars risks are now quite common in the United States, from office and shopping complexes to large manufacturing facilities, sports stadiums, transportation hubs and energy infrastructure not to mention infrastructure such as bridges, tunnels and dams. These exposures exist in every state.

Reinsurance capacity, which was extremely limited in the aftermath of 9/11, is up as well. A 2011 report from reinsurance broker Guy Carpenter noted that there is between $6 billion and $8 billion of terrorism reinsurance capacity available in the U.S. market, but cautions that the market remains vulnerable to a major terrorism loss. The $6 billion to $8 billion in terrorism reinsurance capacity stands in stark contrast to approximately $100 billion in reinsurance capacity available in the market today against traditional risks (mostly property catastrophe risks). A continued cautious approach is clearly required. Indeed, many modeled terrorism loss scenarios result in insured losses in the tens or even hundreds of billions of dollars—some even exceeding the claims paying capital of the entire industry. As noted previously, much of the capacity in the market today is predicated on the existence of the Terrorism Risk Insurance Program. In the absence of the program, reinsurance capacity would be greatly reduced.

Capital Markets and Terrorism Risk

Capital markets are playing an increasingly important role in providing capacity against losses arising from large natural disaster events which are becoming increasingly frequent in the United States and around the world. Capital market reinsurance capacity for U.S. natural catastrophe risks is estimated at $30 billion to $40 billion. However, investor appetite for catastrophe risk is so far limited to natural catastrophes such as hurricanes and earthquakes. Investors are attracted to investments in backing natural disasters risks in part because the performance of these assets is entirely uncorrelated with the performance of traditional financial market instruments such as stocks and bonds. A recession, for example, will impact the value of stocks and corporate bond prices but will have no impact on the likelihood of sustaining a loss on a catastrophe bond.

Investors to date have shown no appetite for terrorism risk because in the event of a major terrorist attack the performance of securitized terrorism risk instruments (such as catastrophe bonds) and tradition equity market and fixed income investment vehicles are likely to be *highly correlated*. For example, a large-scale terrorist attack could cause bonds exposed to the event to lose all or part of their value, leading to large losses for investors while stock markets plunge (as they did in the wake of the September 11, 2001 attack). Investor disinterest in terrorism risk is also a function of the inability to model and therefore price) such risks with anything close to the same degree of precision as tradition natural disaster risk.

CHANGES IN THE TERRORISM THREAT LANDSCAPE AND IMPACTS ON TERRORISM INSURANCE MARKETS

In the immediate aftermath of 9/11 the ability of commercial policyholders to purchase adequate limits of terrorism coverage at affordable prices was severely constrained. Commercial property owners and businesses were faced with substantially reduced protection for terrorism-related risks, in addition to higher property/casualty rates overall. As a result, many were forced to go without coverage or only partly insure their assets.

Today, reports of property owners having problems securing terrorism coverage due to a lack of capacity in the market are no longer making headline news. Indeed, it is therefore tempting to conclude that in the eleven years since TRIA was first implemented that insurance markets have fully adjusted to the post-9/11 environment and that insurers and reinsurers have concluded that terrorism is a fully insurance risk.

The reality is quite different. The fact of the matter is that terrorism risk today is almost every bit as uninsurable as it was a decade ago. Recent major successes in the war on terror, including the killing of al-Qaida leader Osama bin Laden in 2011, do not alter this conclusion. This is because the current stability in the terrorism insurance market in the United States is due almost entirely to two factors:

(i) There has been no successful large-scale terrorist attack on U.S. soil since 2001, and
(ii) TRIA remains in place.

The influence of both of these factors is discussed in the sections that follow.

Absence of Successful Attacks Does Not Imply Terrorism Risk is Inconsequential

The fact that there has been no successful large-scale terrorist attack in the United States in eleven years is a remarkable achievement. It is a testimony to the hard work and dedication of this nation's counterterrorism agencies and the bravery of the men and women in uniform who fought and continue to fight battles abroad to keep us safe here at home.

Unfortunately, the threat from terrorist attack in the United States is both real and substantial and will remain as such for the foreseeable future. Indeed, the U.S. State

Department warned in a recent report that despite the death of bin Laden and other key al-Qaeda figures, the terrorist network's affiliates and adherents remain adaptable and resilient, and constitute "an enduring and serious threat to our national security."[14]

Table 2 below shows that interest in attacking targets within the United States remains undiminished—with four terrorist plots executed or interdicted within the past year alone. Indeed, it is clear from Table 2 that in addition to an ongoing threat from foreign terrorist networks, the United States also faces homegrown (domestic) terrorist threats from radical individuals, who may be inspired by al-Qaida and others, but may have little or no actual connection to militant groups.

Catastrophe modeler Risk Management Solutions (RMS) points to an increase in the number of homegrown plots in the U.S. in recent years.[15] Many of these have been thwarted, such as the 2012 attempt by Quazi Ahsam Nafis to blow up the Federal Reserve Bank of New York and Mohamed Osman Mohamud who targeted a Portland, Oregon, Christmas tree lighting ceremony. Also among the more notable unsuccessful attacks was an April 2013 attempt to blow up an Amtrak train en route between New York and Toronto. Other thwarted attacks against passenger and cargo aircraft, including the Christmas Day 2009 attempt to blow-up a jet over Detroit, are indicative of an ongoing risk to aviation infrastructure.

Table 2 also shows that terrorists are interesting in attacking targets across the United States, not just in large urban areas. Cities such as Springfield, Illinois and Lubbock, Texas, have also been targeted. It also important to note that the largest act of domestic terrorism in United States history was the truck bombing of the Alfred P. Murrah Federal Building in Oklahoma City in April 1995, which killed 166 people and produced insured property losses totaling $189 million (in 2012 dollars).

Another evolving threat is cyber-terrorism. Recent high profile attacks, such as the sabotaging of Iran's nuclear program via the Stuxnet computer worm and malicious infiltration attempts here in the U.S. by foreign entities, underscore the growing threat to both national security and the economy.

All these factors suggest that terrorism risk will be a constant and evolving threat for the foreseeable future.

POTENTIAL IMPACTS IF TRIA IS NOT EXTENDED

Without question, TRIA and its successors are the principal reason for the continued stability in the insurance and reinsurance market for terrorism insurance today. As discussed previously, TRIA is credited with restoring terrorism coverage in commercial insurance policies upon its enactment in late 2002.

Potential macroeconomic effects of allowing TRIA to expire—reduced economic growth and fewer jobs—were discussed earlier. In terms of impacts on insurance markets there is no question that coverage will become more expensive and less available—and in many cases unavailable. The question is not a theoretical one. In 2004, more than a year before the original Act's expiration at year-end 2005, terrorism exclusions once again emerged for policies with exposure extending into 2006. This was an unmistakable indication that insurance and reinsurance markets felt that terrorism risk, at least for larger scale attacks, remained uninsurable in the private sector. After Congress agreed to extend the program for another two years under the Terrorism Risk Insurance Extension Act of 2005 (TRIEA), terrorism coverage remained available and affordable in the market. However, with TRIEA's looming expiration in year-end 2006, terrorism exclusions once again appeared in the market, signaling the market's assessment that terrorism risk remained fundamentally uninsurable. These exclusions largely disappeared following passage of a 7-year extension of the program under the Terrorism Risk Insurance Program Reauthorization Act of 2007 (TRIPRA). With TRIPRA's expiration now a little more than one year away (year-end 2014), it is virtually certain that terrorism exclusions will soon reappear in the market. Indeed, insurance broker Aon estimates that at least 80 percent of the commercial property market will be impacted by these exclusions and other restrictions.

Studies by various organizations, including the University of Pennsylvania's Wharton School Risk Center, the RAND Corporation and the Organization for Economic Co-operation and Development (OECD), have supported the idea of a substantive federal role in terrorism insurance. In particular, the Wharton School found that TRIA has had a positive effect on availability of terrorism coverage and also has significantly contributed to reducing insurance premiums.[16] The OECD notes, however, that the financial (capital) markets have thus far shown little appetite for terrorism risk.

Ratings Implications

Although expiration of TRIA is currently more than a year away, insurance ratings agencies are compelled to take action today by subjecting insurers to "stress tests" to ascertain their ability to absorb losses in the event of a terrorist attack.[17] Ratings agency A.M. Best scenario recently employed in its stress test a deterministic scenario simulating a conventional weapon attack similar to a "five- or six- ton TNT truck bomb, with no restrictions placed on the radius and assuming the attack occurs when the buildings are at their highest occupancy." A.M. Best found that 226 of the 889 "ratings units" it examined had exposure to such a scenario and 34 (3.8%) of these ratings units failed the stress test. Consequently, the companies will be required to "present and action plan detailing the steps they will take to reduce concentration of exposure to terrorism risk, should TRIPRA protection change materially." In the event that the insurer's action plan is deemed to be "insufficient" then the "rating unit will face *negative rating pressure, likely in the form of assigning a negative outlook*." [italics added]

A.M. Best's concerns run deeper still, adding that while private reinsurance is currently available in the market, future availability and affordability of this coverage is "uncertain" in the event TRIA is not renewed or if the program changes significantly.

It is also worth noting that the A.M. Best analysis shows that smaller insurers would be disproportionately impacted by the expiration of TRIA. For those rating units with terrorism exposure under the A.M. Best criteria and with surplus (i.e., effectively net worth) under $500 million, 19 percent failed the stress tests. For those with surplus between $500 million and $1 billion, 11 percent failed.

This finding is notable. An Insurance Information Institute analysis of market share indicates that insurers with less than $500 million in surplus serviced approximately 16.8 percent of TRIA-backed coverages in 2012 while insurers with surplus of under $1 billion accounted for nearly a quarter of the market (23.6 percent).

Table 2. Recent Terrorist Attacks and Attempts in the United States

Date	Location	Event
April 15, 2013	Boston, MA	Brothers Tamerlan and Dzhokhar Tsarnaev detonate two pressure cooker bombs near the finish line of the Boston Marathon, killing 3 and injuring 264
April, 2013	New York City, NY-Toronto	Two suspects with al-Qaida links arrested in Toronto, Canada for alleged plot to blow up Amtrak passenger train en route from New York City to Toronto
November, 2012	New York City, NY	Brothers Raees Alam Qazi and Sheheryar Alam Qazi arrested and charged with conspiring to detonate a weapon of mass destruction targeting a New York City landmark
October, 2012	New York City, NY	Quazi Mohammad Rezwanul Ahsan Nafis arrested in plot to blow up Federal Reserve Bank in New York City
August, 2012	Ludowici, GA	Four U.S. soldiers charged in connection with murder and illegal gang activity, linked to foiled plot to commit domestic acts of terrorism, including overthrowing the government and assassinating the President
May, 2012	TBD	Foiled underwear bomb plot to bring down U.S.-bound commercial airliner around the anniversary of bin Laden's death
July 27, 2011	Fort Hood, TX	U.S. Army Pfc Naser Jason Abdo arrested and charged with plotting bomb attack on fellow soldiers at Fort Hood
June 22, 2011	Seattle, WA	Two men arrested in plot to attack military recruiting station in Seattle
May 11, 2011	New York City, NY	Ahmed Ferhani and Mohamed Mamdouh arrested in plot to attack Manhattan synagogue.
February 23, 2011	Lubbock, TX	Foiled plot to bomb military and political targets, including former President George W. Bush in New York, Colorado and California
December 8, 2010	Baltimore, MD	Attempted bombing of Armed Forces recruiting center by U.S. citizen Antonio Martinez, aka Muhammad Hussain
November 26, 2010	Portland, OR	Attempted bombing at Christmas tree lighting ceremony in downtown Portland by naturalized U.S. citizen Mohamed Osman Mohamud
October, 2010	Washington, D.C.	Attempted plot to bomb D.C.-area metro stations
May 1, 2010	New York City, NY	Attempted SUV bombing in Times Square, New York City, by naturalized U.S. citizen Faisal Shahzad
December 25, 2009	Over Detroit, MI	Attempted bombing of Northwest Airlines passenger jet over Detroit by underwear bomber Umar Farouk Abdulmutallab
September, 2009	New York City, NY	U.S. resident Najibullah Zazi and others charged with conspiracy to use weapons of mass destruction in New York City
September, 2009	Springfield, IL	Attempted plot to detonate a vehicle bomb at the federal building in Springfield.
September, 2009	Dallas, TX	Attempted bombing of skyscraper in Dallas

Date	Location	Event
May, 2009	New York City, NY	Foiled plot to bomb Jewish synagogue and shoot down military planes in New York City
May, 2009	Various U.S. targets	Conviction of Liberty City six for conspiring to plan attacks on U.S. targets, including Sears Tower, Chicago

Source: Federal Bureau of Investigation (FBI); various news reports; Insurance Information Institute.

One corollary to this finding is that many insurers—particularly small and medium-size insurers—are already at or near their maximum exposure to terrorism risk. Changes to the program that would increase their exposure (or an outright end to the program) would not motivate them to write more coverage. Indeed, the opposite is likely to happen. The bottom line is that any dramatic changes to the program are likely to be highly disruptive to a large share of the market.

A.M. Best also found that rating units with large workers compensation exposures were the most vulnerable under the stress test scenario. Because terrorism protection is mandatory under workers compensation policies, "This leaves ratings units with large workers comp terrorism risks even less options when contemplating how to reduce exposure."

Finally, it is important to recognize that the five- to six-ton TNT truck bomb scenario employed in the A.M. Best stress test should by no means me construed as worst-case scenario. Much larger events are possible which would produce greater stress on rating units and likely increase failure rates.

Evidence from Other Countries: Terrorism Risk Insurance Programs Abroad

Additional evidence that terrorism risk is fundamentally uninsurable comes from abroad. A number of countries have established their own terrorism risk insurance programs and these have operated successfully, often for many years. Australia, Austria, Belgium, France, Germany, the Netherlands, Spain, Switzerland and the United Kingdom have all created programs to cover terrorism in the event of an attack on their own soil.[18] None of these countries is considering the discontinuation of its program.

This begs the question as to why—twelve years after the 9/11 attack and a decade after the initial terrorism risk insurance program legislation was enacted—terrorism risk, particularly for large-scale attacks, is still viewed as uninsurable? The answer is surprisingly simple and explains why even the absence of a successful major attack on U.S. soil since 2001 does not alter this assessment.

Obstacles to Insuring Losses Arising from Acts of Terrorism

Simply put, acts of terror violate all four of the basic requirements traditionally associated with insurability of a risk. In situations where these requirements cannot be met, it is difficult or impossible to ascertain the premium to be charged and/or difficult or impossible to achieve the necessary spread of risk to avoid excessive exposure to catastrophic loss, thereby threatening the insurer's solvency. Consequently, such a risk would generally be deemed to be commercially *not* viable (i.e., insurable) in whole or in part.

The four basic requirements for insurability of a risk are detailed below (as well in Exhibits 5A and 5B), with a description of how terrorism risk violates each requirement:

1. **Estimable Frequency:** Insurers require a large number of observations to develop predictive, statistically sound rate-making models (an actuarial concept known as "credibility"). For example, insurers handle millions of auto, home, workers compensation and business property claims every year, providing them with vast amounts of data from which they can reliably estimate the frequency of such claims. For major catastrophic risks such as hurricanes and earthquakes that occur less frequently insurers still maintain databases with hundreds or even thousands of these events, supplemented by sophisticated catastrophe models, that help provide statistically reliable estimates of frequency. Terrorism risk is clearly different in this respect.
   Obstacle: There are very few data points on which to base frequency estimates for acts of terror in the United States, thus estimates lack any true actuarial credibility. The opinions of experts on the likelihood of terrorist attacks, which might be viewed by some as substitutes for actuarially credible data, are also highly subjective. At any given time, there is a wide range of viewpoints among national security experts on the likelihood, location and/or attack modality. Moreover, insurers have no access to data used internally by counterterrorism agencies. Given the paucity of historical data and diversity and shifting nature of expert opinions, catastrophe models used to estimate terrorism risk are relatively undeveloped compared to those used to assess natural hazard risks. The bottom line is that estimating the frequency of terror attacks with any degree of accuracy (credibility) is extraordinarily challenging, if not impossible in many circumstances.
2. **Estimable Severity:** Insurability requires that the maximum possible/probable loss be estimable in order to calculate the insurer's exposure (in dollar terms) and minimize its "probability of ruin." No insurer can expose itself to losses of a magnitude that present an unreasonable risk of insolvency.
   Obstacle: Potential losses arising from terrorist attacks are virtually unbounded. In this sense terrorism risk is akin to war risk, which is almost universally excluded from commercial insurance policies worldwide. Consequently, losses arising from acts of terror can easily exceed an insurer's claims paying capital resources. Workers compensation coverage, which does not permit any exclusions or limitation if injuries or deaths arise from terrorist acts, can lead to extreme losses that on their own could potentially bankrupt an insurer under some attack scenarios. In addition, when it comes to estimating losses from potential terrorist attacks there also appears to be significant variability in outcomes (i.e., disagreement on estimated severity impacts), underscoring the degree of uncertainty associated with potential terrorist attacks.
3. **Diversifiable Risk:** Insurability requires that the losses can be spread across a large number of risks. This is an application of the "Law of Large Numbers" and helps makes losses more manageable and less volatile. Failure to achieve an adequate spread of risk increases the risk of insolvency in the same way that an undiversified portfolio of stocks (or any asset) is riskier than a well-diversified portfolio.

Obstacle: Terrorism attacks are likely to be highly concentrated geographically (e.g., World Trade Center site), concentrated within an industry (e.g., power plants, airports) or within a certain span of time (e.g., coordinated attack).

Exhibit 5A. Terrorism Violates Traditional Requirements for Insurability

Requirement	Definition	Violation
Estimable Frequency	• Insurance requires large number of observations to develop predictive rate-making models (an actuarial concept known as credibility)	• Very few data points • Terror modeling still in infancy, untested. • Inconsistent assessment of threat
Estimable Severity	• Maximum possible/probable loss must be at least estimable in order to minimize "risk of ruin" (insurer cannot run an unreasonable risk of insolvency though assumption of the risk)	• Potential loss is virtually unbounded. • Losses can easily exceed insurer capital resources for paying claims. • Extreme risk in workers compensation and statute forbids exclusions.

Exhibit 5B.

Requirement	Definition	Violation
Diversifiable Risk	• Must be able to spread/distribute risk across large number of risks • "Law of Large Numbers" helps makes losses manageable and less volatile	• Losses likely highly concentrated geographically or by industry (e.g., WTC, power plants)
Random Loss Distribution/ Fortuity	• Probability of loss occurring must be purely random and fortuitous • Events are individually unpredictable in terms of time, location and magnitude	• Terrorism attacks are planned, coordinated and deliberate acts of destruction • Dynamic target shifting from "hardened targets" to "soft targets" • Terrorist adjust tactics to circumvent new security measures • Actions of US and foreign govts. may affect likelihood, nature and timing of attack

Source: Insurance Information Institute.

4. **Random Loss Distribution/Fortuity:** Insurability requires that the probability of a loss occurring be random or fortuitous. This implies that individual events must be unpredictable in terms of timing, location and magnitude.
Obstacle: Terrorism attacks are planned, coordinated and deliberate acts of destruction. Again, they are likely to be highly concentrated geographically (e.g., World Trade Center site) or concentrated within an industry (e.g., power plants). Terrorists engage in "dynamic target shifting" whereby terrorists shift from

"hardened targets" to "soft targets" which implies that losses are not random or fortuitous in nature. The April 2013 Boston Marathon bombing was an example of an attack on a soft target. It is also not difficult to imagine attacks occurring in the United States similar to the September 2013 attack on an upscale shopping mall (another soft target) in Nairobi, Kenya, by al-Shabaab, a Somali-based terrorist group with links to al-Qaeda.

ADDITIONAL ISSUES FOR CONSIDERATION IN CONJUNCTION WITH TRIA REAUTHORIZATION

Certification Deadline: While TRIA spells out a highly detailed set of criteria that must be met for an event to be officially certified as a "terrorist act," TRIA offers no timeline or deadline by which such a certification must be made. Although the Boston Marathon bombings occurred more than five months ago (on April 15, 2013), there has to date been no certification by the Treasury Department nor has there been any statement by Treasury that the event would not be certified. Indeed, Treasury has offered no guidance as to whether any such determination is ever forthcoming. This situation has created some uncertainty and confusion for policyholders, insurers and other impacted parties. A simple and reasonable solution would be to require that a certification determination must be made within a specified number of days after the event.

Cyber Terrorism: The threat both to national security and the economy posed by cyber terrorism is a growing concern for governments and businesses around the world, with critical infrastructure, such as power plants, transportation, and communication infrastructure at risk.[19] The Department of Homeland Security received reports of some 198 attacks on critical infrastructure systems in the U.S. in 2012, a 52 percent increase on 2011.[20]

Former U.S. Homeland Security Secretary Janet Napolitano recently warned that a "cyber 9/11" could happen imminently and noted that critical infrastructure – including water, electricity and gas – is very vulnerable to such a strike.[21]

Earlier, in an October 2012 speech then U.S. Defense Secretary Leon Panetta warned that the United States was facing a possible "cyber Pearl Harbor" scenario, and increasingly vulnerable to foreign cyber attacks on its critical infrastructure networks. Such attacks are targeting the computer control systems that operate chemical, electricity and water plants and transportation networks, Panetta said.

SUMMARY

In the twelve years since the tragedy of the September 11, 2001 terrorist attack on the United States, much has been learned about the nature of terrorism risk and its insurability. There is no question that the Terrorism Risk Insurance Act and its successors brought much needed stability to the market in the aftermath of the most costly insurance loss in global history. In the decade since, private sector insurers, reinsurers and the federal government have successfully partnered with one another in order to maintain that stability, providing tangible benefits for businesses large and small—and their employees—all across America.

The looming expiration of the TRIA at the end of 2014 brings to a head the question of whether terrorism risk is now, or ever will be, a risk that can be managed entirely within the private sector. The evidence, both in the United States and from similar programs abroad, is that market stability in terms of both pricing and availability of terrorism coverage, as well as the ability to maintain adequate and expanding levels of capacity over time, are contingent on the continued existence of the Terrorism Risk Insurance Program. Moreover, based on recent ratings agency "stress test" analyses, significant changes to the program could prove to be very disruptive to markets.

Thank you for you for the opportunity to testify before the Committee today. I would be happy to respond to any questions you may have.

End Notes

[1] Contact information: Tel: (212) 346-5520; Email: bobh@iii.org.

[2] See *Terrorism Risk: A Constant Threat,* Robert P. Hartwig and Claire Wilkinson, Insurance Information Institute, June 2013: http://www.iii.org/white_papers/terrorism-risk-a-constant-threat-2013.html.

[3] The loss totals do not include the March 2010 settlement of up to $657.5 million announced by New York City officials and plaintiffs' lawyers to compensate about 10,000 workers whose health was damaged during the rescue and cleanup at the World Trade Center.

[4] "Unease Over Terrorism Insurance Rattles Market," *Commercial Mortgage Alert*, November 1, 2013.

[5] R. Glenn Hubbard and Bruce Deal, *The Economic Effects of Federal Participation in Terrorism Risk*, Analysis Group, September 14, 2004.

[6] Figures cited in Table 1 are Insurance Information Institute estimates based on findings of the study referenced in footnote 3.

[7] As of July 26 (latest available). P/C insurers also held $1.41 million in reserves for claims associated with the bombings. Figures are from the Massachusetts Division of Insurance as reported in BestWire Services, *P/C Insurers Have Paid $1.18 Million in Boston Marathon Bombing Related Claims,* September 3, 2013.

[8] United States Treasury accessed as of 9/22/13 at http://www.treasury.gov/resource-center/fin- mkts/Documents/TRIAasamended-CompositeTextPost.pdf.

[9] National Conference of Insurance Guaranty Funds accessed September 22, 2013 at: http://www.ncigf.org/media/files/Primer-2012.pdf

[10] Marsh, *2013 Terrorism Risk Insurance Report*, May 2013.

[11] *Market Conditions for Terrorism Risk Insurance 2010*, Report of the President's Working Group on Financial Markets.

[12] *Initial Results on Availability of Terrorism Insurance in Specific Geographic Markets*, GAO-08-919R, July 2008.

[13] *September 11, 2001: One Hundred Minutes of Terror that Changed the Global Insurance Industry Forever*, Robert P. Hartwig, John Liner Review, January 2002.

[14] *Country Reports on Terrorism 2011*, U.S. Department of State, July 31, 2012.

[15] RMS Terrorism Risk Briefing, July 2012.

[16] *Evaluating the Effectiveness of Terrorism Risk Financing Solutions*, Howard C. Kunreuther and Erwann O. Michel-Kerjan, September 2007, National Bureau of Economic Research.

[17] "The Future of TRIPRA Remains Uncertain, Ratings Pressure Intensifies," *Best's Briefing*, October 9, 2013.

[18] In 1993, the British government formed a mutual reinsurance pool for terrorist coverage following acts of terrorism by the Irish Republican Army. Insurance companies pay premiums at rates set by the pool. The primary insurer pays the entire claim for terrorist damage but is reimbursed by the pool for losses in excess was extended to cover all risks, except war, including nuclear and biological contamination, aircraft impact and flooding, if caused by terrorist attacks. The British government acts as the reinsurer of last resort, guaranteeing payments above the industry retention.

[19] *Cyber Risks: The Growing Threat,* Robert P. Hartwig and Claire Wilkinson, Insurance Information Institute, April 2013.

[20] *As Hacking Against U.S. Rises, Experts Try to Pin Down Motive*, the New York Times, March 3, 2013

[21] *Napolitano warns of risk of major cyber attack*, Newsday, January 24, 2013.

INDEX

#

9/11, 2, 11, 66, 67, 68, 69, 76, 80, 84, 97, 110, 111, 113, 132, 135, 137, 138, 139, 144, 145, 149, 152

A

access, 41, 43, 58, 80, 110, 124, 150
accounting, 54, 78, 79, 125, 126
accreditation, 126
accurate models, 106
actuarial methods, 130
adjustment, 102
adverse effects, 69, 82, 96
agencies, 20, 27, 30, 31, 41, 43, 52, 59, 61, 78, 122, 145, 147, 150
aggregation, 35, 111, 113
air carriers, 6, 99, 140
airports, 25, 137, 151
anthrax, 100
appetite, 81, 109, 110, 111, 112, 117, 125, 130, 132, 144, 145, 147
Appropriations Act, 61
assault, 120
assessment, viii, 27, 33, 65, 87, 95, 100, 110, 112, 143, 147, 149, 151
assets, 16, 61, 62, 78, 102, 118, 129, 142, 144, 145
Attorney General, 3, 6, 13, 57, 71, 72, 140
audit(s), 22, 50, 57
Austria, 149
authorities,
authority(s), viii, 2, 4, 7, 8, 16, 29, 42, 53, 58, 59, 70, 71

B

balance sheet, 100
banking, 17, 98, 100, 103
bankruptcy, 9, 124, 125
base, 23, 41, 77, 130, 131, 132, 150
base rate(s), 23
Belgium, 149
benchmarking, 89
benefits, 25, 85, 98, 116, 134, 135, 138, 143
boilers, 25
bomb attack, 148
bond market, 129, 131, 132, 134
bonds, 40, 41, 43, 122, 124, 129, 131, 133, 144, 145
borrowers, 137
bounds, 132
breakdown, 25
businesses, 2, 12, 17, 18, 20, 22, 23, 24, 27, 31, 32, 34, 36, 37, 38, 39, 42, 43, 49, 55, 56, 58, 60, 62, 68, 98, 102, 106, 116, 135, 137, 138, 143, 145, 152
buyers, 96, 101, 120

C

CAP, 142
capital flows, 121
capital markets, 40, 43, 81, 96, 120, 124, 130
cash, 59, 127
catastrophe bonds, 32, 40, 41, 43, 81, 123, 124, 145
catastrophe exposure, 35, 89, 127
catastrophes, 10, 34, 37, 40, 79, 94, 110, 121, 123, 127, 144
certification, 3, 4, 26, 72, 74, 95, 103, 112, 117, 136, 152
CFR, 63
challenges, 10, 40, 41, 50, 59
chaos, 127
chemical(s), 20, 25, 49, 56, 67, 76, 89, 91, 97, 117, 120, 122, 134, 152
Chicago, 67, 86, 149

city(s), 11, 43, 61, 67, 78, 86, 101, 135, 136, 146, 148, 149, 153
clarity, 51, 52, 55, 95
classes, 117, 131, 132
cleanup, 153
clients, 12, 29, 35, 56, 60, 67, 83, 98, 102, 104, 120, 121
Code of Federal Regulations, 25, 63
coercion, 71, 140
coffee, 109
collateral, 125
commerce, 51
commercial bank, 12
communication, 25, 152
communities, 135, 143
compensation, 6, 8, 9, 13, 14, 18, 25, 26, 32, 38, 43, 49, 57, 58, 60, 61, 62, 63, 68, 69, 70, 71, 72, 74, 79, 80, 85, 96, 98, 99, 103, 104, 112, 117, 118, 133, 136, 138, 140, 142, 149, 150, 151
competition, 33, 77, 120, 121
compilation, 26, 59
complement, 83, 124
complexity, 98, 102
composition, 34
computer, 9, 146, 152
congress, vii, viii, 1, 2, 3, 6, 9, 11, 14, 15, 17, 18, 19, 21, 23, 25, 27, 28, 32, 43, 52, 53, 54, 55, 56, 59, 61, 65, 66, 67, 71, 73, 75, 76, 93, 97, 103, 106, 107, 118, 137, 140, 146
Congressional Budget Office, 7, 12, 18, 24, 55, 61
congressional hearings, 21, 56
consensus, 137
conspiracy, 148
construction, 3, 11, 12, 36, 69, 88, 137
consulting, 11
consumer advocates, ix, 65, 82, 100
consumer protection, 69, 125
consumers, 2, 3, 6, 8, 69, 121, 135, 138
contamination, 153
content analysis, 55
correlation(s), 81, 132, 133
cost, vii, 1, 3, 9, 24, 40, 44, 50, 59, 81, 82, 83, 85, 88, 89, 102, 104, 111, 123, 127, 138, 139
counseling, 43
counterterrorism, 41, 77, 111, 145, 150
covering, 20, 21, 34, 35, 37, 39, 40, 41, 42, 51, 60, 80, 83, 112, 131
CPI, 137
credit rating, 59, 67, 78, 80
critical infrastructure, 137, 138, 152
crop, 14, 17, 58, 70
crop insurance, 14, 17, 70
crowding out, 106

crowds, 82
cure, 111, 134
current balance, 102
customers, 113, 120, 122, 125
cyber-attack, 121
cybersecurity, 103

D

data analysis, 55
data collection, 22, 58
data set, 117, 123
deaths, 9, 150
decision makers, 31
Department of Defense, 17
Department of Homeland Security, 152
Department of the Treasury, 8, 20, 21, 53, 58, 59, 60, 61, 62, 97, 103
depression, 127
depth, 27, 55, 124
derivatives, 124, 125
destruction, 112, 151
deterrence, 43
detonation, 81
diminishing returns, 122
directors, 14, 70, 99, 142
disaster, 43, 94
disaster assistance, 43, 94
disaster relief, 44
disclosure, 71
dislocation, 118
distribution, viii, 2, 15, 16, 31
District of Columbia, 27, 57
diversification, 111, 124, 130
diversity, 150
Dodd-Frank Wall Street Reform XE "Reform" and Consumer Protection Act, 8, 58, 70, 97, 107
domestic industry, 58
domestic terrorism, vii, 1, 6, 23, 25, 107, 111, 121, 146
draft, 53, 54, 55, 59
drawing, 59

E

earthquakes, 77, 83, 116, 121, 130, 144, 150
economic activity, 69
economic consequences, 137
economic damage, 3
economic development, 106, 122
economic growth, 139, 146
economic impact, vii, 1, 11, 15

economic losses, 117
economic problem, 98
economic rent, 134
education, 38, 88, 91
electricity, 152
emergency, 43
employees, 85, 98, 152
employers, 43, 61, 85, 98, 104, 106
employment, 12, 69, 85, 122, 139
endowments, 131
energy, 3, 12, 51, 89, 91, 99, 144
environment, 96, 121, 122, 125, 145
equipment, 25, 43
equity, 115, 121, 124, 127, 145
equity market, 145
Europe, 84, 124, 131
evacuation, 43
evidence, 2, 22, 39, 57, 79, 103, 124, 127, 129, 144, 149, 153
evolution, 123
exclusion, 11, 49, 71, 95, 120, 122, 134
executive branch, 3
Executive Order, 103
exercise, 80
expenditures, 43, 141
expertise, 50, 77, 111, 112

F

factories, 137
Fair Access to Insurance Requirement, 18
fat, 123
fears, 3, 11
federal assistance, 24, 43, 59, 79, 141
Federal Bureau of Investigation (FBI), 149
Federal funds, 140
federal government, vii, viii, 1, 6, 19, 21, 23, 24, 28, 30, 31, 43, 50, 52, 56, 57, 58, 59, 62, 65, 67, 73, 78, 94, 96, 106, 110, 137, 139, 143, 152
federal law, 18
Federal Register, viii, 65, 97
Federal Reserve, 4, 58, 97, 125, 146, 148
Federal Reserve Board, 4
fidelity, 62
financial, viii, 12, 14, 17, 20, 21, 31, 33, 35, 38, 41, 45, 52, 58, 59, 60, 63, 65, 70, 74, 76, 77, 81, 88, 89, 91, 111, 115, 116, 117, 126, 127, 136, 138, 139, 142, 144, 147
financial condition, 52, 76
financial crisis, 33, 60
financial data, 58, 59, 63
financial incentives, 126
financial institutions, 12, 38, 138, 139

financial markets, 81
fires, 121
flaws, 133
flooding, 153
floods, 77, 83
fluctuations, 40
food, 12, 89
football, 61
force, 42, 71, 103, 125
foreign person, 13, 72, 80
formation, 130
Fort Hood, 148
foundations, 131
France, 127, 149
fraud, 58, 143
free market economy, 119
funding, 43, 50, 66, 80, 103, 116, 124
funds, 43, 50, 61, 81, 94, 118, 121, 123, 124, 127, 131, 132, 142, 143

G

game theory, 127
garbage, 122
GDP, 139, 140, 143
General Accounting Office (GAO), viii, 4, 9, 17, 19, 20, 25, 26, 28, 35, 45, 47, 48, 55, 58, 59, 60, 61, 62, 63, 76, 95, 97, 98, 100, 103, 126, 127, 143, 153
general insurance policies, vii, 1
geography, 32, 53, 89
geo-political, 112
Germany, 10, 61, 127, 149
global economy, 135
government loss sharing, vii, 1, 21
government policy, 13
government spending, 30
governments, 130, 152
grants, 43
graph, 101
grouping, 86
growth, 46, 51, 79, 119, 123, 124, 132, 137, 143
growth rate, 132
guidance, 36, 51, 53, 54, 112, 152

H

hardness, 33
health, 14, 17, 23, 34, 57, 88, 89, 115, 138, 142, 153
health care, 88, 89, 138
health insurance, 17, 34, 142
historical data, 10, 77, 110, 111, 150

Index

history, 37, 123, 130, 136, 146, 152
homeowners, 57, 68, 121, 130, 142
homes, 17
hospitality, 12, 88, 89
hotels, 137
House, viii, ix, 2, 3, 4, 5, 17, 18, 21, 61, 67, 80, 97, 105, 106, 109, 115, 119, 129, 135
House of Representatives, 5, 21, 97
Housing and Urban Development, 11
human, 10, 25, 71, 122, 127, 134, 140
human agency, 122
human behavior, 127
Hurricane Andrew, 130, 131
Hurricane Katrina, 44, 127
hurricanes, 9, 83, 116, 121, 130, 144, 150

I

ID, 98, 100, 102, 103, 104
ideal, 10
identification, 58
improvements, 35, 76, 77, 112
income, 33, 115, 125, 127, 145
increased competition, 77
individuals, 17, 41, 43, 57, 69, 71, 72, 131, 140, 146
infancy, 127, 151
inflation, 106, 137
infrastructure, 25, 43, 71, 119, 135, 139, 140, 144, 146, 152
injury(s), 25, 68, 138, 142, 150
insurance industry, vii, 1, 3, 6, 8, 21, 27, 28, 29, 32, 46, 49, 51, 53, 58, 59, 60, 63, 67, 78, 79, 94, 106, 110, 111, 112, 116, 117, 118, 131, 135, 140, 142
insurance policy, ix, 9, 11, 41, 66, 68, 76, 77, 95, 100, 141
intelligence, 41, 59, 110, 116, 122
interest rates, 40
intervention, 110, 120, 122, 123
investment(s), 33, 40, 41, 60, 61, 125, 129, 131, 133, 144, 145
investors, 41, 61, 81, 111, 121, 122, 124, 127, 130, 131, 132, 133, 145
Iran, 146
IRI, 84
Irish Republican Army, 10, 153
issues, 41, 93, 122, 123, 125, 126, 127, 132, 133, 135
Italy, 127

J

jurisdiction, 8, 85, 125
justification, 32

K

Kenya, 110, 152

L

landscape, 136
law enforcement, 77, 122
laws, 8, 13, 15, 22, 25, 54, 62, 95, 112, 125, 127
lawyers, 153
lead, 4, 11, 80, 103, 111, 120, 139, 150
legislation, 6, 8, 9, 15, 17, 23, 54, 106, 124, 125, 126, 136, 149
legislative proposals, 3
lending, 11, 137
liability insurance, 2, 70, 71, 99
liberty, 126
life sciences, 89
light, 54, 66, 68, 84, 85, 125
liquidity, 44, 45, 113, 124
livestock, 17, 70
loan guarantees, 43
loans, 11, 12, 18, 43
local government, 43, 138
love, 133

M

machinery, 25, 38, 70
magnitude, 22, 28, 30, 31, 46, 53, 59, 60, 63, 111, 122, 150, 151
major disaster declaration, 43
majority, 39, 58, 60, 67, 129, 143
man, 136
management, 44, 76, 129
manufacturing, 89, 91, 144
market penetration, 143
market share, 31, 47, 48, 57, 115, 121, 122, 147
marketplace, 4, 8, 12, 15, 24, 62, 68, 74, 75, 80, 99, 106, 115, 143
marsh, 102, 104
masking, 12
mass, 134
matter, 16, 120, 121, 126, 145
measurement, 76
media, 18, 36, 38, 67, 89, 91, 153
median, 12, 36, 60, 79, 86, 87, 89, 98, 102, 122
medical, 14, 17, 25, 62, 70, 85, 142
medical care, 25
membership, 4
methodology, 22
metropolitan areas, 81, 104, 118, 137, 143

Mexico, 127
Middle East, 120
militancy, 133
military, 116, 148, 149
mission(s), 13, 99, 135, 140
misunderstanding, 132
mixing, 132
models, 2, 9, 10, 35, 41, 50, 59, 77, 100, 102, 122, 123, 125, 130, 131, 134, 150, 151
modifications, 22, 40, 55, 68, 72, 93, 94
mortality, 41, 61, 134
mortality risk, 134
mortgage-backed securities, 12
multiple factors, 72
murder, 148

N

national security, 135, 139, 146, 150, 152
natural disaster(s), 2, 41, 144, 145
negative effects, 134
Netherlands, 149
neutral, 21
niche market, 124
North Africa, 120
North America, 80
Northridge Earthquake, 130, 131
Northwest Airlines, 148
nuclear program, 146

O

objectivity, 103
obstacles, 50
OECD, 123, 147
Office of Management and Budget, 16
officials, 26, 28, 29, 30, 31, 51, 55, 58, 59, 61, 153
Oklahoma, 146
operations, 26, 43, 63, 142
opportunities, 115
oversight, 26, 51
ownership, 60
ownership structure, 60

P

pairing, 133
paralysis, 111
participants, viii, 19, 20, 22, 29, 31, 33, 38, 39, 40, 42, 45, 51, 55, 56, 58, 59, 65, 77, 106
peer review, 27
permission, 58

permit, 38, 58, 62, 69, 75, 150
Philadelphia, 60, 87
plants, 152
platform, 125
playing, 118, 144
policy, 2, 11, 14, 25, 28, 30, 31, 34, 36, 39, 40, 49, 51, 58, 60, 61, 62, 63, 68, 69, 71, 77, 83, 85, 95, 104, 121, 127, 140, 144
policymakers, 21
pollution, 95
pools, 9, 50, 123
population, 13, 61, 71, 140
portfolio, 78, 111, 117, 129, 150
potential benefits, 126
power plants, 151, 152
precedent, 111
president, v, vi, viii, ix, 3, 4, 12, 10, 17, 18, 20, 26, 55, 58, 61, 62, 63, 65, 97, 103, 107, 119, 135, 143, 148, 153
President Obama, 3
prevention, 41, 123
principles, 23, 49
private banks, 131
private industry, vii, viii, 1, 2, 24, 44
private insurers, vii, 1, 21, 24, 43, 106, 139, 143
private investment, 123
private sector, viii, 19, 31, 44, 46, 62, 76, 80, 94, 105, 107, 111, 113, 118, 136, 137, 139, 143, 146, 152, 153
probability, 9, 10, 41, 53, 117, 123, 150, 151
professionals, 77, 130, 131
profitability, 84
proposition, 101
protection, 43, 80, 83, 104, 116, 135, 140, 145, 147, 149
public interest, 103
public policy, 31, 82, 96, 119

Q

questioning, 3
questionnaire, 22, 33, 35, 38, 39, 40, 42, 44, 46, 50, 51, 54, 55, 56, 59, 60, 63

R

radiation, 122
radius, 147
rating agencies, 22, 43, 55, 96, 124
real estate, 3, 11, 12, 69, 90, 104, 112
reality, 145
reasoning, 133

recession, 133, 137, 139, 144
recognition, 59, 69, 123
recommendations, 20, 53
recovery, 43, 76, 96, 113, 139, 142, 143
recruiting, 148
reform(s), 3, 4, 5, 8, 58, 70, 97, 107
regulations, 14, 22, 26, 29, 53, 54, 58, 95, 125
regulatory framework, 125
regulatory oversight, 27
rehabilitation, 25
reimburse, 23
reliability, 21, 57, 60, 61
reputation, 109
requirements, 18, 27, 29, 52, 99, 103, 125, 126, 127, 142, 149, 150
reserves, 50, 126, 127, 153
resilience, 4, 124
resolution, 126
resources, 40, 43, 50, 51, 59, 142, 150, 151
response, ix, 11, 35, 43, 54, 60, 61, 65, 66, 67, 75, 77, 85, 96, 101, 106, 109, 116, 130
restoration, 43
restrictions, 147
retail, 88
rights, 71
risk factors, 15
risk management, 118
risk perception, 92
risk profile, 83
rules, 4, 99
rural areas, 15

signs, 11, 122, 138
soccer, 61
solution, 10, 152
Spain, 10, 127, 149
speech, 152
spending, 20, 26, 30, 31, 32, 46, 59
Spring, 125
stability, 104, 112, 137, 138, 145, 146, 152, 153
stakeholders, viii, ix, 65, 66, 75, 82, 94
state(s), ix, 2, 6, 8, 11, 12, 18, 20, 27, 28, 29, 30, 31, 38, 42, 43, 49, 52, 57, 58, 59, 61, 65, 68, 69, 71, 78, 79, 81, 82, 85, 95, 96, 98, 99, 103, 116, 120, 123, 125, 126, 127, 129, 130, 132, 135, 137, 142, 144
state laws, 9, 27, 38, 68
state regulators, 2, 8, 27, 28, 95
statistics, 55, 57
statutes, 125
stock, 133, 145
stock markets, 145
storms, 77, 121
stress, 45, 100, 101, 138, 147, 149, 153
stress test, 45, 100, 101, 147, 149, 153
structure, 32, 37, 56, 111, 122, 127, 140, 143
subsidy(s), 94, 101
substitutes, 150
supplier(s), 104, 124
surplus, 12, 43, 44, 45, 46, 48, 57, 58, 61, 62, 67, 78, 79, 80, 94, 99, 100, 127, 147
Switzerland, 127, 149
systemic risk, 125

S

scaling, 3
scarcity, 12
scope, 2, 22, 66, 68, 70, 72, 80, 83, 85, 93, 99, 117
Secretary of Homeland Security, 4, 107
Secretary of the Treasury, vii, 2, 3, 4, 6, 8, 13, 14, 15, 53, 57, 58, 66, 97, 107, 141
security(s), 32, 39, 40, 43, 56, 60, 61, 81, 95, 119, 124, 125, 127, 139, 151
Senate, viii, 2, 4, 5, 67, 97, 106
September 11, vii, viii, 1, 2, 10, 11, 17, 18, 19, 21, 40, 41, 43, 48, 58, 61, 66, 67, 97, 98, 101, 106, 109, 116, 120, 121, 135, 136, 137, 145, 152, 153
service provider, 102
services, ix, 58, 65, 68, 89, 100, 102
settlements, 136
shock, 61, 120, 137
shoot, 149
shortage, 66
showing, 11, 98, 138

T

tactics, 151
tangible benefits, 152
target, 81, 127, 151
taxation, 125, 126
taxes, 33
taxpayers, 21, 24, 107, 112, 113, 123, 138, 139, 142
technical assistance, 43
technical comments, 53
techniques, 111, 117, 118, 131
technology(s), 51, 131
telecommunications, 138
temporary housing, 43
tensions, 112
territory, 121
terrorism insurance, vii, viii, 5, 8, 9, 10, 11, 12, 19, 20, 21, 22, 23, 28, 29, 30, 32, 33, 34, 36, 37, 38, 39, 41, 43, 44, 49, 50, 52, 53, 54, 55, 56, 58, 60, 100, 106, 107, 119, 120, 123, 124, 129, 130, 135, 136, 138, 143, 145, 146, 147

Index

Terrorism Risk Insurance Act, i, iii, vii, viii, 1, 3, 5, 13, 16, 20, 21, 25, 26, 35, 45, 47, 54, 58, 59, 61, 63, 65, 66, 68, 97, 98, 100, 101, 105, 107, 109, 116, 119, 137, 152
terrorist acts, 10, 11, 25, 41, 106, 137, 138, 142, 150
terrorists, 23, 41, 127, 146, 151
textbook, 10
theft, 14, 26, 71, 142
thoughts, 123
threats, 42, 51, 52, 110, 112, 127, 134, 146
time frame, 21, 95, 103
Title I, 5
Title II, 5
Title V, 70
tornadoes, 121
trade, ix, 22, 40, 55, 66, 100, 120, 135
transaction costs, 134
transactions, vii, 1, 61, 69, 81, 125, 127
transference, 32, 39
transparency, 95, 103
transport, 25
transportation, 3, 12, 25, 51, 88, 89, 90, 144, 152
transportation infrastructure, 51
Treasury, v, vii, viii, 4, 8, 14, 19, 20, 21, 22, 23, 24, 25, 26, 27, 28, 29, 30, 31, 34, 38, 49, 50, 51, 52, 53, 54, 55, 58, 59, 60, 61, 62, 65, 67, 69, 70, 74, 75, 95, 96, 97, 100, 103, 106, 107, 123, 140, 152, 153
Treasury Secretary, 8, 58, 107, 140
treaties, 61
treatment, 5, 51, 52, 125, 126
triggers, 123, 125, 127

U

U.S. Department of the Treasury, viii, 16, 54, 65, 97, 103
U.S. history, 121
U.S. Treasury, 16, 62
underwriting, 10, 22, 28, 33, 35, 37, 49, 50, 55, 117, 120, 136
uniform, 12, 90, 125, 145
uninsured, 143
United, v, 2, 6, 9, 10, 11, 12, 13, 16, 19, 22, 27, 39, 41, 56, 57, 71, 78, 80, 83, 84, 99, 111, 112, 115, 121, 124, 127, 129, 135, 136, 137, 140, 144, 145, 146, 148, 149, 150, 152, 153
United Kingdom (UK), 10, 84, 111, 127, 131, 149
United States, v, 2, 6, 9, 10, 11, 12, 13, 16, 19, 22, 27, 39, 41, 56, 57, 71, 78, 80, 83, 84, 99, 111, 112, 115, 121, 124, 129, 135, 136, 137, 140, 144, 145, 146, 148, 150, 152, 153
urban, 15, 40, 67, 77, 78, 95, 96, 106, 110, 146
urban areas, 40, 67, 77, 96, 106, 110, 146
urbanization, 112
USA, 84

V

validation, 123
vandalism, 25, 68
variables, 32, 53
variations, 126
vehicles, 101, 123, 131, 145
venue, 123
vessels, 6, 25, 99, 140
Vice President, 101
victims, 143
vision, 130, 131
volatility, 82, 93, 124
vote, viii, 2, 4, 5
vulnerability, 117, 127

W

wages, 25
war, 2, 11, 13, 17, 68, 71, 120, 138, 140, 145, 150, 153
Washington, 43, 58, 59, 60, 61, 63, 67, 86, 148
water, 25, 51, 152
wealth, 124, 131
weapon of mass destruction, 148
weapons, 20, 25, 49, 77, 78, 97, 148
weapons of mass destruction, 148
web, 26
White House, 17
wholesale, 88, 120
wildfire, 131
witnesses, 105
workers, 9, 11, 13, 14, 18, 25, 32, 38, 43, 49, 57, 58, 60, 61, 62, 63, 68, 69, 70, 80, 85, 96, 98, 99, 103, 104, 118, 136, 137, 138, 140, 142, 149, 150, 151, 153
World Bank, 129
World Trade Center, 144, 151, 153
World War I, 11
worldwide, 101, 129, 136, 150

Y

yield, 122, 124, 133